LANGUAGE!

The Comprehensive Literacy Curriculum

Jane Fell Greene, Ed.D.

 SOPRIS WEST Educational Services
A Cambium Learning Company

BOSTON, MA • NEW YORK, NY • LONGMONT, CO

08 07 06 05   10 9 8 7 6 5 4 3 2 1

Editorial Director: Nancy Chapel Eberhardt
Word and Phrase Selection: Judy Fell Woods
English Learners: Jennifer Wells Greene
Lesson Development: Sheryl Ferlito, Donna Lutz, Isabel Wesley
Morphology: John Alexander, Mike Minsky, Bruce Rosow
Text Selection: Sara Buckerfield, Jim Cloonan
Decodable and Independent Text: Jenny Hamilton, Steve Harmon

ISBN 1-59318-376-3

Printed in the United States of America

Published and distributed by

SOPRIS
WEST
EDUCATIONAL SERVICES

4093 Specialty Place • Longmont, CO 80504 • (303) 651-2829
www.sopriswest.com

Table of Contents

Lesson Checklist
Lessons 1–2

Check off the activities you complete with each lesson. Evaluate your accomplishments at the end of each lesson. Pay attention to teacher evaluations and comments.

Unit Objectives	Lesson 1 (Date:_____)	Lesson 2 (Date:_____)
STEP 1 **Phonemic Awareness and Phonics** • Identify conditions for soft **c** and soft **g**. • Say the sound for -**dge**. • Write the sound-spelling correspondence -**dge** for / j /. • Identify the conditions for the multiple spellings of / j /: **j**, **g**, or -**dge**.	❑ Exercise 1: Sort It: Two Sounds for **s** ❑ Exercise 2: Discover It: Conditions for Soft **c**	❑ Exercise 1: Discover It: Conditions for Soft **g**
STEP 2 **Word Recognition and Spelling** • Read and spell multisyllable words. • Read and spell the **Essential Words:** *carriage, machine, marriage, pigeon, shoe, surgeon.* • Spell words with prefixes, suffixes, and roots.	❑ Exercise 3: Spelling Pretest 1 ❑ Memorize It	❑ Exercise 2: Sort It: Soft **c** and **g** ❑ Exercise 3: Write It: Essential Words ❑ Word Fluency 1
STEP 3 **Vocabulary and Morphology** • Identify attributes. • Identify and define adjective suffixes. • Use the meaning of prefixes, suffixes, and roots to define words.	❑ Unit Vocabulary ❑ Explore It (T) ❑ Expression of the Day	❑ Exercise 4: Choose It: Affixed Words ❑ Write It: Journal Entry
STEP 4 **Grammar and Usage** • Identify adjectives and nouns. • Identify past participles of regular and irregular verbs. • Identify phrases and clauses • Use semicolons to write compound sentences. • Identify the four basic sentence types.	❑ Exercise 4: Write It: Past and Past Participle Forms of Verbs ❑ Exercise 5: Identify It: Functions of Past Participles	❑ Exercise 5: Choose It: Adjective Suffixes ❑ Exercise 6: Identify It: Confusing Verbs
STEP 5 **Listening and Reading Comprehension** • Interpret visual information. • Use context-based strategies to define words. • Identify thought and form in poetry. • Identify, understand, and answer questions that use different types of signal words.	❑ Independent Text: "Stonehenge: Secrets of an Ancient Circle" ❑ Exercise 6: Phrase It ❑ Exercise 7: Use the Clues	❑ Passage Fluency 1 ❑ Exercise 7: Using Visuals: Illustrations and Photographs
STEP 6 **Speaking and Writing** • Use visual and text information to answer questions. • Write responses to sentences using signal words. • Organize information in a graphic organizer for a compare-and-contrast paragraph. • Write a compare-and-contrast paragraph and essay.	❑ Exercise 8: Rewrite It	❑ Exercise 8: Answer It
Self-Evaluation (5 is the highest) **Effort** = I produced my best work. **Participation** = I was actively involved in tasks. **Independence** = I worked on my own.	**Effort:** 1 2 3 4 5 **Participation:** 1 2 3 4 5 **Independence:** 1 2 3 4 5	**Effort:** 1 2 3 4 5 **Participation:** 1 2 3 4 5 **Independence:** 1 2 3 4 5
Teacher Evaluation	**Effort:** 1 2 3 4 5 **Participation:** 1 2 3 4 5 **Independence:** 1 2 3 4 5	**Effort:** 1 2 3 4 5 **Participation:** 1 2 3 4 5 **Independence:** 1 2 3 4 5

(T) = Template

Lesson 3 (Date:_____)	**Lesson 4** (Date:_____)	**Lesson 5** (Date:_____)
❑ Exercise 1: Listening for Sounds in Words ❑ Exercise 2: Discover It: Position-Spelling Pattern for **-dge**	❑ Exercise 1: Sort It: Soft **c** and Soft **g** ❑ Exercise 2: Identify It: Stressed Syllables and Rhyme	❑ Content Mastery: Soft **c** and Soft **g**
❑ Build It: Words With **-dge** ❑ Divide It ❑ Word Fluency 2	❑ Make a Mnemonic ❑ Present It: Mnemonics for Confusing Word Pairs	❑ Content Mastery: Spelling Posttest 1 ❑ Present It: Mnemonics for Confusing Word Pairs
❑ Vocabulary Focus ❑ Use the Clues ❑ Expression of the Day	❑ Exercise 3: Match It: Affixed Words	❑ Exercise 1: Define It: Prefixes, Roots, and Suffixes
❑ Identify It: Adjectives, Prepositional Phrases, and Predicate Adjectives	❑ Exercise 4: Identify It: Phrase or Independent Clause ❑ Exercise 5: Combine It: Compound Sentences	❑ Exercise 2: Identify It: Kinds of Sentences ❑ Exercise 3: Rewrite It: Sentences
❑ Instructional Text: "Circle Poems Take Many Forms"	❑ Take Note: "Circle Poems Take Many Forms"	❑ Take Note: Studying Poems
❑ Exercise 3: Answer It	❑ Map It: Compare and Contrast (T) ❑ Challenge Text: "Living in a Circle"	❑ Exercise 4: Write It: Compare and Contrast (T) ❑ Challenge Text: "Living in a Circle" ❑ Exercise 5: Challenge Writing: Write a Haiku
Effort: 1 2 3 4 5 **Participation:** 1 2 3 4 5 **Independence:** 1 2 3 4 5	**Effort:** 1 2 3 4 5 **Participation:** 1 2 3 4 5 **Independence:** 1 2 3 4 5	**Effort:** 1 2 3 4 5 **Participation:** 1 2 3 4 5 **Independence:** 1 2 3 4 5
Effort: 1 2 3 4 5 **Participation:** 1 2 3 4 5 **Independence:** 1 2 3 4 5	**Effort:** 1 2 3 4 5 **Participation:** 1 2 3 4 5 **Independence:** 1 2 3 4 5	**Effort:** 1 2 3 4 5 **Participation:** 1 2 3 4 5 **Independence:** 1 2 3 4 5

Check off the activities you complete with each lesson. Evaluate your accomplishments at the end of each lesson. Pay attention to teacher evaluations and comments.

Unit Objectives	Lesson 6 (Date:_____)	Lesson 7 (Date:_____)
STEP 1 **Phonemic Awareness and Phonics** • Identify conditions for soft <u>c</u> and soft <u>g</u>. • Say the sound for -<u>dge</u>. • Write the sound-spelling correspondence -<u>dge</u> for /j/. • Identify the conditions for the multiple spellings of /j/: <u>j</u>, <u>g</u>, or -<u>dge</u>.	❑ Content Mastery: Using Student Performance	❑ Listening for Word Parts: Prefixes
STEP 2 **Word Recognition and Spelling** • Read and spell multisyllable words. • Read and spell the **Essential Words:** *carriage, machine, marriage, pigeon, shoe, surgeon*. • Spell words with prefixes, suffixes, and roots.	❑ Exercise 1: Spelling Pretest 2 ❑ Word Fluency 3	❑ Build It: Words With Suffixes ❑ Word Fluency 4
STEP 3 **Vocabulary and Morphology** • Identify attributes. • Identify and define adjective suffixes. • Use the meaning of prefixes, suffixes, and roots to define words.	❑ Exercise 2—Word Line: Degrees of Meaning ❑ Expression of the Day	❑ Vocabulary Focus ❑ Use the Clues ❑ Expression of the Day
STEP 4 **Grammar and Usage** • Identify adjectives and nouns. • Identify past participles of regular and irregular verbs. • Identify phrases and clauses. • Use semicolons to write compound sentences. • Identify the four basic sentence types.	❑ Exercise 3: Identify It: Kinds of Sentences ❑ Exercise 4: Combine It: Compound Sentences With Semicolons	❑ Identify It: Adjectives in Poetry
STEP 5 **Listening and Reading Comprehension** • Interpret visual information. • Use context-based strategies to define words. • Identify thought and form in poetry. • Identify, understand, and answer questions that use different types of signal words.	❑ Instructional Text: "Circles in Nature"	❑ Take Note: "Circles in Nature"
STEP 6 **Speaking and Writing** • Use visual and text information to answer questions. • Write responses to sentences using signal words. • Organize information in a graphic organizer for a compare-and-contrast paragraph. • Write a compare-and-contrast paragraph and essay.	❑ Exercise 5: Answer It	❑ Exercise 1: Map It: Compare and Contrast

Self-Evaluation (5 is the highest)
  Effort = I produced my best work.
  Participation = I was actively involved in tasks.
  Independence = I worked on my own.
	Effort: 1 2 3 4 5
	Participation: 1 2 3 4 5
	Independence: 1 2 3 4 5
		Effort: 1 2 3 4 5
		Participation: 1 2 3 4 5
		Independence: 1 2 3 4 5

Teacher Evaluation	**Effort:** 1 2 3 4 5 **Participation:** 1 2 3 4 5 **Independence:** 1 2 3 4 5	**Effort:** 1 2 3 4 5 **Participation:** 1 2 3 4 5 **Independence:** 1 2 3 4 5

(T) = Template

Lesson 8 (Date:_____)	**Lesson 9** (Date:_____)	**Lesson 10** (Date:_____)
❏ Exercise 1: Listening for Word Parts: Suffixes		
❏ Exercise 2: Divide It: Morpheme Parts	❏ Drop It: Drop <u>e</u> Rule (T)	❏ Content Mastery: Spelling Posttest 2
❏ Exercise 3: Write It: Attributes ❏ Explore It: (T)	❏ Content Mastery: Attributes ❏ Content Mastery: Affixed Words	❏ Content Mastery: Using Student Performance ❏ Using a Dictionary: Word Origins ❏ Find It: Word Derivations ❏ Write a Mini-Dialog: Idioms
❏ Exercise 4: Combine It: Compound Sentences With Semicolons ❏ Exercise 5: Diagram It: Compound Sentences (T)	❏ Content Mastery	❏ Content Mastery: Using Student Performance
❏ Present It: Poetry	❏ Present It: Poetry	❏ "Instructional Text: "Circles in Nature" ❏ Exercise 1: Answer It: Multiple Choice
❏ Exercise 6: Write It: Compare-and-Contrast Essay	❏ Exercise 1: Write It: Images in a Poem	❏ Write It: Response to Poetry
Effort: 1 2 3 4 5 **Participation:** 1 2 3 4 5 **Independence:** 1 2 3 4 5	**Effort:** 1 2 3 4 5 **Participation:** 1 2 3 4 5 **Independence:** 1 2 3 4 5	**Effort:** 1 2 3 4 5 **Participation:** 1 2 3 4 5 **Independence:** 1 2 3 4 5
Effort: 1 2 3 4 5 **Participation:** 1 2 3 4 5 **Independence:** 1 2 3 4 5	**Effort:** 1 2 3 4 5 **Participation:** 1 2 3 4 5 **Independence:** 1 2 3 4 5	**Effort:** 1 2 3 4 5 **Participation:** 1 2 3 4 5 **Independence:** 1 2 3 4 5

Exercise 1 · Sort It: Two Sounds for s

▶ Read each word in the first column.

▶ Listen for the pronunciation of **s** at the end of each word.

▶ Mark an X under the heading that indicates the correct pronunciation of **s** in that word.

	/ s /	/ z /
Example: songs		
1. stirs		
2. forms		
3. thinks		
4. poems		
5. drifts		
6. shapes		
7. words		
8. thinks		
9. combines		
10. poets		

Exercise 2 · Discover It: Conditions for Soft c

▶ Write the rule for the sound-spelling pattern for soft **c**.

_____

_____

▶ Write two examples for each soft **c** pattern:

ce = / s /   ci = / s /   cy = / s /

_____   _____   _____

_____   _____   _____

Exercise 3 · Spelling Pretest 1

▶ Write the word your teacher repeats.

1. _____   6. _____   11. _____

2. _____   7. _____   12. _____

3. _____   8. _____   13. _____

4. _____   9. _____   14. _____

5. _____   10. _____   15. _____

Unit 25 · Lesson 1

Exercise 4 · Write It: Past and Past Participle Forms of Verbs

▶ Read each verb form that is written in the chart.

▶ Refer to the *Student Text*, page 9, for past participle forms of these verbs.

▶ Complete the grid with the correct past and past participle forms of each verb.

Present	Past	Past Participle
charge		
change		
win		
circle		
come		
hide		
trace		
force		
lie		
pay		

Exercise 5 · Identify It: Functions of Past Participles

▸ Do the first two examples with your teacher.

▸ Read each sentence and underline the past participle.

▸ Decide if the past participle is part of a verb phrase or is acting as an adjective.

▸ Copy the participle under the correct heading.

▸ Follow the same procedure to complete the activity independently.

Sentence	Past Participle That Is Part of a Verb Phrase	Past Participle That Is Acting as an Adjective
Example: The rhymed poem had a regular beat.		
Example: The teacher has taught her students many poems.		
1. The poet has used words sparingly.		
2. Poems have given happiness to many people.		
3. Stressed syllables give poems rhythm.		
4. The spoken words sound like music.		
5. The students have read many different poems.		

Unit 25 · Lesson 1

Exercise 6 · Phrase It

▶ Use the penciling strategy to "scoop" the phrases in each sentence.

▶ Read the sentences as you would speak them.

> ### based on "Stonehenge: Secrets of an Ancient Circle"
>
> This circle of large, upright stones in southern England is one of the world's great mysteries. It holds secrets of an ancient people. Over time, discoveries have been made about how it was built. Why it was built remains a puzzle.

Exercise 7 · Use the Clues

▶ Read the excerpt below.

▶ Reread the underlined word **picks**.

▶ Reread the text before **picks**.

▶ Circle the words that give clues to the meaning of **picks** in this excerpt.

▶ Write a definition for the word **picks** as it is used here.

▶ Write a sentence using the word **picks**.

> ### from "Stonehenge: Secrets of an Ancient Circle"
>
> Within the bank, fifty-six holes were dug. These holes may have held wooden posts. The digging was done using deer antler picks.

Define It:

picks: _____

Sentence: _____

_____

Exercise 8 · Rewrite It

▶ Read the following groups of sentences.

▶ Rewrite each group by combining sentences and adding a conjunction to contrast the ideas.

▶ Check that each sentence uses sentence signals—capital letters, commas, and end punctuation.

1. Some scientists believe that Stonehenge was used to study the moon. Other scientists do not believe this theory.

   _____

   _____

   _____

2. The ancient builders had no modern tools. They were still able to lift the huge stones.

   _____

   _____

3. Many have studied the circle. The ancient circle still remains a mystery.

   _____

   _____

4. The huge stones were incredibly heavy. They could be moved easily on rafts.

   _____

   _____

5. Stonehenge is built aligned to the midsummer sunrise. No one is sure whether ancient people used that particular sunrise to mark the ends and beginnings of years.

   _____

   _____

   _____

   _____

Exercise 1 · Discover It: Conditions for Soft *g*

▸ Write the rule for the **sound-spelling pattern** for soft **g**.

_____

_____

▸ Write two examples for each soft **g** pattern below.

<u>ge</u> = / *j* /   <u>gi</u> = / *j* /   <u>gy</u> = / *j* /

_____   _____   _____

_____   _____   _____

Exercise 2 · Sort It: Soft <u>c</u> and <u>g</u>

▶ Read each word in the **Word Bank**.

Word Bank

city	closed	regular	origin	energy
again	imagine	except	nice	count
fancy	gym	dance	age	huge

▶ Identify the sound for <u>c</u> or **g** in the word.

▶ Write the word under the correct heading.

<u>c</u> = / k /	<u>c</u> = / s /	<u>g</u> = / g /	<u>g</u> = / j /

Unit 25 · Lesson 2

Exercise 3 · Write It: Essential Words

▶ Review the **Essential Words** in the **Word Bank**.

Word Bank

shoe	surgeon	carriage	pigeon	machine	marriage

▶ Put the words in alphabetical order and write them on the lines.

▶ Write one sentence for each **Essential Word**.

▶ Check that each sentence uses sentence signals—correct capitalization, commas, and end punctuation.

1. _____

   _____

2. _____

   _____

3. _____

   _____

4. _____

   _____

5. _____

   _____

6. _____

   _____

Exercise 4 · Choose It: Affixed Words

▸ Read each sentence.

▸ Choose the correct word to complete the sentence and write it in the blank.

▸ Circle each prefix and suffix, then underline the root of the word chosen.

▸ Write the word and its definition on the line. Use your **Morphemes for Meaning Cards** and a dictionary as resources.

1. The student's story about accidentally dropping his homework into a swiftly flowing

   river was _____.
   a. credible   b. creditable   c. incredible

   _____
   word   definition

2. The gymnast was able to twist and turn her very _____ body in every direction.
   a. pliers   b. pliable   c. complex

   _____
   word   definition

3. The woman claimed to be a doctor, but she had not studied medicine and so was a/an

   _____.
   a. postal carrier   b. poster   c. impostor

   _____
   word   definition

4. After studying ecology, the student became a strong _____ of laws to protect the environment.
   a. poster   b. proponent   c. postpone

   _____
   word   definition

5. The directions to the playing field were very _____, and I got lost trying to get there.
   a. pliant   b. implicated   c. complicated

   _____
   word   definition

Unit 25 · Lesson 2

Exercise 5 · Choose It: Adjective Suffixes

▸ Read each sentence and the word choices below the sentence.

▸ Use what you know about adjective suffixes to choose the correct word.

▸ Copy the word into the blank and circle the suffix.

▸ Reread the sentence to make sure it makes sense.

1. The pillars at Stonehenge appear _____.
   a. destructing   b. indestruct   c. indestructible

2. The Stonehenge circle is _____ from a great distance.
   a. visit   b. visible   c. visiting

3. The old man had an _____ memory for poetry.
   a. incredibly   b. incredible   c. credit

4. The poem had a _____ theme.
   a. comprehending   b. comprehends   c. comprehensible

5. Julia learned about several _____ explanations for the arrangement of the stones at Stonehenge.
   a. possibly   b. possible   c. possessive

Exercise 6 · Identify It: Confusing Words

▶ Read each sentence and the word choices below the sentence.

▶ Use what you know about the pronunciation and function of each word to choose the correct word to complete the sentence.

▶ Copy the word into the blank.

▶ Use your dictionary as a resource if you need help.

1. At Stonehenge scientists have found that the smaller bluestones _____ the larger sandstone pillars.
   a. preceded   b. proceeded

2. The ancient builders _____ a way for the stones to be brought from far away.
   a. deviced   b. devised

3. It is not known whether the builders used a _____ to hoist the stones in place.
   a. device   b. devise

4. Today at Stonehenge, people can _____ along the avenue and into the circle.
   a. precede   b. proceed

5. Sometimes it is hard to accept _____.
   a. advice   b. advise

6. The teacher will _____ students on what electives to select.
   a. advice   b. advise

(continued)

Exercise 6 (continued) · Identify It: Confusing Verbs

7. Each year the students _____ a new plan for celebrating the end of exams.

   a. device   b. devise

8. At the ceremony, the student council president's speech will _____ the other speeches.

   a. precede   b. proceed

9. Inventors are creating new _____ all the time.

   a. devices   b. devises

10. You should _____ down Main Street, and then turn left onto Brook Street.

    a. precede   b. proceed

Exercise 7 · Using Visuals: Illustrations and Photographs

▸ Highlight all of the headings on the chart.

▸ Use information from **"Stonehenge: Secrets of an Ancient Circle"** to complete the chart.

▸ Write a title above the chart.

Title: _____

	Start Date	Types of Stones Added	Number of Circles	Major Achievement
Stage One	3100 BC		2	ditch digging, holes
Stage Two		bluestones		
Stage Three			7	giant sandstone pillars set up, with stones laid across the top

Exercise 8 · Answer It

▸ Use information from the text and the illustrations in **"Stonehenge: Secrets of an Ancient Circle"** to answer each of these questions. Write complete sentences.

▸ Circle whether the answer can be found in the text, an illustration, or both.

1. Stonehenge was built over a period of how many years?   text   illustrations   both

_____

_____

2. Where is Stonehenge located?   text   illustrations   both

_____

_____

3. What type of stones were added in the final stage?   text   illustrations   both

_____

_____

4. During what stage of construction was the path to the circle added?   text   illustrations   both

_____

_____

5. In the final stage, were there only five sets of pillars that had top stones?   text   illustrations   both

_____

_____

Exercise 1 · Listening for Sounds in Words

▶ Listen to each word that your teacher says.

▶ Use the **position-spelling pattern** for / *f* /, / *l* /, / *s* /, / *z* /, or / *ch* / to write each word.

1. _____   6. _____

2. _____   7. _____

3. _____   8. _____

4. _____   5. _____

5. _____   10. _____

▶ When do you use the **position-spelling patterns** -**ff**, -**ll**, -**ss**, -**zz**, and -**tch**?

_____

_____

_____

Exercise 2 · Discover It: Position-Spelling Pattern for -dge

▶ Write the rule for the position-spelling pattern for **-dge**.

_____

_____

▶ In numbers 1–5, listen to each word that your teacher says.

▶ Use the position-spelling pattern for / j / to write each word.

▶ In numbers 6–10, work with a partner to write five more words that follow the **-dge** pattern. (Hint: Think of a word that rhymes with each word in numbers 1–5).

1. _____   6. _____

2. _____   7. _____

3. _____   8. _____

4. _____   5. _____

5. _____   10. _____

Exercise 3 · Answer It

▶ Underline the signal word in each item.

▶ Write the answer in complete sentences.

1. Summarize the poem "The Life of a Man Is a Circle."

_____

_____

_____

_____

_____

_____

2. Hypothesize what types of things the author is talking about when he refers to "everything/Where power moves" in "The Life of a Man Is a Circle."

_____

_____

_____

_____

3. Contrast the form of "Outwitted" with the form of "The Life of a Man Is a Circle."

_____

_____

_____

_____

(continued)

Exercise 3 (continued) · **Answer It**

4. Compare the forms of the two Richard Wright haikus, "#745" and "#716."

_____

_____

_____

5. All of the Unit 25 poems involve circles. How can you distinguish the elements of thought and form in these poems?

_____

_____

_____

_____

_____

_____

_____

_____

_____

Exercise 1 · Sort It: Soft c and g

▸ Read each word in the **Word Bank**.

Word Bank

exercise	precede	hinge	principal	strategy
excite	legislate	reduce	charge	emerge
apologize	manage	policy	civilize	celebrate

▸ Underline the letters that indicate the position-spelling pattern for soft **c** or soft **g** in each word.

▸ Write the word under the correct heading for soft **c** or soft **g**.

/ s /	/ j /

▸ Think about the word **circle**. It has two **c**'s.
Why is the second **c** in **circle** not pronounced / s / ?

_____

_____

Exercise 2 · Identify It: Stressed Syllables and Rhyme

▸ Read the poem below with your teacher.

▸ Underline the stressed syllables you hear in each line.

▸ Count the number of stressed syllables in each line.

▸ Answer questions 1–5 below.

---

from "Circle Poems Take Many Forms"

"Outwitted" by Edwin Markham

He drew a circle that shut me out—

Heretic, a rebel, a thing to flout. (heretic, not heretic)

But Love and I had the wit to win:

We drew a circle that took him in!

---

1. How many stressed syllables do you hear in each line? _____

2. What is the pattern of the stressed syllables? _____

   _____

3. What is the pattern for words that rhyme in this poem? _____

   _____

4. Circle the two words that rhyme at the end of lines 1 and 2. Write four more words that rhyme with **out** and **flout**.

   _____   _____

   _____   _____

5. Circle the two words that rhyme at the end of lines 3 and 4. Write four more words that rhyme with **win** and **in**.

   _____   _____

   _____   _____

Exercise 3 · Match It: Affixed Words

▸ Listen to the directions and do the first example with your teacher.

▸ Read each remaining word in each set.

▸ Match each word to its definition.

▸ Use a dictionary and your knowledge of prefixes, roots, and suffixes as resources.

▸ Answer the questions on the next page.

Word	Definition
1. expressible	a. marked by force
2. objective	b. to put off till later
3. creative	c. being able to create
4. postpone	d. able to be expressed
5. forcible	e. based on facts, not influenced by personal feelings

Word	Definition
1. postscript	a. to put a date later than the actual date on a document
2. incredible	b. characterized by action
3. reproducible	c. hard to believe
4. active	d. a note added to a completed letter
5. postdate	e. able to be produced again

(continued)

Exercise 3 (continued) · Match It: Affixed Words

▶ Circle the answer to each of the following questions:

1. What word means the opposite of **incredible**?
   a. incredulous   b. credible   c. unbelievable

2. What word means the opposite of **postdate**?
   a. dating   b. date   c. predate

3. What word means the opposite of **active**?
   a. inactive   b. activate   c. action

▶ Write two sentences using two different words from this exercise.

1. _____

_____

2. _____

_____

Exercise 4 · Identify It: Phrase or Independent Clause

▸ Read each group of words.

▸ Decide if it is a phrase or an independent clause, and underline the correct answer.

▸ Rewrite each independent clause with correct capitalization and punctuation.

▸ Label the subject **S** and predicate **P**.

▸ Expand each phrase into an independent clause and write it on the line.

1. a poet chooses words carefully

    a. phrase   b. independent clause

_____

2. the word's last phonemes

    a. phrase   b. independent clause

_____

3. we wrote the poem in a circle

    a. phrase   b. independent clause

_____

4. haiku originated in Japan

    a. phrase   b. independent clause

_____

5. a closed form poem

    a. phrase   b. independent clause

_____

Exercise 5 · Combine It: Compound Sentences

▶ Read each pair of independent clauses.

▶ Decide whether to use **and**, **but**, or **or** to join the clauses.

▶ Write the compound sentence on the line.

▶ Add sentence signals—capital letters, commas, and end punctuation.

▶ Circle the conjunction used to join the independent clauses.

1. My father loves reading poetry.
My mother prefers to read science journals.

_____

_____

2. The class went to a play.
They also went backstage to meet the actors.

_____

_____

3. The student may start to write his poem tonight.
He may postpone his work until the weekend.

_____

_____

4. The poem had an organized rhythm.
It had a regular rhyme pattern, too.

_____

_____

5. The students could choose to read their poems aloud.
They could choose to post their poems on the bulletin board.

_____

_____

Lesson 5

Exercise 1 · Define It: Prefixes, Roots, and Suffixes

▶ Read each sentence.

▶ Use your knowledge of morphemes to select the meaning of the word part.

▶ Copy the underlined word and write its meaning on the line.

▶ Refer to your **Morphemes for Meaning Cards** and a dictionary as needed.

1. The teacher <u>impounded</u> the student's electronic game.
    What does the root of the underlined word mean?
    a. give   b. open   c. place   d. cover

    _____

2. Some poems have a very <u>complicated</u> rhythm.
    What does the root of the underlined word mean?
    a. pick   b. twist   c. easy   d. fast

    _____

3. The end of the mystery story was unexpected and <u>incredible</u>.
    What does the root of the underlined word mean?
    a. false   b. full   c. very   d. believe

    _____

4. The game was <u>postponed</u> till Monday.
    What does the prefix of the underlined word mean?
    a. before   b. after   c. never   d. always

    _____

5. The final math test had many very <u>complex</u> problems to solve.
    What does the root of the underlined word mean?
    a. twist   b. easy   c. put   d. few

    _____

Exercise 2 · Identify It: Kinds of Sentences

▶ Read each sentence.

▶ Think about its purpose and decide if the sentence is declarative, interrogative, imperative, or exclamatory.

▶ Select the correct answer.

▶ Place the correct punctuation mark at the end of the sentence.

1. Poetry is best read aloud
   a. declarative   b. interrogative   c. imperative   d. exclamatory

2. Learn this poem
   a. declarative   b. interrogative   c. imperative   d. exclamatory

3. Are you entering the poetry contest
   a. declarative   b. interrogative   c. imperative   d. exclamatory

4. Closed form poetry has a regular rhythm
   a. declarative   b. interrogative   c. imperative   d. exclamatory

5. What beautiful images this poem creates
   a. declarative   b. interrogative   c. imperative   d. exclamatory

Unit 25 • Lesson 5

Exercise 3 • Rewrite It: Sentences

▸ Read the paragraph below with your teacher.

▸ Underline any past participles that are used incorrectly and correct them.

▸ Revise each sentence using Stages 4, 5, and 6 of your **Masterpiece Sentence Cue Chart**.

▸ Proofread for spelling and punctuation, paying special attention to the past participles.

> The class had went to the poetry performance. Everyone had learn a poem.
>
> Some poems didn't have rhymes. I liked them.

_____

_____

_____

_____

_____

_____

Exercise 4 • Write It: Compare and Contrast Paragraph

▶ Follow the directions below to write sentences you can use in your compare and contrast paragraph.

1. Write an introductory sentence.	
2. Describe the topic of the first poem.	
3. Describe the topic of the second poem.	
4. Describe how the poems are alike.	
5. Describe how the poems are different.	
6. Write a concluding sentence.	

(continued)

Exercise 4 (continued) · Write It: Compare and Contrast

▶ Copy the sentences on the previous page into the lines provided below to complete your compare and contrast paragraph.

_____

_____

_____

_____

_____

_____

_____

_____

_____

Exercise 5 · Challenge Writing: Write a Haiku

The Task: Write a haiku poem that consists of three lines and has a 5-7-5 syllable pattern. Your haiku should convey a powerful feeling or a unique image that has to do with a time of year. It should also include a *kigo*, or season word. This word should indicate what season the haiku is set in, or what season you are thinking about as you write.

How to Plan a Haiku Poem

1. Pick a season to write about. Choose a *kigo* that communicates something about that season. It can be a word or a phrase. Here are some to get you started. Add your own on the lines below.

Spring	Summer	Fall	Winter
daffodils	buzzing insects	flying geese	short days
baseball	ice cream	full moon	icicles
tadpoles	lake shore	pile of leaves	glistening streets
_____	_____	_____	_____
_____	_____	_____	_____

2. Think about the feeling or mood you want to convey. Then think of an image that can help you convey that mood or feeling. Write your ideas below.

Example

feeling: loneliness _____ image: bare tree in winter _____

feeling: _____ image: _____

feeling: _____ image: _____

3. Write a draft of your haiku. Use a pencil so you can make changes later. Remember to keep each line short. Try to have five syllables in the first line, seven in the second, and five in the third.

lines   **syllables**

_____   _____

_____   _____

_____   _____

(continued)

Exercise 5 (continued) · Challenge Writing: Write a Haiku

4. Use this list to revise your haiku:

- Think carefully about your choice of words. Circle one word or phrase that could be improved.

- Think about whether your haiku communicates a powerful feeling or includes a unique image. Circle one word or phrase that could be changed to strengthen the feeling or image your haiku is communicating.

- Check to see that each line ends at a natural pause. If any lines do not end with a natural pause, circle the words you could change to fix this.

- Count syllables to make sure your haiku has the 5-7-5 syllable pattern. Circle any lines that do not fit the pattern.

Now write your revised haiku on the lines below.

_____

_____

_____

5. Read your poem to a partner. Ask him or her to describe the thoughts and feelings that the poem brings to mind. Then ask your partner to give you suggestions on how to make the poem better.

6. Use your partner's reactions and ideas to revise your haiku, if you like. Give your finished haiku a title. Then make a clean copy of it on another sheet of paper.

Exercise 1 · Spelling Pretest 2

▶ Write the word your teacher repeats.

1. _____   6. _____   11. _____

2. _____   7. _____   12. _____

3. _____   8. _____   13. _____

4. _____   9. _____   14. _____

5. _____   10. _____   15. _____

Unit 25 · Lesson 6

Exercise 2 · Word Line—Degrees of Meaning

▸ Study the words on the word line.

▸ Read the words in the **Word Bank**.

Word Bank

minute	big	enormous	gigantic	great	vast
average	miniscule	bulky	massive	giant	petite
miniature	middling	puny	median	little	microscopic

▸ Use a dictionary to define unfamiliar words.

▸ Write each word from the **Word Bank** under the word on the word line that has the same degree of meaning.

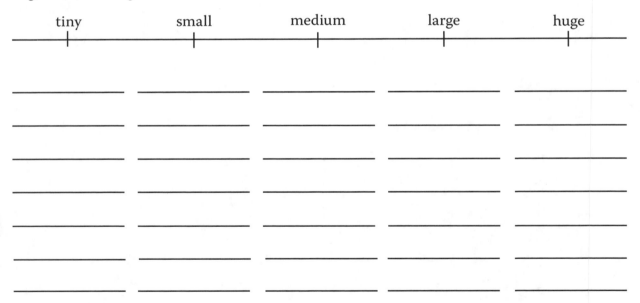

tiny	small	medium	large	huge

(continued)

Exercise 2 (continued) · Word Line—Degrees of Meaning

▶ Read each sentence below.

▶ Fill in the blank with the word from below the word line that makes the best sense in the sentence. There may be more than one correct answer.

1. Scientists use microscopes to study _____ living things.

2. Because I am fairly tall, I will need a _____ overcoat.

3. Stonehenge is a group of _____ blocks of stone arranged in a circle.

4. My sister is neither short nor tall; she is of _____ size.

5. A dancer who is small will need a _____ costume.

▶ Locate the word **huge** in the thesaurus.

▶ Select two more synonyms for **huge** and add them to the correct column above.

Unit 25 · Lesson 6

Exercise 3 · Identify It: Kinds of Sentences

▶ Read each sentence.

▶ Think about its purpose and decide if the sentence is declarative, interrogative, imperative, or exclamatory.

▶ Select the correct answer.

▶ Place the correct punctuation mark at the end of the sentence.

1. Experimental poetry can be difficult to understand

   a. declarative   b. interrogative   c. imperative   d. exclamatory

2. Is this poem about the earth, or about the sky

   a. declarative   b. interrogative   c. imperative   d. exclamatory

3. Take your time

   a. declarative   b. interrogative   c. imperative   d. exclamatory

4. What is your opinion of this poem

   a. declarative   b. interrogative   c. imperative   d. exclamatory

5. What a fantastic poem this is

   a. declarative   b. interrogative   c. imperative   d. exclamatory

Exercise 4 · Combine It: Compound Sentences With Semicolons

▸ Read each pair of sentences.

▸ Decide if they are independent clauses.

▸ Decide if the ideas in the two sentences are closely related.

▸ Rewrite the sentences to form a compound sentence using a semicolon.

1. Barbara Juster Esbensen wrote an experimental poem.
She combined different patterns in it.

_____

_____

2. Experimental poems generally sound like conversational talk.
They do not sound like closed form poetry.

_____

_____

3. Hearing the poem "Circles" is not enough.
It needs to be seen.

_____

_____

4. My friend likes poetry by E.E. Cummings.
I prefer poetry by Esbensen.

_____

_____

5. Read the three poems.
Choose the one you like best.

_____

_____

Exercise 1 · Map It: Compare and Contrast

▶ Use this chart to record information about the two poems in **"Circles in Nature."** Use the poems "who knows if the moon's" and "#745."

Poem #1			Poem #2		
Title: _____			Title: _____		
Author: _____			Author: _____		
Poem's Theme (stated as a universal truth)			**Poem's Theme** (stated as a universal truth)		
Yes	**No**		**Yes**	**No**	
❏	❏	Does it rhyme?	❏	❏	Does it rhyme?
❏	❏	Does it have verses?	❏	❏	Does it have verses?
❏	❏	Is there a pattern to the number of syllables in a line?	❏	❏	Is there a pattern to the number of syllables in a line?
❏	❏	Is it concrete?	❏	❏	Is it concrete?
❏	❏	Is it experimental?	❏	❏	Is it experimental?

Lesson 8

Exercise 1 · Listening for Word Parts: Suffixes

▸ Listen to each word your teacher says.

▸ Repeat the word.

▸ Mark **Yes** or **No** to tell if you hear a suffix.

▸ If you mark **Yes**, write the suffix.

	Do you hear a suffix on the word?		If **Yes**, what is the suffix?
	Yes	**No**	
1.			
2.			
3.			
4.			
5.			
6.			
7.			
8.			
9.			
10.			
11.			
12.			
13.			
14.			
15.			

Unit 25 · Lesson 8

Exercise 2 · Divide It: Morpheme Parts

▶ Read each word.

▶ Break the word into its morpheme parts.

▶ Write these word parts in the blank, being careful to spell each word part correctly.

1. invisible = _____

2. pliable = _____

3. explicit = _____

4. compound = _____

5. discredit = _____

6. credible = _____

7. excessive = _____

8. intercede = _____

9. deposit = _____

10. provide = _____

Exercise 3 · Write It: Attributes

▶ Complete the chart by filling in each blank with a word from the **Unit Vocabulary** list in the *Student Text*, page 6, that completes the attribute pair.

1. _____ :   seat

2. _____ :   jazz

3. candy: _____

4. parrot: _____

5. pumpkin: _____

▶ Write a sentence that demonstrates the relationship of each attribute pair.

1. _____

2. _____

3. _____

4. _____

5. _____

Unit 25 · Lesson 8

Exercise 4 · Combine It: Compound Sentences With Semicolons

▶ Complete this exercise with your teacher.

▶ Read each pair of sentences.

▶ Decide if they are independent clauses.

▶ Decide if the ideas in each sentence are closely related.

▶ Select the appropriate answer.

▶ Rewrite each pair of sentences with related ideas as a compound sentence, using a semicolon to join them.

▶ Leave each pair of sentences with unrelated ideas as two sentences.

1. Experimental poetry tries something new.
   The form and typography can look different.
   a. related   b. unrelated

   _____

   _____

2. Some poetry follows a defined pattern.
   We learn nursery rhymes when we are young.
   a. related   b. unrelated

   _____

   _____

(continued)

Exercise 4 (continued) · Combine It: Compound Sentences With Semicolons

3. Experimental poems are different in form.
   All poetry is meant to be heard.
   a. related   b. unrelated

   _____

   _____

4. Read some experimental poems.
   Note the differences from other forms.
   a. related   b. unrelated

   _____

   _____

5. My class intends to write some poems.
   We have already started one.
   a. related   b. unrelated

   _____

   _____

Exercise 5 · Diagram It: Compound Sentences

▶ Complete the first example with your teacher.

▶ Read each remaining sentence.

▶ Find the two complete sentences in the compound sentence and underline them.

▶ Circle the semicolon.

▶ Diagram the compound sentence.

1. Experimental poets write poetry; they use different forms.

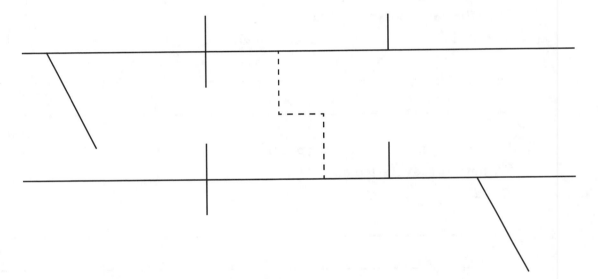

2. My friend likes poetry; I prefer prose.

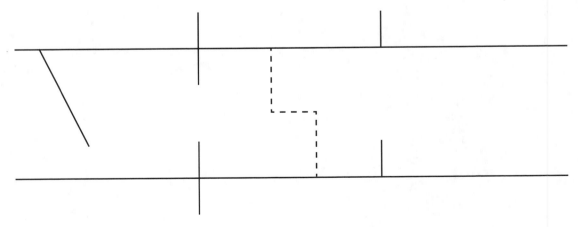

(continued)

Exercise 5 (continued) · Diagram It: Compound Sentences

3. The student read three poems; he learned his favorite.

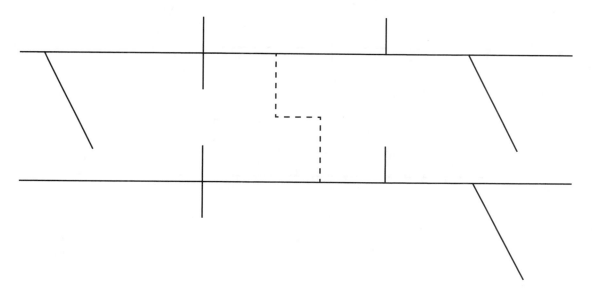

4. The student presented her poem; she was impressive.

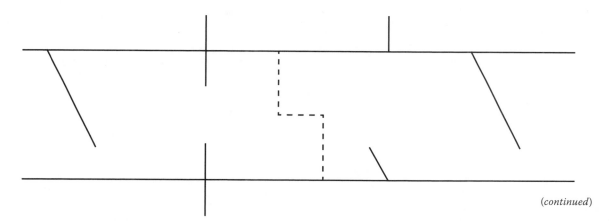

(continued)

Exercise 5 (continued) · Diagram It: Compound Sentences

5. Nursery rhymes are poetry; they have a defined form.

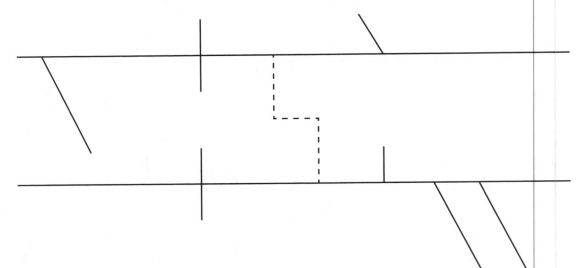

Exercise 6 · Write It: Compare and Contrast Essay

▸ Follow the directions below to write sentences you can use in your comparison essay.

Introduction

1. Write an introductory sentence.	
2. Write a sentence or two introducing the elements of the poems you will compare.	

Second Paragraph

1. Write an introductory sentence.	
2. Describe the topic of the first poem.	
3. Describe the topic of the second poem.	
4. Describe how the poems are alike.	
5. Describe how the poems are different.	
6. Write a concluding sentence.	

(continued)

Exercise 6 (continued) · Write It: Compare and Contrast Essay

Third Paragraph

1. Write an introductory sentence.	
2. Describe the form of the first poem.	
3. Describe the form of the second poem.	
4. Describe how the poems are alike.	
5. Describe how the poems are different.	
6. Write a concluding sentence.	

Conclusion

1. Write two sentences restating your introduction.	

(continued)

Exercise 6 (continued) · Write It: Compare and Contrast Essay

▶ Copy your sentences in the space provided below to build a full essay, or use a computer to word process a final draft of your essay.

_____

_____

_____

_____

_____

_____

_____

_____

_____

_____

_____

_____

_____

_____

_____

_____

_____

_____

_____

_____

_____

Exercise 1 • Write It: Images in a Poem

▶ Reread the poem "who knows if the moon's."

▶ Work with your teacher to identify the first image in the poem and complete the sentences about it.

▶ Work independently to identify three other images in the poem. Complete the sentences about each one.

First Image

1. The first image in this poem is _____

   _____

2. This image makes me feel _____

   _____

3. This image makes me imagine that _____

   _____

Second Image

4. The second image in this poem is _____

   _____

5. This image makes me feel _____

   _____

6. This image makes me imagine that _____

   _____

(continued)

Exercise 1 (continued) · Write It: Images in a Poem

Third Image

7. The third image in this poem is _____

_____

8. This image makes me feel _____

_____

9. This image makes me imagine that _____

_____

Fourth Image

10. The fourth image in this poem is _____

_____

11. This image makes me feel _____

_____

12. This image makes me imagine that _____

_____

Exercise 1 • Answer It: Multiple Choice

▸ Work independently to identify the correct answer to each question below.

▸ Circle or underline the correct answer.

▸ Discuss the correct answers with your teacher.

1. In the poem "who knows if the moon's" by E.E. Cummings, the moon is described as _____.

   A. a keen city

   B. pretty people

   C. a balloon

   D. love

2. What unusual thing do the flowers in the poem do at the end of "who knows if the moon's"?

   A. They grow up to the moon.

   B. They fly in a balloon.

   C. They water themselves.

   D. They pick themselves.

3. In the poem "circles" by Barbara Juster Esbensen, what are the rings of a tree called?

   A. a round calendar

   B. a compass-rose

   C. a medallion

   D. a disk

(continued)

Exercise 1 · (continued) Answer It: Multiple Choice

4. In the poem "circles," why do the musk oxen mentioned in the poem stand in a circle?

    A. to figure out which way is north

    B. to protect themselves from wolves

    C. to hide from danger

    D. to sleep on cold nights

5. In the poem "circles," the sun is called a _____.

    A. solid globe

    B. widening ring

    C. blazing disk

    D. circular bear

Check off the activities you complete with each lesson. Evaluate your accomplishments at the end of each lesson. Pay attention to teacher evaluations and comments.

	Unit Objectives	Lesson 1 (Date:_____)	Lesson 2 (Date:_____)
STEP 1	**Phonemic Awareness and Phonics** • Say the sounds for **oo** (/ōō/ and /o̅o̅/). • Say the sounds for **ue**, **ui**, and **ou**. • Write the sound-spelling correspondences for / ōō / and / o̅o̅ /.	❑ Discover It: Sounds for _oo_ ❑ Vowel Chart (T)	❑ Exercise 1: Sort It: Sounds for _oo_
STEP 2	**Word Recognition and Spelling** • Read and spell multisyllable words. • Read and spell the **Essential Words**: _four, lose, move, movement, movie, prove._ • Read and spell words with prefixes, suffixes, and roots.	❑ Exercise 1: Spelling Pretest 1 ❑ Memorize It	❑ Exercise 2: Write It: Essential Words ❑ Word Fluency 1
STEP 3	**Vocabulary and Morphology** • Identify antonyms and synonyms. • Identify and define noun and adjective suffixes. • Use the meanings of prefixes, suffixes, and roots to define words.	❑ Unit Vocabulary ❑ Explore It (T) ❑ Write It: Journal Entry	❑ Exercise 3: Choose It: Affixed Words ❑ Expression of the Day
STEP 4	**Grammar and Usage** • Identify subordinating conjunctions, participial phrases, and adverbial clauses. • Identify past participles of regular and irregular verbs. • Identify the four basic sentence types. • Use a colon to introduce a list.	❑ Exercise 2: Identify It: Functions of Participles ❑ Exercise 3: Identify It: Participial Phrases ❑ Exercise 4: Rewrite It: Coordinating Conjunctions	❑ Exercise 4: Identify It: Phrase or Independent Clause ❑ Exercise 5: Identify It: Subordinating Conjunctions ❑ Exercise 6: Identify It: Adverbial Clauses
STEP 5	**Listening and Reading Comprehension** • Interpret visual information. • Use context-based strategies to define words. • Identify setting. • Identify, understand, and answer questions that use different types of signal words.	❑ Independent Text: "Tsunamis" ❑ Exercise 5: Phrase It ❑ Exercise 6: Use the Clues	❑ Passage Fluency 1 ❑ Exercise 7: Using Visuals: Diagrams
STEP 6	**Speaking and Writing** • Use visuals and text to answer questions. • Write responses using signal words. • Organize information in a graphic organizer for a compare and contrast paragraph. • Write a compare-and-contrast paragraph and essay.	❑ Exercise 7: Rewrite It	❑ Exercise 8: Answer It
	Self-Evaluation (5 is the highest) **Effort** = I produced my best work. **Participation** = I was actively involved in tasks. **Independence** = I worked on my own.	**Effort:** 1 2 3 4 5 **Participation:** 1 2 3 4 5 **Independence:** 1 2 3 4 5	**Effort:** 1 2 3 4 5 **Participation:** 1 2 3 4 5 **Independence:** 1 2 3 4 5
	Teacher Evaluation	**Effort:** 1 2 3 4 5 **Participation:** 1 2 3 4 5 **Independence:** 1 2 3 4 5	**Effort:** 1 2 3 4 5 **Participation:** 1 2 3 4 5 **Independence:** 1 2 3 4 5

Lesson 3 (Date:_____)	**Lesson 4** (Date:_____)	**Lesson 5** (Date:_____)
❑ Discover It: Vowel Digraphs _ue_, _ui_, and _ou_ ❑ Vowel Chart (T)	❑ Exercise 1: Sort It: Spellings for _oo_	❑ Content Mastery: Vowel Digraphs
❑ Build It: Words With _oo_ ❑ Divide It: Compound Words ❑ Word Fluency 2	❑ Make a Mnemonic ❑ Present It: Mnemonics for Confusing Word Pairs	❑ Content Mastery: Spelling Posttest 1 ❑ Present It: Mnemonics for Confusing Word Pairs
❑ Vocabulary Focus ❑ Use the Clues ❑ Expression of the Day	❑ Exercise 2: Combine It: Prefix Plus Root ❑ Exercise 3: Match It: Affixed Words	❑ Exercise 1: Rewrite It: Affixed Words ❑ Exercise 2: Build It: Using Morphemes
❑ Identify It: Participles and Participial Phrases	❑ Exercise 4: Identify It: Independent and Dependent Clauses ❑ Masterpiece Sentences: Stage 2	❑ Exercise 3: Rewrite It: Sentences
❑ Instructional Text: "The House on Mango Street"	❑ Comprehend It ❑ Take Note: Details of a Setting	❑ Take Note: Details of a Setting
❑ Exercise 1: Answer It	❑ Map It: Compare and Contrast (T) ❑ Challenge Text: "Savion Glover: The Man Can Move"	❑ Exercise 4: Compare-and-Contrast Paragraph: Outline ❑ Write It: Compare-and-Contrast Paragraph ❑ Challenge Text: "Savion Glover: The Man Can Move" ❑ Exercise 5: Challenge Writing: Write an Autobiographical Essay

Effort:	1	2	3	4	5	**Effort:**	1	2	3	4	5	**Effort:**	1	2	3	4	5
Participation:	1	2	3	4	5	**Participation:**	1	2	3	4	5	**Participation:**	1	2	3	4	5
Independence:	1	2	3	4	5	**Independence:**	1	2	3	4	5	**Independence:**	1	2	3	4	5
Effort:	1	2	3	4	5	**Effort:**	1	2	3	4	5	**Effort:**	1	2	3	4	5
Participation:	1	2	3	4	5	**Participation:**	1	2	3	4	5	**Participation:**	1	2	3	4	5
Independence:	1	2	3	4	5	**Independence:**	1	2	3	4	5	**Independence:**	1	2	3	4	5

Check off the activities you complete with each lesson. Evaluate your accomplishments at the end of each lesson. Pay attention to teacher evaluations and comments.

Unit Objectives	Lesson 6 (Date:_____)	Lesson 7 (Date:_____)
STEP 1 **Phonemic Awareness and Phonics** • Say the sounds for <u>oo</u> (/ $\overline{oo}$ / and / $\overline{oo}$ /). • Say the sounds for <u>ue</u>, <u>ui</u>, and <u>ou</u>. • Write the sound-spelling correspondences for / $\overline{oo}$ / and / $\overline{oo}$ /.	❑ Content Mastery: Using Student Performance	❑ Exercise 1: Using a Dictionary
STEP 2 **Word Recognition and Spelling** • Read and spell multisyllable words. • Read and spell the **Essential Words**: *four, lose, move, movement, movie, prove*. • Read and spell words with prefixes, suffixes, and roots.	❑ Exercise 1: Spelling Pretest 2 ❑ Word Fluency 3	❑ Build It: Words With Suffixes ❑ Word Fluency 4
STEP 3 **Vocabulary and Morphology** • Identify antonyms and synonyms. • Identify and define noun and adjective suffixes. • Use the meanings of prefixes, suffixes, and roots to define words.	❑ Vocabulary Focus ❑ Use the Clues ❑ Expression of the Day	❑ Exercise 2: Word Line—Degrees of Meaning ❑ Expression of the Day
STEP 4 **Grammar and Usage** • Identify subordinating conjunctions, participial phrases, and adverbial clauses. • Identify past participles of regular and irregular verbs. • Identify the four basic sentence types. • Use a colon to introduce a list.	❑ Exercise 2: Identify It: Types of Sentences ❑ Exercise 3: Identify It: Colons Before a List ❑ Exercise 4: Identify It: Confusing Words	❑ Identify It: Adverbs, Adverbial Phrases, and Adverbial Clauses
STEP 5 **Listening and Reading Comprehension** • Interpret visual information. • Use context-based strategies to define words. • Identify setting. • Identify, understand, and answer questions that use different types of signal words.	❑ Instructional Text: "Rules of the Game" ❑ Comprehend It	❑ Comprehend It ❑ Take Note: Details of a Setting
STEP 6 **Speaking and Writing** • Use visuals and text to answer questions. • Write responses using signal words. • Organize information in a graphic organizer for a compare and contrast paragraph. • Write a compare-and-contrast paragraph and essay.	❑ Map It: Venn Diagram (T)	❑ Map It: Venn Diagram (T)

Self-Evaluation (5 is the highest)
  Effort = I produced my best work.
  Participation = I was actively involved in tasks.
  Independence = I worked on my own.
	Effort: 1 2 3 4 5
	Participation: 1 2 3 4 5
	Independence: 1 2 3 4 5
		Effort: 1 2 3 4 5
		Participation: 1 2 3 4 5
		Independence: 1 2 3 4 5

Teacher Evaluation	**Effort:** 1 2 3 4 5 **Participation:** 1 2 3 4 5 **Independence:** 1 2 3 4 5	**Effort:** 1 2 3 4 5 **Participation:** 1 2 3 4 5 **Independence:** 1 2 3 4 5

(T) = Template

Lesson 8 (Date:_____)	Lesson 9 (Date:_____)	Lesson 10 (Date:_____)
❑ Exercise 1: Listening for Word Parts: Prefixes and Suffixes	❑ Listening for Stressed Syllables	
❑ Exercise 2: Divide It: Morpheme Parts	❑ Discover It: Adding -ic	❑ Content Mastery: Spelling Posttest 2
❑ Exercise 3: Relate It: Synonyms and Antonyms ❑ Explore It (T)	❑ Content Mastery: Synonyms and Antonyms ❑ Content Mastery: Morphology	❑ Content Mastery: Using Student Performance ❑ Using a Dictionary: Word Origins ❑ Find It: Word Derivations ❑ Write a Mini-Dialog: Idioms
❑ Exercise 4: Combine It: Colons Used Before a List ❑ Exercise 5: Identify It: Confusing Verbs ❑ Exercise 6: Diagram It: Sentences With Adverbial Clauses (T)	❑ Content Mastery	❑ Content Mastery: Using Student Performance
❑ Comprehend It ❑ Exercise 7: Answer It: Multiple Choice	❑ Comprehend It ❑ Map It: Venn Diagram (T)	❑ Revise It: Compare-and-Contrast Essay
❑ Map It: Venn Diagram (T) ❑ Exercise 8: Write It: Shaping the Topic ❑ Exercise 9: Write It: Outline	❑ Write It: Compare-and-Contrast Essay ❑ Challenge Text: "The Women's Suffrage Movement"	❑ Revise It: Compare-and-Contrast Essay ❑ Challenge Text: "The Women's Suffrage Movement"
Effort: 1 2 3 4 5 **Participation:** 1 2 3 4 5 **Independence:** 1 2 3 4 5	**Effort:** 1 2 3 4 5 **Participation:** 1 2 3 4 5 **Independence:** 1 2 3 4 5	**Effort:** 1 2 3 4 5 **Participation:** 1 2 3 4 5 **Independence:** 1 2 3 4 5
Effort: 1 2 3 4 5 **Participation:** 1 2 3 4 5 **Independence:** 1 2 3 4 5	**Effort:** 1 2 3 4 5 **Participation:** 1 2 3 4 5 **Independence:** 1 2 3 4 5	**Effort:** 1 2 3 4 5 **Participation:** 1 2 3 4 5 **Independence:** 1 2 3 4 5

Exercise 1 · Spelling Pretest 1

▶ Write the word your teacher repeats.

1. _____   6. _____   11. _____

2. _____   7. _____   12. _____

3. _____   8. _____   13. _____

4. _____   9. _____   14. _____

5. _____   10. _____   15. _____

Exercise 2 · Identify It: Functions of Participles

▶ Do the first two examples with your teacher.

▶ Read each remaining sentence and underline the present participle or past participle in it.

▶ Decide if the participle is part of a verb phrase or is acting as an adjective.

▶ Copy the participle under the correct heading.

▶ Follow the same procedure to complete the activity independently.

▶ Answer the question at the end of the exercise.

Sentence	Participle Acting as a Verb	Participle Acting as an Adjective
Example 1 A tsunami has struck the coastline of South Asia.		
Example 2 The force of the wave was overwhelming.		
1. The devastating tsunami killed more than a hundred thousand people.		
2. In the past, earthquakes have shaken this region many times.		
3. Some local people had recognized the signs of danger.		
4. Those frightened people rushed for higher ground.		
5. Most families had not taken anything with them.		
6. They had lost their possessions, but they were alive and safe.		
7. A towering wave destroyed everything in its path.		
8. Many people are contributing to tsunami relief funds.		
9. Scientists are finding better ways to predict tsunamis.		
10. They will build better warning systems.		

(continued)

Exercise 2 (continued) · Identify It: Functions of Participles

Find the past participles used in the exercise on the previous page and copy them on the line below. Use your *Student Text*, page 46, to identify which of these past participles are irregular.

_____

Exercise 3 · Identify It: Participial Phrases

▸ Read each sentence.

▸ Identify and label the simple subject (**S**) and predicate (**V**).

▸ Identify the participial phrase and underline it.

▸ Draw an arrow from the participial phrase to the noun it modifies.

▸ Place a comma after the participial phrase if it is at the beginning of the sentence.

1. Racing across the ocean the tsunami threatened coastal cities.

2. A seagull sitting on a wave does not move forward.

3. A wave is water moving forward.

4. Driven by wind waves form in the ocean.

5. Waves formed by wind are not as powerful as tsunamis.

Exercise 4 · Rewrite It: Coordinating Conjunctions

▶ Read each pair of sentences.

▶ Choose a coordinating conjunction, **and**, **or**, or **but**, to combine the sentences into one sentence.

▶ Write the new sentence on the line.

▶ Circle the coordinating conjunction.

1. The seagull doesn't move forward.
   It moves up and down.

   _____

   _____

2. Tsunamis can be caused by undersea landslides.
   Tsunamis can be caused by undersea volcanic eruptions.

   _____

   _____

3. Special devices sense undersea earthquakes.
   Scientists use this information to send out tsunami warnings.

   _____

   _____

4. There is a tsunami warning system on some Pacific Ocean beaches.
   There has not been a warning system along the shores of the Indian Ocean until recently.

   _____

   _____

   _____

5. The tsunami hit the coastline of South Asia.
   It also struck the east coast of Africa.

   _____

   _____

Exercise 5 · Phrase It

▸ Use the penciling strategy to "scoop" the phrases in each sentence.

▸ Read the sentences as you would speak them.

from "Tsunamis"

On December 26, 2004, there was a huge 9.0 earthquake. It happened under the Indian Ocean. Soon after, a tsunami slammed into the coastlines of South Asia. It hit India and Africa. This deadly wave couldn't be stopped. Some people saw what was happening. They knew a tsunami was coming. They saved lives. Sadly, thousands of people also died.

Exercise 6 · Use the Clues

▶ Read the excerpt below.

▶ Reread the underlined word **plates**.

▶ Reread the text before and after the word.

▶ Circle the word **these** in the second sentence.

▶ Underline the words in the first sentence that **these** refers back to.

▶ Draw an arrow connecting the word **these** with the words it represents.

▶ Draw a box around the meaning signal that connects **plates** to the words that definite it.

▶ Write a definition for the word **plates** as it is used here.

▶ Answer the question that follows, using the information from the text.

---

from "Tsunamis"

The earth's crust is divided into several large pieces. These are called <u>plates</u>.

Plates make up the continents. They make up the seafloor.

Define It:

plates: _____

What two parts of Earth's crust are made up of **plates**?

_____

Unit 26 · Lesson 1

Exercise 7 · Rewrite It

▸ Read the following pairs of sentences.

▸ Look at each boldface noun in the first sentence.

▸ Look at each underlined phrase in the second sentence.

▸ Combine each pair of sentences by adding the underlined phrase beginning with a participle from the second sentence after the boldface noun in the first.

> **Example: Waves** blow across the water. They are <u>driven by the wind</u>.
> Waves driven by the wind blow across the water.

1. Imagine a **seagull**. The seagull is <u>sitting on a wave</u>.

   _____

   _____

2. The earth's crust is divided into **pieces**. These are <u>called plates</u>.

   _____

   _____

3. Along the coast there were massive **waves**. They were <u>caused by displaced water</u>.

   _____

   _____

4. Fishermen did not notice the **tsunami**. The tsunami was <u>speeding through the open sea</u>.

   _____

   _____

5. A **girl** saw signs of the tsunami and warned others. The girl was <u>walking on the beach</u>.

   _____

   _____

Exercise 1 · Sort It: Sounds for <u>oo</u>

▶ Read each word in the **Word Bank**.

Word Bank

shook	bloom	brook	good	food
moon	stood	proof	wood	troop
loose	hood	room	foot	smooth

▶ Mark each word with the correct diacritical mark, / ŏŏ /, as in **took**, or / ōō /, as in **moo**.

▶ Write the word under the correct heading, according to the sound for <u>oo</u>.

<u>oo</u> = / ŏŏ /	<u>oo</u> = / ōō /

▶ Find a word that has a homophone. What is it? _____

What is the homophone? _____

Exercise 2 · Write It: Essential Words

▸ Review the **Essential Words** in the **Word Bank**.

Word Bank

move	lose	four	prove	movement	movie

▸ Put the words in alphabetical order and write them on the lines.

▸ Write one sentence for each **Essential Word**.

▸ Check that each sentence uses sentence signals—correct capitalization, commas, and end punctuation.

1. _____

_____

2. _____

_____

3. _____

_____

4. _____

_____

5. _____

_____

6. _____

_____

Exercise 3 · Choose It: Affixed Words

▶ Read each sentence.

▶ Choose the correct word to complete the sentence, and write it in the blank.

▶ Circle each prefix and suffix of the word chosen, and underline its root or base word.

▶ Write the word and its definition on the line. Use your **Morphemes for Meaning Cards** and a dictionary as needed.

1. The people who survived the tsunami will always _____ the images of the wave in their memories.

   a. detain   b. pertain   c. retain

   _____
   word   definition

2. The _____ of the destruction caused by the tsunami had to be seen to be believed.

   a. total   b. totality   c. totaling

   _____
   word   definition

3. Scientists could not _____ and hold back the tsunami.

   a. intercept   b. deceptive   c. percept

   _____
   word   definition

4. The movement of a tsunami is barely _____ in the deep ocean.

   a. deceptive   b. perceptible   c. except

   _____
   word   definition

5. The tsunami disaster generated much _____ and information about the countries affected.

   a. public   b. publish   c. publicity

   _____
   word   definition

Unit 26 · Lesson 2

Exercise 4 · Identify It: Phrase or Independent Clause

▶ Read each group of words.

▶ Determine if the group of words has a subject and predicate. Label the subject **S** and predicate **P**.

▶ Decide if it is a phrase or an independent clause, and circle the answer.

▶ Rewrite each independent clause with correct capitalization and punctuation.

▶ Expand each phrase into an independent clause by adding necessary parts. Ask yourself **what did it?** and **what did it do?** to help.

▶ Write the independent clause on the line. Check for capital letters and punctuation.

1. the house on Mango Street is small and red

    a. phrase   b. independent clause

_____

2. a house with peeling paint

    a. phrase   b. independent clause

_____

3. one day I will own my own house

    a. phrase   b. independent clause

_____

4. the house will be on a hill

    a. phrase   b. independent clause

_____

5. then out of nowhere

    a. phrase   b. independent clause

_____

Exercise 5 · Identify It: Subordinating Conjunctions

▶ Read each sentence.

▶ Identify the subordinating conjunction and circle it.

▶ Underline the clause that follows the subordinating conjunction.

▶ Circle the question the dependent clause answers.

1. The family bought the house on Mango Street because they could afford it.
   a. how?   b. when?   c. where?   d. why?   e. under what condition?

2. Our family was happy, although we were poor.
   a. how?   b. when?   c. where?   d. why?   e. under what condition?

3. My mother sings while she is cooking oatmeal.
   a. how?   b. when?   c. where?   d. why?   e. under what condition?

4. The family would stay poor unless they won the lottery.
   a. how?   b. when?   c. where?   d. why?   e. under what condition?

5. The girl will get new clothes if her family has some extra money.
   a. how?   b. when?   c. where?   d. why?   e. under what condition?

Exercise 6 · Identify It: Adverbial Clauses

▸ Read each sentence with your teacher.

▸ Identify the subordinating conjunction and circle it.

▸ Underline the clause that comes after the subordinating conjunction.

▸ Decide which question the adverbial clause answers and circle it.

1. The girl stares out the window while she does her homework.
   a. how?   b. when?   c. where?   d. why?   e. under what condition?

2. Although I love my sister, she is not my best friend.
   a. how?   b. when?   c. where?   d. why?   e. under what condition?

3. The family lived at the edge of town because the houses cost less there.
   a. how?   b. when?   c. where?   d. why?   e. under what condition?

4. The boy would not be happy unless his father came to the game.
   a. how?   b. when?   c. where?   d. why?   e. under what condition?

5. We will succeed if we all work hard.
   a. how?   b. when?   c. where?   d. why?   e. under what condition?

Exercise 7 · Using Visuals: Diagrams

▶ Read the titles of the two charts below.

▶ Use information from **"Tsunamis"** in the *Student Text*, pages 54–55, to complete the charts.

The Beginnings of a Tsunami

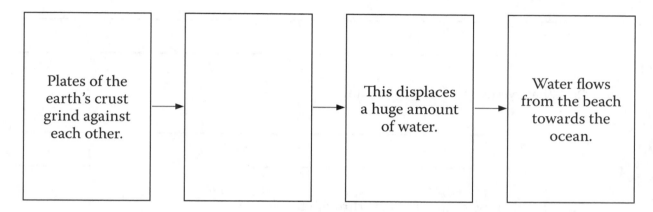

How Tsunami Waves Change in Size and Shape

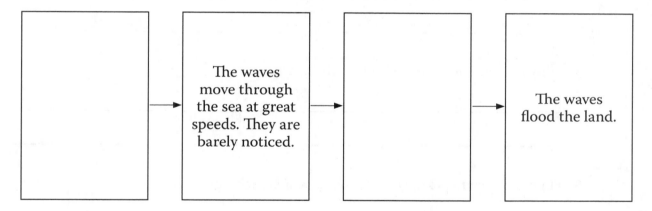

Unit 26 · Lesson 2

Exercise 8 · Answer It

▶ Use information from the text and the diagram in **"Tsunamis"** to answer each of these questions. Write complete sentences.

1. What parts of the world did the tsunami hit on December 26, 2004?

   _____

   _____

2. What events can cause a tsunami?

   _____

   _____

3. What do waves move forward through the water?

   _____

   _____

4. Why is a tsunami hard to spot on the open sea?

   _____

   _____

5. How can scientists know if a tsunami is approaching?

   _____

   _____

Exercise 1 · Answer It

▶ Underline the signal word in the question.

▶ Write the answer in complete sentences.

1. Make a generalization about Esperanza's relationship with her sister Nenny.

_____

_____

_____

_____

2. In **"Meme Ortiz,"** the narrator describes her house as looking like a cat with "its feet tucked under." Describe the image that is created by that comparison.

_____

_____

_____

_____

_____

_____

3. In **"Alicia and I Talking on Edna's Steps,"** Alicia says to Esperanza, "Like it or not, you are Mango Street, and one day you'll come back, too." Paraphrase Alicia's words.

_____

_____

_____

_____

(continued)

Exercise 1 (continued) · **Answer It**

4. In **"Mango Says Goodbye Sometimes,"** the narrator announces, "I am going to tell you a story about a girl who didn't want to belong." Explain the meaning of that line.

_____

_____

_____

_____

_____

_____

_____

5. Summarize how writing helps Esperanza feel better about where she comes from.

_____

_____

_____

_____

_____

_____

Exercise 1 · Sort It: Spellings for / o͞o /

▶ Read each word in the **Word Bank**.

Word Bank

troupe	bruise	youth	due	choose
scoop	sue	cruise	route	suit
spool	blue	roof	clue	wound

▶ Underline the letters that represent the / o͞o / sound in each word.

▶ Sort the words according to their sound-spelling correspondence.

▶ Read each column with a partner.

oo	ue	ui	ou

▶ Six of the words are homophones. Write at least two of them.

_____   _____

▶ Three of the words have two different pronunciations: **route**, **wound**, and **roof**.
  Use a dictionary to write the pronunciation variations for each word.

route = _____

wound = _____

roof = _____

▶ The Unit 26 target word is **movement**. Write the vowel sound for the first syllable. _____

Exercise 2 · Combine It: Prefix Plus Root

▶ Read each prefix and root or base word.

▶ Underline the last letter of the prefix.

▶ Underline the first letter of the root or base word and write it on the line.

▶ Decide if the last letter of the prefix should change to the first letter of the root or base word.

▶ Combine the prefix and root or base word and write the whole word on the line.

	Prefix		Root or Base Word	First Letter of Root or Base Word	Whole Word
1.	ob-	+	pose		
2.	ob-	+	fer		
3.	ob-	+	tain		
4.	ob-	+	serve		
5.	ob-	+	press		
6.	ob-	+	lige		
7.	ob-	+	cupy		
8.	ob-	+	solete		
9.	ob-	+	ponent		
10.	ob-	+	clude		

Exercise 3 · Match It: Affixed Words

▸ Read each word.

▸ Match the word to its definition.

▸ Use your knowledge of prefixes, roots, and suffixes, your **Morphemes for Meaning Cards**, and a dictionary as needed.

▸ Answer the questions at the bottom.

1. containment
2. opposing
3. prehistoric
4. retentive
5. discontinue

a. pertaining to the time before recorded history
b. characterized by holding back
c. the state of holding within
d. not able to go on with an action or condition
e. to be against or in conflict with

▸ Circle the answers to the following questions:

1. What word means the opposite of **discontinue?**
   a. discern   b. continue   c. contain

2. What does the root in **contain** mean?
   a. give   b. twist   c. hold

3. What does the prefix in the word **prehistoric** mean?
   a. before   b. after   c. through

▸ Write the answers to the following questions.

1. Write each morpheme in the word **containment**.

   _____

2. What does the suffix in the word **prehistoric** mean?

   _____

Exercise 4 · Identify It: Independent and Dependent Clauses

▸ Read each group of words and decide if they express a complete thought.

▸ Underline **independent clause** if the words express a complete thought.

▸ Rewrite each of the independent clauses using correct capitalization, commas, and end punctuation.

▸ Underline the answer **dependent clause** if the words do not express a complete thought.

▸ Circle the subordinating conjunction and expand the dependent clause into a complete sentence by adding an independent clause.

1. our home has two bedrooms

   a. independent clause   b. dependent clause

   _____

2. the stairs in our house are narrow

   a. independent clause   b. dependent clause

   _____

3. because we were moving constantly

   a. independent clause   b. dependent clause

   _____

   _____

4. if the family arrives before noon

   a. independent clause   b. dependent clause

   _____

   _____

5. on some evenings my sister and I sit in front of the fireplace

   a. independent clause   b. dependent clause

   _____

   _____

Lesson 5

Exercise 1 · Rewrite It: Affixed Words

▶ Read the words in the **Word Bank**.

Word Bank

legality	tenant	contained	continue
opposed	captive	symbolic	

▶ Read each sentence.

▶ Replace the underlined phrase in the sentence with a word from the **Word Bank**.

▶ Use your **Morphemes for Meaning Cards** and a dictionary as references as needed.

▶ Reread each sentence to check your work.

Sentence With Underlined Phrase:	Sentence With Phrase Changed to a Single Word:
1. The garden <u>held within</u> only weeds.	The garden _____ only weeds.
2. The other students were <u>placed against</u> my plan.	The other students were _____ to my plan.
3. The boarded up laundromat was <u>pertaining to a symbol</u> of the state of the neighborhood.	The boarded up laundromat was _____ of the state of the neighborhood.
4. The <u>state of being legal</u> of the house sale is now unclear.	The _____ of the house sale is now unclear.
5. The girl felt she was <u>in a state of being held</u> in the house.	The girl felt she was a _____ in the house.

Exercise 2 · Build It: Using Morphemes

▶ Read the directions for each example.

▶ Build a word that matches the definition, using the given morphemes.

▶ Write the word on the line.
Hint: Remember to assimilate the prefix when spelling the word.

1. Use two of these morphemes to build a word meaning "to delay or hold back."

con-	de-	tain	-ing	-ed

_____

2. Use three of these morphemes to build a word meaning "not able to hold."

ob-	un-	ten	-ive	-able

_____

3. Use three of these morphemes to build a word meaning "placed against."

ob-	dis-	pos	-ing	-ed

_____

4. Use two of these morphemes to build a word meaning "hold within."

pre-	con-	tain	-ive	-ed

_____

5. Use three of these morphemes to build a word meaning "placed in."

in-	de-	pound	-or	-ed

_____

Exercise 3 · Rewrite It: Sentences

▶ Read the paragraph with your teacher.

▶ Underline each past participle that is used incorrectly, and write the correct form above it.

▶ Revise each sentence using the stages on the **Masterpiece Sentence Cue Chart**.

▶ Proofread for spelling and punctuation, paying special attention to the past participles.

> Her family had choosed a new house. She had tooken a look at it. She was not happy. Because she wanted a bigger house. She has to live there. She will move one day.

_____

_____

_____

_____

_____

_____

_____

Unit 26 · Lesson 5

Exercise 4 · Compare-and-Contrast Paragraph: Outline

▸ To write a good paragraph, you should first create an outline.

▸ Use the chart below to plan how you will organize your ideas for a paragraph comparing and contrasting the two houses in **"The House on Mango Street."**

1. Introductory sentence		
2. Describe		
3. Describe		
4. Describe		
5. Describe		
6. Concluding sentence		

Exercise 5 · Challenge Writing: Write an Autobiographical Essay

The Task: Write an autobiographical essay about an important experience or event in your own life. Choose one of the following ideas, or think of your own:

• an important transition, such as a move to a new city or school

• a time when you learned that you could do something you thought you could not do

• an incident in which your feelings toward another person changed for the better

Talk with a partner about the experience. Explain what happened and why the experience was important. Next, fill out the **Story Map template** with basic information about where and when the experience took place. Then complete the **Planning Guide** below.

Planning Guide

• Write the important experience or event on the line below.

• In the first column of the charts on the following pages, write the main events that took place at the beginning, middle, and end of the experience.

• In the second column, write what you thought and felt as the experience unfolded.

• In the third column, include some dialog that took place during each part of the experience. If you do not remember the exact words that were said, make up the dialog based on what you do remember.

Experience: _____

(continued)

Exercise 5 (continued) · Challenge Writing: Write an Autobiographical Essay

Events	How I Felt	Dialog
Beginning	How did I feel as the experience began to unfold?	
Answer the following questions to tell how the event began. Use sequence words such as **last February** or **one year ago** to show when the event took place.		
1. Where and when did this experience take place?		
2. Who else was involved?		
3. What was the first event in the sequence?		

(continued)

Exercise 5 (continued) · Challenge Writing: Write an Autobiographical Essay

Events	How I Felt	Dialog
Middle Write the main events. Use transition words to help readers follow the sequence.	How did I feel as the events were unfolding?	

(continued)

Exercise 5 (continued) · Challenge Writing: Write an Autobiographical Essay

Events	How I Felt	Dialog
End Write how the event ended. Use transition words to make the sequence of events clear. **1.** How did the experience end? _____ _____ _____ _____ _____ _____ _____ **2.** Is this the ending I predicted? Why or why not? _____ _____ _____ _____ _____ _____ _____	**1.** How did I feel at the end of the experience? _____ _____ _____ _____ _____ _____ _____ _____ _____ **2.** What did I learn as a result of the experience? _____ _____ _____ _____ _____ _____ _____ _____	

Exercise 1 · Spelling Pretest 2

▶ Write the word your teacher repeats.

1. _____   6. _____   11. _____

2. _____   7. _____   12. _____

3. _____   8. _____   13. _____

4. _____   9. _____   14. _____

5. _____   10. _____   15. _____

Unit 26 · Lesson 6

Exercise 2 · Identify It: Types of Sentences

▶ Read each sentence.

▶ Think about its purpose and decide if the sentence is declarative, interrogative, imperative, or exclamatory.

▶ Underline the correct answer.

▶ Place the correct punctuation at the end of the sentence.

1. Who said this word
   a. declarative   b. interrogative   c. imperative   d. exclamatory

2. My brothers have keen ears
   a. declarative   b. interrogative   c. imperative   d. exclamatory

3. What a great victory
   a. declarative   b. interrogative   c. imperative   d. exclamatory

4. The missionary ladies put together the gifts
   a. declarative   b. interrogative   c. imperative   d. exclamatory

5. Why can't the pawns move more steps
   a. declarative   b. interrogative   c. imperative   d. exclamatory

Exercise 3 · Identify It: Colons Before a List

▶ Read each sentence.

▶ Identify the list of items and underline it.

▶ Confirm that the first part of the sentence is an independent clause by writing an **S** over the subject and **P** over the predicate.

▶ Place the colon in the correct position.

1. At the party the children received the following presents a chess set, a large coloring book, a vial of lavender water, and a tin globe.

2. Vincent chose the flavors of the candy wild cherry, peppermint, and strawberry.

3. A chess set has sixteen pieces for each side one king, one queen, two bishops, two knights, two castles, and eight pawns.

4. Several good smells come from the bakery downstairs red beans, sesame balls, and curried chicken.

5. Waverly had many sponsors a bakery, a florist, and an engraver.

Unit 26 · Lesson 6

Exercise 4 · Identify It: Confusing Words

▸ Read each sentence and the word choices below the sentence.

▸ Use what you know about the meaning and function of each word to choose the correct word.

▸ Refer to the *Student Text*, page 46, if necessary.

▸ Copy the word into the blank.

1. Waverly's mother had _____ to the vegetable market.
   a. gone   b. went

2. The baby _____ on the floor.
   a. lies   b. lays

3. Yesterday, Waverly _____ all the chess pieces on the board.
   a. laid   b. lay

4. Last summer my brother _____ in a hammock and slept.
   a. laid   b. lay

5. Waverly _____ to many chess tournaments.
   a. gone   b. went

Exercise 1 · Using a Dictionary

▶ Turn to the **Vocabulary** section in the back of the *Student Text*.

▶ Locate each word and its diacritical markings.

▶ Write the diacritical markings for the word on the line next to the word.

▶ Use the markings to read the word aloud.

Word	Pronunciation (diacritical markings)
1. ache	_____
2. attic	_____
3. tactics	_____
4. retort	_____
5. humility	_____

▶ Bonus: Use a classroom or personal dictionary to find the diacritical markings of these words.

6. acoustic	_____
7. theorize	_____
8. recruit	_____
9. joule	_____
10. bivouac	_____

Unit 26 · Lesson 7

Exercise 2 · Word Line—Degrees of Meaning

▸ Study the words on the word line.

▸ Discuss the meanings of the words **start**, **continue**, and **finish** with your teacher.

▸ Read the words in the **Word Bank**.

Word Bank

maintain	end	begin	pursue	complete
terminate	commence	open	enter	resume

▸ Use a dictionary to define unfamiliar words.

▸ Sort and record each word under the word on the word line that has the same degree of meaning.

start   **continue**   **finish**

_____   _____   _____

_____   _____   _____

_____   _____   _____

_____   _____   _____

_____   _____   _____

(continued)

Exercise 2 (continued) · Word Line—Degrees of Meaning

▶ Read each pair of sentences below.

▶ Fill in each blank with the word from below the word line that makes the best sense according to the context of the sentence. Words may be used more than once.

1. It is important to understand the rules before you _____ playing a game. The game will _____ when the first person guesses all the clues.

2. A new school year will _____ after Labor Day. School will _____ after the Thanksgiving holidays.

3. He is going to _____ a degree in marketing. After he graduates, he will _____ working for a living.

4. _____ the track through the gate. _____ your warm-up before the meet begins.

5. Try to _____ a constant speed for two more minutes. Then it will be time for you to _____ your workout and go to the locker room.

Exercise 1 · Listening for Word Parts: Prefixes and Suffixes

▶ Listen to each word your teacher says.

▶ Repeat the word.

▶ Mark **Yes** or **No** to tell if you hear a prefix or a suffix.

▶ If yes, write the prefix or suffix you hear under the correct heading.

	Do you hear a prefix or suffix on the word?		If **Yes**, write the prefix or suffix.	
	Yes	No	Prefix	Suffix
1.				
2.				
3.				
4.				
5.				
6.				
7.				
8.				
9.				
10.				

(continued)

Exercise 1 (continued) · Listening for Word Parts: Prefixes and Suffixes

	Do you hear a prefix or suffix on the word?		If **Yes**, write the prefix or suffix.	
	Yes	No	Prefix	Suffix
11.				
12.				
13.				
14.				
15.				
16.				
17.				
18.				
19.				
20.				

Exercise 2 · Divide It: Morpheme Parts

▸ Read each word. Think about its morphemes—its meaning units.

▸ Break each word into its morpheme parts.

▸ Write the word parts in the blank. Put plus signs between morphemes. Be careful to spell each word correctly.

1. observer = _____

2. discontent = _____

3. acidity = _____

4. poetic = _____

5. finality = _____

6. retainer = _____

7. object = _____

8. deceitful = _____

9. classic = _____

10. concept = _____

Exercise 3 · Relate It: Synonyms and Antonyms

▸ Read the words in the **Word Bank**.

Word Bank

reject	acceptable	select	activate	remain
accurate	unpleasant	top	false	base

▸ Choose a synonym and antonym for each unit word in the chart.

▸ Complete the chart.

Unit Word	Synonym	Antonym
1. foot		
2. move		
3. good		
4. choose		
5. true		

Exercise 4 · Combine It: Colons Used Before a List

▶ Read each independent clause and list.

▶ Write a new sentence in which you combine the clause and the list, using a colon.

▶ Circle the colon.

▶ Underline the conjunction before the last item in the list.

▶ Check the sentence for correct capitalization, commas, and end punctuation.

1. **Independent clause:** On her way home, Waverly saw many places.
   List: the alley, the shops, the tourists, the playground.

   _____

   _____

2. **Independent clause:** The girl still had some chess pieces on the board.
   List: the king, the queen, two pawns.

   _____

   _____

3. **Independent clause:** Waverly dreamed of several different images.
   List: a chessboard, her mother, a cliff.

   _____

   _____

4. **Independent clause:** Waverly learned necessary chess tactics.
   List: attack, defense, foresight.

   _____

   _____

5. **Independent clause:** For each competition, Waverly wore the same outfit.
   List: a dress, barrettes, shoes.

   _____

   _____

Exercise 5 · Identify It: Confusing Words

▸ Read each sentence and the word choices below the sentence.

▸ Use what you know about the function of each word to choose the correct word to complete the sentence.

▸ Copy the word into the blank.

1. The tourists had _____ into the Chinese restaurant.
   a. gone   b. went

2. At night Waverly _____ on her bed and planned chess strategies.
   a. lie   b. lay

3. Her mother is _____ down and taking a rest.
   a. lying   b. laying

4. The children _____ to a Christmas party.
   a. gone   b. went

5. Vincent always _____ the chess pieces on the table carefully.
   a. lies   b. lays

Exercise 6 · Diagram It: Sentences With Adverbial Clauses

▶ Do the first item with your teacher.

▶ Read each remaining sentence.

▶ Circle the subordinating conjunction.

▶ Find the dependent clause and underline it.

▶ Diagram the sentence.

1. Waverly improved her chess game because she studied the tactics.

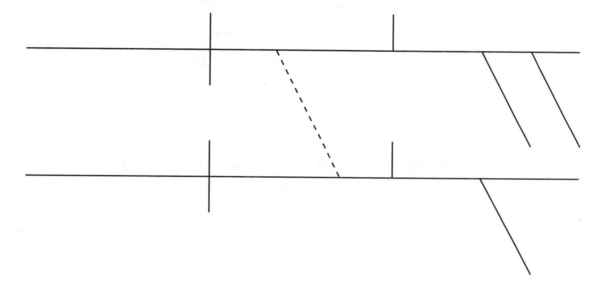

2. She plays chess on weekends if she has a competition.

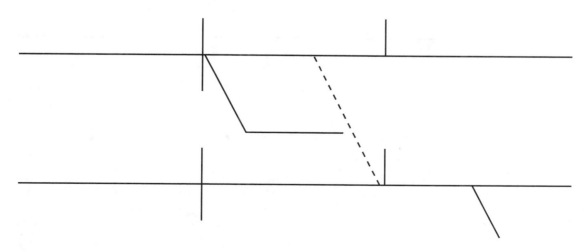

(continued)

Exercise 6 (continued) · Diagram It: Sentences With Adverbial Clauses

3. The competition will be cancelled unless more competitors enroll.

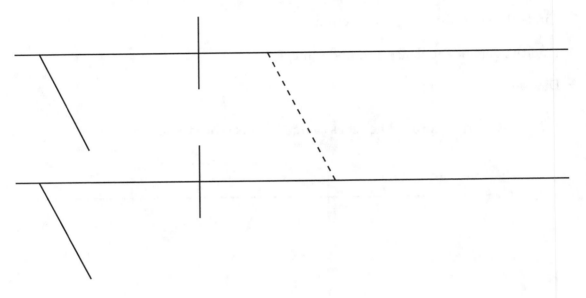

4. Waverly's mother cooked while she monitored Waverly's practice.

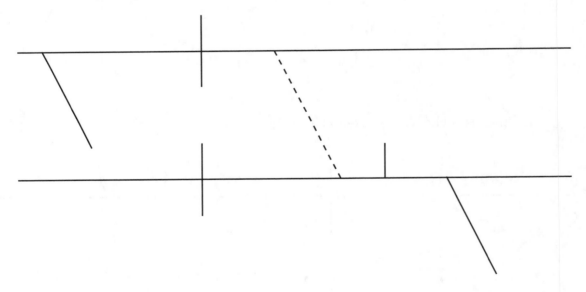

(continued)

5. Although she played well, Waverly lost the match.

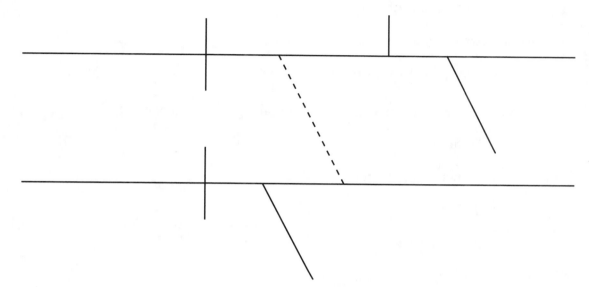

Unit 26 · Lesson 8

Exercise 7 · Answer It: Multiple Choice

▶ Read each question and its answer choices.

▶ Turn to **Text Connection 4**, **"Rules of the Game,"** in the *Interactive Text*, pages C22–C37, if you need to check story information.

▶ Underline the correct answer.

▶ Discuss the answers with your teacher.

1. Who teaches Waverly to become a really good chess player?

   A. her mother

   B. her brother Vincent

   C. Lau Po

   D. her father

2. What does the name Meimei mean?

   A. little sister

   B. older sister

   C. chess player

   D. invisible strength

3. What does it mean to "rise above one's circumstances"?

   A. to become proud and boastful

   B. to acquire a better position in life than one had as a child

   C. to become a chess champion

   D. to immigrate to a foreign country

(continued)

4. According to the story, Waverly's mother is proud when Waverly wins but tells everyone it was due to luck. Why does she say this?

   A. because in Chinese custom it is rude to brag about the achievements of oneself or one's family

   B. because she believes that how her daughter plays is only due to good luck or bad luck, not to skill

   C. because her mother doesn't really believe that Waverly won fairly

   D. because her mother believes that Waverly could not play as well in another game

5. Waverly can best be described as _____.

   A. smart and observant

   B. selfish and cruel

   C. careless and reckless

   D. anxious and shy

Unit 26 · Lesson 8

Exercise 8 · Write It: Shaping the Topic

▶ To write your four-paragraph compare-and-contrast essay, you will need to choose two aspects of the neighborhoods in **"The House on Mango Street"** and **"Rules of the Game"** that you would like to compare and contrast. Here are some options:

1. The physical aspects of the neighborhood

2. The people and the sense of community in the neighborhood

3. The activities in the neighborhood (for example, children playing or store owners selling things)

4. The narrator's attitude toward her neighborhood

▶ Choose two of the topics above, or identify another topic relating to the neighborhoods.

▶ Record your choices below.

In my essay, I will compare and contrast two aspects of the neighborhoods. In one of the middle paragraphs, I will focus on _____. In the other middle paragraph, I will focus on _____.

Exercise 9 · Write It: Outline

▶ Creating an outline can help you write a good essay. Use the chart below to plan how you will organize your ideas for an essay comparing the neighborhoods in **"The House on Mango Street"** and **"Rules of the Game."**

Introduction

1.	
2.	

Second Paragraph

1. Introductory sentence	
2. Describe	
3. Describe	
4. Describe	
5. Describe	
6. Concluding sentence	

(continued)

Third Paragraph

1. Introductory sentence	
2. Describe	
3. Describe	
4. Describe	
5. Describe	
6. Concluding sentence	

Conclusion

1.
2.

Check off the activities you complete with each lesson. Evaluate your accomplishments at the end of each lesson. Pay attention to teacher evaluations and comments.

Unit Objectives	Lesson 1 (Date:_____)	Lesson 2 (Date:_____)
STEP 1 **Phonemic Awareness and Phonics** • Say the sounds for the vowel digraphs: **ui** (/ ī / as in **guide**), **ou** (/ ō / as in **soul**), **ey** (/ ā / as in **they**), **ei** (/ ē / as in **either** and / ā / as in **vein**). • Write the letters for the sounds / ā /, / ē /, / ī /, and / ō / using vowel digraphs.	❏ Discover It: Vowel Digraphs <u>ei</u>, <u>ey</u>, <u>ou</u>, and <u>ui</u> ❏ Vowel Chart (T)	❏ Exercise 1: Listening for Sounds in Words: Spelling Patterns for / sh /
STEP 2 **Word Recognition and Spelling** • Read and spell multisyllable words. • Read and spell the **Essential Words:** billion, million, opinion, region, religion, union. • Spell words with prefixes, suffixes, and roots.	❏ Exercise 1: Spelling Pretest 1 ❏ Memorize It	❏ Exercise 2: Add It ❏ Exercise 3: Write It: Essential Words ❏ Word Fluency 1
STEP 3 **Vocabulary and Morphology** • Identify synonyms. • Identify and define noun suffixes. • Use the meaning of prefixes, suffixes, and roots to define words.	❏ Unit Vocabulary ❏ Explore It (T) ❏ Write It: Journal Entry	❏ Exercise 4: Combine It: Prefix Plus Root ❏ Exercise 5: Choose It: Affixed Words ❏ Write It: Thank You Note
STEP 4 **Grammar and Usage** • Identify subordinating conjunctions. • Identify participial phrases. • Identify adverbial clauses. • Identify past participles. • Use a colon to introduce a list.	❏ Exercise 2: Identify It: Functions of Participles and Participial Phrases ❏ Exercise 3: Identify It: Subordinating Conjunctions	❏ Exercise 6: Identify It: Phrase or Independent Clause ❏ Exercise 7: Identify It: Subordinating Conjunctions and Adverbial Clauses
STEP 5 **Listening and Reading Comprehension** • Interpret visual information. • Use context-based strategies to define words. • Identify setting and rising action. • Identify, understand, and answer questions that use different types of signal words.	❏ Independent Text: "Wolf Society" ❏ Exercise 4: Phrase It ❏ Exercise 5: Use the Clues	❏ Passage Fluency 1 ❏ Exercise 8: Using Visuals: Diagrams
STEP 6 **Speaking and Writing** • Use visual and text information to answer questions. • Write responses to sentences using signal words. • Organize information in a graphic organizer for a narrative composition. • Write a narrative composition.	❏ Exercise 6: Rewrite It	❏ Exercise 9: Answer It
Self-Evaluation (5 is the highest) **Effort** = I produced my best work. **Participation** = I was actively involved in tasks. **Independence** = I worked on my own.	**Effort:** 1 2 3 4 5 **Participation:** 1 2 3 4 5 **Independence:** 1 2 3 4 5	**Effort:** 1 2 3 4 5 **Participation:** 1 2 3 4 5 **Independence:** 1 2 3 4 5
Teacher Evaluation	**Effort:** 1 2 3 4 5 **Participation:** 1 2 3 4 5 **Independence:** 1 2 3 4 5	**Effort:** 1 2 3 4 5 **Participation:** 1 2 3 4 5 **Independence:** 1 2 3 4 5

Lesson 3 (Date:_____)	**Lesson 4** (Date:_____)	**Lesson 5** (Date:_____)
❑ Discover It: Sounds for <u>ei</u> ❑ Vowel Chart (T)	❑ Exercise 1: Listening for Sounds in Words: / *sh* / and / *zh* / ❑ Exercise 2: Discover It: Loan Words from Romance Languages	❑ Content Mastery: Vowel Digraphs
❑ Exercise 1: Sort It: Words With Long Vowels ❑ Divide It ❑ Word Fluency 2	❑ Make a Mnemonic ❑ Present It: Mnemonics for Confusing Word Pairs	❑ Content Mastery: Spelling Posttest 1 ❑ Present It: Mnemonics for Confusing Word Pairs
❑ Vocabulary Focus ❑ Use the Clues ❑ Expression of the Day	❑ Exercise 3: Combine It: Prefix Plus Root ❑ Exercise 4: Match It: Affixed Words	❑ Exercise 1: Rewrite It: Affixed Words ❑ Exercise 2: Build It: Using Morphemes
❑ Identify It: Participles and Participial Phrases	❑ Exercise 5: Identify It: Independent and Dependent Clauses ❑ Masterpiece Sentences: Stage 2	❑ Exercise 3: Rewrite It: Sentences
❑ Instructional Text: "David Copperfield" ❑ Comprehend It	❑ Comprehend It ❑ Take Note: Introduction	❑ Comprehend It ❑ Story Map
❑ Exercise 2: Answer It	❑ Story Map (T) ❑ Challenge Text: "Youth Activists Work for Social Change"	❑ Exercise 4: Write It: Outline ❑ Present It: Story Summary ❑ Challenge Text: "Youth Activists Work for Social Change
Effort: 1 2 3 4 5 **Participation:** 1 2 3 4 5 **Independence:** 1 2 3 4 5	**Effort:** 1 2 3 4 5 **Participation:** 1 2 3 4 5 **Independence:** 1 2 3 4 5	**Effort:** 1 2 3 4 5 **Participation:** 1 2 3 4 5 **Independence:** 1 2 3 4 5
Effort: 1 2 3 4 5 **Participation:** 1 2 3 4 5 **Independence:** 1 2 3 4 5	**Effort:** 1 2 3 4 5 **Participation:** 1 2 3 4 5 **Independence:** 1 2 3 4 5	**Effort:** 1 2 3 4 5 **Participation:** 1 2 3 4 5 **Independence:** 1 2 3 4 5

Check off the activities you complete with each lesson. Evaluate your accomplishments at the end of each lesson. Pay attention to teacher evaluations and comments.

Unit Objectives	Lesson 6 (Date:_____)	Lesson 7 (Date:_____)
STEP 1 **Phonemic Awareness and Phonics** • Say the sounds for the vowel digraphs: <u>ui</u> (/ ī / as in **guide**), <u>ou</u> (/ ō / as in **soul**), <u>ey</u> (/ ā / as in **they**), <u>ei</u> (/ ē / as in **either** and / ā / as in **vein**). • Write the letters for the sounds / ā /, / ē /, / ī /, and / ō / using vowel digraphs.	❑ Content Mastery: Using Student Performance	❑ Exercise 1: Using a Dictionary
STEP 2 **Word Recognition and Spelling** • Read and spell multisyllable words. • Read and spell the **Essential Words:** *billion, million, opinion, region, religion, union.* • Spell words with prefixes, suffixes, and roots.	❑ Exercise 1: Spelling Pretest 2 ❑ Word Fluency 3	❑ Build It: Words With Suffixes ❑ Word Fluency 4
STEP 3 **Vocabulary and Morphology** • Identify synonyms. • Identify and define noun suffixes. • Use the meaning of prefixes, suffixes, and roots to define words.	❑ Vocabulary Focus ❑ Use the Clues ❑ Expression of the Day	❑ Exercise 2: Rewrite It: Using Synonyms ❑ Expression of the Day
STEP 4 **Grammar and Usage** • Identify subordinating conjunctions. • Identify participial phrases. • Identify adverbial clauses. • Identify past participles. • Use a colon to introduce a list.	❑ Exercise 2: Rewrite It: Colons Used When Writing Time ❑ Exercise 3: Identify It: Confusing Words	❑ Exercise 3: Identify It: Confusing Words ❑ Identify It: Adverbs, Adverbial Phrases, and Adverbial Clauses
STEP 5 **Listening and Reading Comprehension** • Interpret visual information. • Use context-based strategies to define words. • Identify setting and rising action. • Identify, understand, and answer questions that use different types of signal words.	❑ Instructional Text: "David Copperfield" ❑ Map It: Plot Analysis (T) ❑ Comprehend It	❑ Comprehend It
STEP 6 **Speaking and Writing** • Use visual and text information to answer questions. • Write responses to sentences using signal words. • Organize information in a graphic organizer for a narrative composition. • Write a narrative composition.	❑ Exercise 4: Write It: Shaping the Topic	❑ Map It: Plot Analysis (T)
Self-Evaluation (5 is the highest) **Effort** = I produced my best work. **Participation** = I was actively involved in tasks. **Independence** = I worked on my own.	**Effort:** 1 2 3 4 5 **Participation:** 1 2 3 4 5 **Independence:** 1 2 3 4 5	**Effort:** 1 2 3 4 5 **Participation:** 1 2 3 4 5 **Independence:** 1 2 3 4 5
Teacher Evaluation	**Effort:** 1 2 3 4 5 **Participation:** 1 2 3 4 5 **Independence:** 1 2 3 4 5	**Effort:** 1 2 3 4 5 **Participation:** 1 2 3 4 5 **Independence:** 1 2 3 4 5

Lesson 8 (Date:_____)	Lesson 9 (Date:_____)	Lesson 10 (Date:_____)
☐ Exercise 1: Listening for Word Parts: Prefixes and Suffixes		
☐ Exercise 2: Divide It: Morpheme Parts	☐ Exercise 1: Sort It: Sounds for **-sion**	☐ Content Mastery: Spelling Posttest 2
☐ Exercise 3: Replace It: Synonyms ☐ Explore It (T)	☐ Content Mastery: Synonyms ☐ Content Mastery: Morphology	☐ Content Mastery: Using Student Performance ☐ Using a Dictionary: Word Origins ☐ Find It: Word Derivations ☐ Write a Mini-Dialog: Idioms
☐ Exercise 4: Rewrite It: Colon Usage ☐ Exercise 5: Diagram It: Sentences With Adverbial Clauses (T)	☐ Content Mastery	☐ Content Mastery: Using Student Performance
☐ Take Note: Plot Analysis	☐ Instructional Text: "David Copperfield" ☐ Exercise 2: Answer It: Multiple Choice	☐ Content Mastery: Answering Questions ☐ Revise It: Narrative Essay
☐ Exercise 6: Write It: Narrative Outline	☐ Write It: Narrative ☐ Challenge Text: "Stand Alone or Join the Crowd"	☐ Revise It: Narrative Essay ☐ Challenge Text: "Stand Alone or Join the Crowd"
Effort: 1 2 3 4 5 **Participation:** 1 2 3 4 5 **Independence:** 1 2 3 4 5	**Effort:** 1 2 3 4 5 **Participation:** 1 2 3 4 5 **Independence:** 1 2 3 4 5	**Effort:** 1 2 3 4 5 **Participation:** 1 2 3 4 5 **Independence:** 1 2 3 4 5
Effort: 1 2 3 4 5 **Participation:** 1 2 3 4 5 **Independence:** 1 2 3 4 5	**Effort:** 1 2 3 4 5 **Participation:** 1 2 3 4 5 **Independence:** 1 2 3 4 5	**Effort:** 1 2 3 4 5 **Participation:** 1 2 3 4 5 **Independence:** 1 2 3 4 5

Exercise 1 · Spelling Pretest 1

▸ Write the word your teacher repeats.

1. _____   6. _____   11. _____

2. _____   7. _____   12. _____

3. _____   8. _____   13. _____

4. _____   9. _____   14. _____

5. _____   10. _____   15. _____

Exercise 2 · Identify It: Functions of Participles and Participial Phrases

▸ Read each sentence.

▸ Find and underline the participle.

▸ Determine the function of the underlined word.

▸ Check the correct column.

	Participle in Verb Phrase	Participle as Adjective	Participle in Participial Phrase
1. David had lived with his mother and Peggotty for ten years.			
2. Trembling from head to toe, David walked with Mr. Quinion.			
3. Mr. Micawber wore a shirt with an imposing collar.			
4. David, filled with hunger, looked in bakery windows.			
5. Writing from experience, Charles Dickens detailed the dreadful conditions of child labor.			
6. Mr. Murdstone had removed David from school.			
7. The decaying floors of the old house were dangerous.			
8. Taking his few belongings, David moved in with the Micawbers.			
9. The Micawbers had an unoccupied room at the back of the house.			
10. Mingling his tears with the water, David began to wash bottles.			

Unit 27 • Lesson 1

Exercise 3 • Identify It: Subordinating Conjunctions

▸ Read each sentence.

▸ Identify the subordinating conjunction and circle it.

▸ Underline the clause that includes the subordinating conjunction.

▸ Circle the question the dependent clause answers.

1. Although David was poor, he preserved his dignity.
   a. how?   b. when?   c. where?   d. why?   e. under what condition?

2. Mr. Micawber was imprisoned because he was in debt.
   a. how?   b. when?   c. where?   d. why?   e. under what condition?

3. At first, David sobbed while he washed bottles.
   a. how?   b. when?   c. where?   d. why?   e. under what condition?

4. Mr. Micawber would stay in prison forever, unless he paid his debts.
   a. how?   b. when?   c. where?   d. why?   e. under what condition?

5. If David's mother had not married Mr. Murdstone, David's life would have been different.
   a. how?   b. when?   c. where?   d. why?   e. under what condition?

Exercise 4 · Phrase It

▶ Use the penciling strategy to "scoop" the phrases in each sentence.

▶ Read the sentences as you would speak them.

From "Wolf Society"

Imagine that you are watching a pack of wild wolves. At first, some of their actions might seem strange. Why do some wolves growl like bullies? Why do others keep their tails between their legs and whine? Why does the pack seem to pick on one wolf? The answers to these questions are complex. Wolf packs have rules. These rules govern the behavior of each pack member.

Exercise 5 · Use the Clues

▶ Read the excerpt from **"Wolf Society"** below.

▶ Reread the underlined words **alpha pair**.

▶ Circle the word **these** in the same sentence.

▶ Reread the first sentence.

▶ Underline the word that **these** refers back to.

▶ Draw an arrow connecting the word **these** with the word it represents.

▶ Draw a box around the meaning signal that connects **alpha pair** to the words that definite it.

▶ Write a definition for **alpha pair**.

> Every wolf pack has two leaders. One is male. One is female. These are called the <u>alpha pair</u>.

Define It:

alpha pair: _____

Exercise 6 · Rewrite It

The verbs in **"Wolf Society"** are in present tense. That is because the story presents facts that are true all the time. Imagine you were writing a story about two particular wolves. You might use past tense verbs to tell what they did at some time in the past. Follow the steps below to practice rewriting sentences by changing verbs from present tense to past tense.

▶ Read each sentence below.

▶ Look at each underlined verb.

▶ Rewrite the sentence by changing each verb to its simple past tense form.

▶ Reread each sentence and check your spelling.

▶ Remember to check for irregular verb forms.

> **Example:** The wolf <u>walks</u> towards the leader of the pack.
> The wolf walked towards the leader of the pack.

1. The wolf <u>is</u> a beta male.

   _____

2. The beta wolf <u>keeps</u> its ears flat.

   _____

3. The beta wolf <u>puts</u> its tail between its legs.

   _____

4. The alpha wolf <u>growls</u> to show it <u>is</u> the boss.

   _____

5. This <u>shows</u> the alpha wolf's higher rank.

   _____

Exercise 1 · Listening for Sounds in Words: Spelling Patterns for / *sh* /

▶ Repeat each word in the chart as your teacher says it.

▶ Locate the position of the / *sh* / sound.

▶ Underline the letters that represent / *sh* /.

▶ Label each column with the letters that represent / *sh* / in the words in the column.

_____ = / sh /	_____ = / sh /	_____ = / sh /	_____ = / sh /
official	mansion	direction	anxious
social	mission	partial	complexion
sufficient	session	patient	obnoxious

Exercise 2 · Add It

▶ Read the words listed below.

▶ Underline the last consonant in each root or base word.

▶ Add the correct spelling of the suffix pronounced / *shun* / to each word; write the new word on the line provided.

▶ Read the new word to a partner.

1. educate _____

2. express _____

3. revise _____

4. electric _____

5. elect _____

Exercise 3 · Write It: Essential Words

▸ Review the **Essential Words** in the **Word Bank**.

Word Bank

region	million	union	opinion	religion	billion

▸ Put the words in alphabetical order and write them on the lines.

▸ Write one sentence for each **Essential Word**.

▸ Check that each sentence uses sentence signals—correct capitalization, commas, and end punctuation.

1. _____

    _____

2. _____

    _____

3. _____

    _____

4. _____

    _____

5. _____

    _____

6. _____

    _____

Exercise 4 · Combine It: Prefix Plus Root

▶ Read each prefix and root or base word.

▶ Underline the last letter of the prefix.

▶ Underline the first letter of the root or base word and write it on the line provided.

▶ Decide if the last letter of the prefix should change to the first letter of the root or base word.

▶ Combine the prefix and root or base word and write the word on the line.

	Prefix	Root or Base Word	Suffix	First Letter of Root or Base Word	Whole Word
1.	ad- +	loc +	ate		
2.	ad- +	fect			
3.	ad- +	tain			
4.	ad- +	range			
5.	ad- +	pend			
6.	ad- +	tune			
7.	ad- +	cede			
8.	ad- +	set			
9.	ad- +	lure			
10.	ad- +	nul			

Exercise 5 · Choose It: Affixed Words

▶ Read each sentence.

▶ Choose the correct word to complete the sentence and write it in the blank.

▶ Circle each prefix and suffix, and underline the root of the word chosen.

▶ Write the word and its definition on the line below the word choices. Use your **Morphemes for Meaning Cards** and a dictionary as resources.

1. Despite enormous difficulties, David Copperfield _____ in learning the hard work of the counting-house.

   a. consisted   b. subsisted   c. persisted

   _____
   word   definition

2. David's day _____ of very long hours and very little food.

   a. desisted   b. consisted   c. resisted

   _____
   word   definition

3. The Micawber family had no money and lived in a state of _____.

   a. restitution   b. superstition   c. destitution

   _____
   word   definition

4. David Copperfield faced many _____.

   a. spectacles   b. obstacles   c. pinnacles

   _____
   word   definition

5. David tried to _____ the Micawbers as best he could.

   a. consist   b. subsist   c. assist

   _____
   word   definition

Unit 27 · Lesson 2

Exercise 6 · Identify It: Phrase or Independent Clause

▶ Read each group of words.

▶ Determine if it has a subject and a predicate. If it does, label the subject **S** and predicate **P**.

▶ Indicate whether the group of words is a phrase or an independent clause by underlining the answer.

▶ Rewrite each independent clause with correct capitalization and punctuation.

▶ Expand each phrase into an independent clause by adding necessary parts. Ask yourself **Who/What did it?** and **What did he/she/it do?** to help.

▶ Write the independent clause on the line. Check for correct capitalization and punctuation.

1. David had lodgings in a small dark room
   a. phrase   b. independent clause

   _____

2. washing bottles for long hours every day
   a. phrase   b. independent clause

   _____

3. the Micawber family rented a room to David
   a. phrase   b. independent clause

   _____

4. Mr. Micawber was taken off to the debtors' prison
   a. phrase   b. independent clause

   _____

5. rats scuttling everywhere
   a. phrase   b. independent clause

   _____

Exercise 7 · Identify It: Subordinating Conjunctions and Adverbial Clauses

▶ Read each sentence.

▶ Identify the subordinating conjunction and circle it.

▶ Underline the adverbial clause that includes the subordinating conjunction.

▶ Circle the question the adverbial clause answers or the relationship it shows.

1. David worked far more hours than he was paid for.

    a. how?   b. when?   c. where?   d. why?   e. under what condition?   f. comparison

2. David had lived with the Micawbers since he had arrived in London.

    a. how?   b. when?   c. where?   d. why?   e. under what condition?   f. comparison

3. When he had extra money, David bought some special food treat.

    a. how?   b. when?   c. where?   d. why?   e. under what condition?   f. comparison

4. Looking at Dickens' biographical data, one can see where he got his information about debtors.

    a. how?   b. when?   c. where?   d. why?   e. under what condition?   f. comparison

5. David lived with the Micawbers until Mr. Micawber went to prison.

    a. how?   b. when?   c. where?   d. why?   e. under what condition?   f. comparison

6. Since Mr. Micawber owed money to many people, most visitors to the house were creditors.

    a. how?   b. when?   c. where?   d. why?   e. under what condition?   f. comparison

7. David decided not to treat the other boys as they treated him.

    a. how?   b. when?   c. where?   d. why?   e. under what condition?   f. comparison

(continued)

Exercise 7 (continued) • Identify It: Subordinating Conjunctions and Adverbial Clauses

8. The Micawbers were kinder to David than his stepfather was.
   a. how? b. when? c. where? d. why? e. under what condition? f. comparison

9. When the Micawber house had no food in it, David offered money to Mrs. Micawber.
   a. how? b. when? c. where? d. why? e. under what condition? f. comparison

10. The story of David Copperfield was important, as it drew attention to major social issues.
    a. how? b. when? c. where? d. why? e. under what condition? f. comparison

Exercise 8 • Using Visuals: Diagrams

▸ Read the title of the diagram below.

▸ Read the parts of the diagram that have already been completed.

▸ Use information from **"Wolf Society"** on *Student Text* page 107 to complete the diagram.

How a New Wolf Pack Is Formed

An alpha male and alpha female have pups.

↓

↓

A pup that is neither the strongest pup nor the weakest grows into a beta wolf.

↓

↓

This alpha pair has pups.

Exercise 9 · Answer It

▶ Use information from the text and the diagram in **"Wolf Society"** to answer each of these questions. Write complete sentences.

1. What are the leaders of a wolf pack called?

   _____

   _____

   _____

2. How does a beta wolf show its lower rank?

   _____

   _____

   _____

3. Omega wolves are not allowed to get close to the rest of the pack. Why do they not go off on their own?

   _____

   _____

   _____

4. How might a new pack of wolves be formed from two existing packs?

   _____

   _____

   _____

5. How are the games that pups play important in wolf society?

   _____

   _____

Exercise 1 · Sort It: Words With Long Vowels

▶ Read each word in the **Word Bank**.

Word Bank

seize	guide	soul	they	veil	street
guise	tails	show	place	mould	grey

▶ Identify the vowel sound in the word.

▶ Write the word under the heading for the vowel sound in the word.

/ ā /	/ ē /	/ ī /	/ ō /

Exercise 2 · Answer It

▶ Underline the signal word in the question.

▶ Write the answer in complete sentences.

1. Summarize the events that have happened so far in David's life.

_____

_____

_____

_____

_____

2. Make a generalization about Murdstone and Grinby's warehouse.

_____

_____

3. Paraphrase David's description of his feelings about his new life, lines 77–88.

_____

_____

_____

_____

4. Describe Mr. Micawber's manner of speaking.

_____

_____

5. Make an inference about why the only visitors to Mr. Micawber's house were creditors.

_____

_____

Exercise 1 · Listening for Sounds in Words: / sh / and / zh /

▶ Listen to each word your teacher says.

▶ Identify the sound of / sh / or / zh / in each word.

▶ Mark an X in the column for / sh / or / zh /, depending on the sound you hear.

	/ sh /	/ zh /
1.		
2.		
3.		
4.		
5.		
6.		
7.		
8.		
9.		
10.		

Exercise 2 · Discover It: Loan Words from Romance Languages

▶ Work with a partner.

▶ Select one of the **Word Bank** lists.

Word Bank

	List 1	List 2	List 3
1.	chili	bravo	gourmet
2.	macaroni	enchilada	allegro
3.	police	llama	valet
4.	unique	salsa	sauté
5.	piano	taco	suede

▶ Locate each word on the selected list in a dictionary.

▶ Look at the pronunciation for the word and decide what is unusual about the sound-spelling correspondence.

▶ Write the word under the heading that matches your discovery.

▶ Write the word's origin (the language from which it was borrowed).

▶ Share your findings with the class.

	$\underline{i}$ = / $\bar{e}$ /	Word Origin	$\underline{a}$ = / $\ddot{a}$ /	Word Origin	$\underline{e}$ or $\underline{et}$ = / $\bar{a}$ /	Word Origin
1.						
2.						
3.						
4.						
5.						

Exercise 3 · Combine It: Prefix Plus Root

▸ Read each prefix and root.

▸ Underline the last letter of the prefix.

▸ Underline the first letter of the root or base word and write it on the line provided.

▸ Decide if the last letter of the prefix should change to the first letter of the root or base word.

▸ Combine the prefix and root or base word and write the word on the line.

	Prefix	Root or Base Word	1st Letter of Root or Base Word	Whole Word
1.	sub- +	ply		
2.	sub- +	fer		
3.	sub- +	gest		
4.	sub- +	cess		
5.	sub- +	press		

Exercise 4 · Match It: Affixed Words

▶ Read each word.

▶ Match each word to its definition.

▶ Use your knowledge of prefixes, roots, and suffixes, your **Morpheme for Meaning Cards**, and a dictionary as resources.

▶ Answer the questions at the bottom.

Word	**Definition**
1. submission	**a.** to feel or carry pain
2. leakage	**b.** an assurance to do or not do something
3. remit	**c.** to send money
4. promise	**d.** a state of putting oneself under the will of another
5. suffer	**e.** an amount lost as a result of leaks

▶ Circle the answer to each of the following questions:

1. What word means the same as **suffer**?

a. enjoy   b. hurt   c. please

2. What word means the opposite of **submission**?

a. surrender   b. meekness   c. resistance

3. What word means the opposite of **remit**?

a. retain   b. pay   c. forward

▶ Select two words from this exercise. Write a sentence for each word.

1. _____

_____

2. _____

_____

Unit 27 · Lesson 4

Exercise 5 · Identify It: Independent and Dependent Clauses

▸ Read each group of words and decide if they express a complete thought.

▸ Underline **independent clause** if the words express a complete thought.

▸ Rewrite each independent clause using correct capitalization and punctuation.

▸ Underline **dependent clause** if the words do not express a complete thought.

▸ Circle the subordinating conjunction and expand the dependent clause into a complete sentence by adding an independent clause.

1. one creditor edged himself into the passageway early in the morning
   a. independent clause   b. dependent clause

   _____

2. where David was working
   a. independent clause   b. dependent clause

   _____

3. as he could afford nothing else
   a. independent clause   b. dependent clause

   _____

4. the Micawber family was kind to David
   a. independent clause   b. dependent clause

   _____

5. since the creditors came at all hours of the day.
   a. independent clause   b. dependent clause

   _____

Exercise 1 · Rewrite It: Affixed Words

▶ Read the words in the **Word Bank**.

Word Bank

supporter	permission	drainage	destitute
omitting	emitted	insisting	

▶ Read each sentence.

▶ Replace the underlined phrase in the sentence with a word from the **Word Bank**.

▶ Use your **Morphemes for Meaning Cards** and a dictionary as references.

▶ Reread each sentence to check your work.

Sentence With Underlined Phrase:	Sentence With Phrase Changed to a Single Word:
1. The dirty water <u>gave out</u> a foul smell.	The dirty water _____ a foul smell.
2. The city of London had a very poor <u>collection of drains</u> system.	The city of London had a very poor _____ system.
3. Dickens was a <u>person who stood below</u> the rights of individuals.	Dickens was a _____ of the rights of individuals.
4. Mr. Micawber gave his <u>act of letting go through</u> to David to visit him in prison.	Mr. Micawber gave his _____ to David to visit him in prison.
5. Mr. Murdstone kept <u>standing in</u> that David work in London.	Mr. Murdstone kept _____ that David work in London.

Exercise 2 · Build It: Using Morphemes

▶ Read the directions for each item.

▶ Use the given morphemes to build a word that matches the definition.

▶ Write the word on the line. Remember to assimilate the prefix and apply spelling rules when writing the word.

1. Use this set of morphemes to build a word meaning "the act of sending to."

   | de-   ad-   mis   -ing   -sion |

   _____

2. Use this set of morphemes to build a word meaning "something that sends across."

   | trans-   ad-   mit   -tion   -er |

   _____

3. Use this set of morphemes to build a word meaning "stood near."

   | sub-   ad-   sist   -tion   -ed |

   _____

4. Use this set of morphemes to build a word meaning "the state of standing under."

   | ad-   sub-   sta   -ive   -tion |

   _____

5. Use this set of morphemes to build a word meaning "a collection of miles."

   | mile   -or   -age |

   _____

Exercise 3 · Rewrite It: Sentences

▶ Read the paragraph with your teacher.

▶ Underline any past participle that is used incorrectly and write the correct form above it.

▶ Revise each sentence as directed, using the **Masterpiece Sentence Cue Chart**. Remember that Stage 4, **Paint Your Subject**, can be used to paint any noun.

▶ Proofread for spelling and punctuation, paying special attention to the past participles.

> 1. David lived with mother and Peggotty. 2. He leaved for London. 3. He meeted the kind but shabby Mr. Micawber. 4. David washed bottles. 5. He didn't like his job.

Item	Use these **Masterpiece Sentence** stages to expand each sentence.	Make this change.
1.	Stage 2 and Stage 3	Write an adverbial clause answering the question **when**?
2.	Stage 2	Write an adverbial clause answering the question **why**?
3.	Stages 2 and Stage 4	Write an adverbial phrase telling **when** and a participial phrase describing Mr. Micawber.
4.	Stage 4	Write a participial phrase describing David, and an adverbial clause answering the question **when**?
5.	Stage 2 and Stage 5	Write an adverbial clause answering the question **why**? Find another word for "didn't like."

_____

_____

_____

_____

_____

_____

Unit 27 · Lesson 5

Exercise 4 · Write It: Outline

▸ Use the chart below to plan your summary of **"David Copperfield."**

▸ To conclude your summary, speculate on whether you think things are going to get better or worse for Mr. and Mrs. Micawber.

Introduce the story (include the title, author, and setting)	
First event	At the beginning of Chapter 11,
Next event	Then
Problem	
Speculate on what will happen next. (Do you think things are going to get better or worse for Mr. and Mrs. Micawber? Why?)	

Exercise 5 · Challenge Writing: Synthesize to Support a Thesis

The Task: Write a five-paragraph essay that supports this thesis: **Individuals can make a difference in the world**. To support this thesis, describe people who have made a difference in the world by working for human rights, improving health and safety, and working for the environment. Draw on information you have read in several different sources.

First, make a list of the people you will describe and the area in which each has made a difference. Then complete the outlining activity below to help you organize and write a first draft of your essay.

Plan the Body of Your Essay
Write the main ideas and details you will include in the three paragraphs that will make up the body of your essay. Go back to the sources you used to add details. Include the names of the sources, too.

I. **Human Rights**

   MAIN IDEA _____

   _____

Individual(s)	Accomplishments
_____	_____
_____	_____
_____	_____
_____	_____
_____	_____

   name(s) of source(s): _____

   _____

(continued)

Exercise 5 *(continued)* · Challenge Writing: Synthesize to Support a Thesis

II. **Health and Safety**

MAIN IDEA _____

_____

Individual(s)	Accomplishments
_____	_____
_____	_____
_____	_____
_____	_____
_____	_____
_____	_____

name(s) of source(s): _____

_____

III. **The Environment**

MAIN IDEA _____

_____

Individual(s)	Accomplishments
_____	_____
_____	_____
_____	_____
_____	_____
_____	_____
_____	_____

name(s) of source(s): _____

_____

(continued)

Exercise 5 *(continued)* · Challenge Writing: Synthesize to Support a Thesis

Write Your Essay

Write the Body of Your Essay: Use the outline above to write the body of your essay. It will have three paragraphs:

1. Individuals who have made a difference in human rights

2. Individuals who have made a difference in health and safety

3. Individuals who have made a difference in the environment

• Write your draft on another sheet of paper.

Write an Introduction: After you have written the body of your essay, add an introduction. Use the thesis statement as the first or last sentence of the introduction. The other sentences should tell readers how you are going to support this thesis.

Last but Not Least: Your essay also needs a conclusion. The conclusion can be short. It should restate the thesis in a new way. You might also include a sentence that encourages readers to make a difference in the world by tackling an issue that is important to them!

Exercise 1 · Spelling Pretest 2

▶ Write the word your teacher repeats.

1. _____   6. _____   11. _____

2. _____   7. _____   12. _____

3. _____   8. _____   13. _____

4. _____   9. _____   14. _____

5. _____   10. _____   15. _____

Exercise 2 · Rewrite It: Colons Used When Writing Time

▶ Read each line.

▶ Rewrite the time in numerals, placing the colon in its correct position.

▶ Add the appropriate initials, indicating either after midnight and before noon (a.m.), or after noon and before midnight (p.m.).

1. ten minutes after eight in the evening

2. half past six in the morning

3. eight forty-five in the morning

4. twelve noon

5. five minutes after ten at night

Exercise 3 · Identify It: Confusing Words

▸ Read each sentence and the word choices below the sentence.

▸ Use what you know about the meaning and function of each word to choose the correct word.

▸ Refer to the *Student Text*, page 100, if you need help.

▸ Copy the word into the blank.

1. David arrived in London and _____ had to find a room.
   a. then   b. than

2. Fortunately David met nice people _____ Mr. Micawber.
   a. like   b. as

3. David listened carefully _____ he entered the house.
   a. like   b. as

4. _____ he was walking home, David looked in bakery windows.
   a. like   b. as

5. David was smaller _____ the other boys at the factory.
   a. then   b. than

6. David did not feel he was _____ the other boys.
   a. like   b. as

7. David received his wages and _____ had to pay for food.
   a. then   b. than

8. Mr. Micawber was a kinder person _____ Mr. Murdstone.
   a. then   b. than

9. David looked for letters from Peggotty, _____ he wanted news from home.
   a. like   b. as

10. Dickens wrote "**David Copperfield**" _____ a way to bring attention to child labor.
    a. like   b. as

Unit 27 · Lesson 6

Exercise 4 · Write It: Shaping the Topic

▶ Read the writing task below:

Think of a time when you found yourself facing some kind of challenge or predicament. It may be something that was unusual, funny, or dramatic. Write a narrative in which you describe the challenge you faced and what led up to it or what happened as a result of it. How did things end up? Did you solve a problem, or did things turn out in a surprising way?

▶ Think of three challenging, surprising, or unusual situations you have been in. Write them here:

_____

_____

_____

▶ Tell the three ideas to a partner.

▶ Think about which idea you would like most to write about. Put an X next to that idea in the above list.

▶ Would you prefer to tell the event exactly as it happened? Or would you prefer to fictionalize it—that is, to make up some details about it? Check one.

❏ tell it exactly as it happened   ❏ fictionalize it

Exercise 1 · Using a Dictionary

▸ Turn to the **Vocabulary** section in the back of the *Student Text*.

▸ Locate the first word and its diacritical markings.

▸ Write the diacritical markings for the word on the line next to the word.

▸ Use the markings to help you read the word aloud with correct pronunciation.

▸ Complete numbers 2–5 using the same process.

Word	Pronunciation (diacritical markings)
1. auspiciously	
2. agony	
3. genteel	
4. mortification	
5. consolation	

▸ Use a classroom dictionary or yourDictionary.com to complete numbers 6–10.

6. portfolio	
7. patriotic	
8. antique	
9. quarantine	
10. pandemonium	

Exercise 2 · Rewrite It: Using Synonyms

▸ Read the first phrase below. (The phrases are all taken from **"David Copperfield."**)

▸ Turn to **"David Copperfield"** in the *Student Text*, page 115, and locate this phrase on the line indicated.

▸ Read the sentence or paragraph that includes the phrase.

▸ Use a dictionary or thesaurus to find a synonym or a phrase with the same meaning for each of the underlined words.

▸ Rewrite the phrase, replacing the underlined words with these synonyms or phrases in a way that makes sense.

▸ Reread the sentence or paragraph in the *Student Text* from which the phrase came, substituting the paraphrased version for the original.

▸ Follow these steps for each of the remaining phrases.

1. was <u>fond</u> of <u>wandering</u>   (*Student Text*, line 25)

fond: _____   wandering: _____

new phrase: _____

2. <u>scantiness</u> of my <u>resources</u>   (*Student Text*, line 33)

scantiness: _____   resources: _____

new phrase: _____

3. <u>lounged</u> about the streets   (*Student Text*, line 38)

lounged: _____

new phrase: _____

4. <u>distressed</u> <u>state</u> of my mind   (*Student Text*, line 50)

distressed: _____   state: _____

new phrase: _____

5. <u>forlorn</u> <u>state</u>   (*Student Text*, line 50)

forlorn: _____   state: _____

new phrase: _____

Exercise 3 · Identify It: Confusing Words

▶ Read each sentence and the word choices below the sentence.

▶ Use what you know about the meaning and function of each word to choose the correct word to complete the sentence.

▶ Copy the word into the blank.

1. David roamed the streets _____ a little vagabond.
   a. like   b. as

2. All alone in London, David had no one he could ask for _____.
   a. advice   b. advise

3. After David had _____ to visit Mr. Micawber, he would walk home slowly.
   a. gone   b. went

4. _____ David had to buy his own food, he was very careful with his money.
   a. like   b. as

5. With the Micawbers, David tried to look happier _____ he felt.
   a. then   b. than

6. Because he was alone in London, David _____ to become very independent.
   a. preceded   b. proceeded

7. The young boy would _____ on his bed at night and imagine a different life.
   a. lie   b. lay

8. David would rise early _____ and have breakfast with the Micawbers.
   a. then   b. than

9. After that, he _____ to work.
   a. gone   b. went

10. Mr. Micawber began to _____ a plan involving presenting a petition to Parliament.
    a. device   b. devise

Lesson 8

Exercise 1 · Listening for Word Parts: Prefixes and Suffixes

▶ Listen to each word your teacher says.

▶ Repeat the word.

▶ Mark **Yes** or **No** to tell if you hear a prefix or suffix.

▶ If **yes**, write the prefix or suffix you hear under the correct heading.

	Do you hear a prefix or suffix on the word?		If **Yes**, write the prefix or suffix.	
	Yes	No	Prefix	Suffix
1.				
2.				
3.				
4.				
5.				
6.				
7.				
8.				
9.				
10.				
11.				
12.				
13.				
14.				
15.				

Exercise 2 · Divide It: Morpheme Parts

▶ Read each word.

▶ Break the word into its morpheme parts.

▶ Write these word parts in the blank. Put a plus sign (+) between morphemes in the word.

1. address = _____

2. subcontract = _____

3. admit = _____

4. subjection = _____

5. consist = _____

6. insist = _____

7. station = _____

8. stature = _____

9. remiss = _____

10. omit = _____

Exercise 3 · Replace It: Synonyms

▶ Read each sentence below, noting the underlined word.

▶ Complete each word pair by choosing a synonym for the underlined word from the **Unit Vocabulary** box in the *Student Text*, page 95.

▶ Write the synonym on the line.

1. I have been chosen to watch the <u>exclusive</u> interview.

   exclusive: _____

2. Our teacher will <u>show</u> us through the park.

   show: _____

3. Do you have <u>ample</u> information to finish the report?

   ample: _____

4. My <u>first</u> reaction was confusion.

   first: _____

5. I was really <u>nervous</u> during try-outs.

   nervous: _____

6. What is the <u>measurement</u> of the height of your speakers?

   measurement: _____

7. Exercise should be part of one's daily <u>habit</u>.

   habit: _____

8. The omega wolf is at the bottom of the <u>group</u> structure.

   group: _____

9. Be careful that the clues don't <u>mislead</u> you.

   mislead: _____

10. Drivers have to <u>follow</u> traffic rules.

    follow: _____

Exercise 4 · Rewrite It: Colon Usage

▸ Read each line.

▸ In item 1 and item 4, rewrite the time in numerals, using a colon and appropriate initials.

▸ In items 2, 3, and 5, place colons where needed, and circle them.

1. fifteen minutes past seven in the morning

2. Dear Mr. President

3. I have read four books by Charles Dickens *Great Expectations, David Copperfield, Oliver Twist,* and *Nicholas Nickleby.*

4. three twenty-five in the afternoon

5. I will take six classes in the fall English, Algebra I, World History, General Science, Physical Education, and Mechanical Drawing.

Exercise 5 · Diagram It: Sentences With Adverbial Clauses

▸ Read each sentence.

▸ Circle the subordinating conjunction.

▸ Find the dependent clause in each sentence and underline it.

▸ Diagram the sentence.

1. David lived with the Micawbers until Mr. Micawber went to prison.

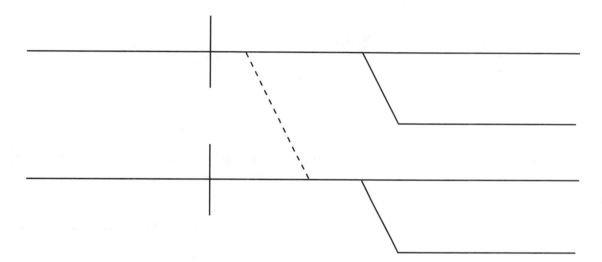

2. David bought extra food if he had spare money.

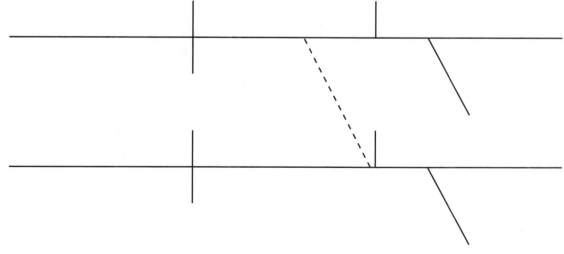

(*continued*)

Exercise 5 (continued) · Diagram It: Sentences With Adverbial Clauses

3. Mr. Murdstone did not understand why a child needed kindness.

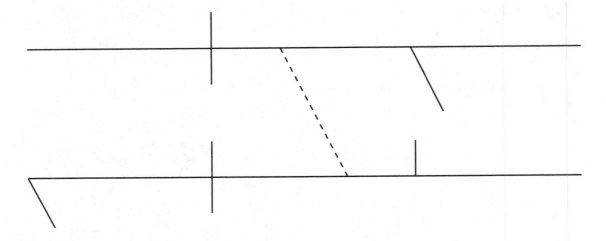

4. When David heard about the signing ceremony, he left work early.

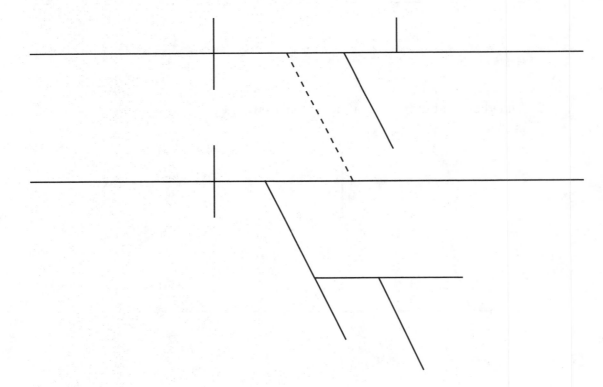

(continued)

5. Although David was young, he was very independent.

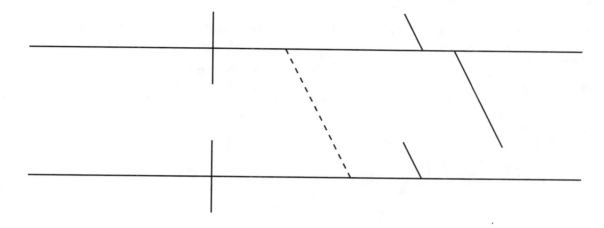

Unit 27 · Lesson 8

Exercise 6 · Write It: Narrative Outline

▸ Use the outline below to plan how you will organize your ideas in your narrative.

▸ List each main story event. Then, under each event, list key details that will make your story interesting to readers.

▸ Remember that your outline should include rising action and build to a climax.

Introduction: Initiating Event

Event that started the whole story:	

Second Paragraph: Rising Action

Another event:	
Detail:	
Detail:	
Detail:	

(continued)

Exercise 6 (continued) · Write It: Narrative Outline

Third Paragraph: Rising Action

Another event:	
Detail:	
Detail:	
Detail:	

Fourth Paragraph: Climax

Turning point or most exciting moment:	
Detail:	
Detail:	
Detail:	

(continued)

Exercise 6 (continued) · Write It: Narrative Outline

Resolution/Conclusion

How things turned out:	

Exercise 1 · Sort It: Sounds for *-sion*

▶ Read each word in the **Word Bank**.

Word Bank

confusion	expression	decision	possession	erosion
division	permission	collision	commission	admission

▶ Identify the sound for **-sion**.

▶ Write the word under the correct heading for the sound you hear.

/ shun /	/ zhun /

Unit 27 · Lesson 9

Exercise 2 · Answer It: Multiple Choice

▸ Work independently to identify the correct answer to each question below. If you need help, refer to **Text Connection 6, "David Copperfield,"** in the *Interactive Text*, pages C46–C53.

▸ Underline the correct answer.

▸ Discuss the correct answers with your teacher.

1. David can best be described as _____.

   A. inactive and bored

   B. optimistic and excited

   C. heartbroken and miserable

   D. fearful and shy

2. Which of the following statements best describes how David manages in his new situation?

   A. He relies on the goodwill of Mr. Quinion.

   B. The other boys at the warehouse offer helpful tips.

   C. He relies mostly on himself.

   D. The Micawbers provide for him financially.

3. Mrs. Micawber says, "Master Copperfield, I make no stranger of you," and tells David about Mr. Micawber's difficulties. What does this show about the relationship between the Micawbers and David?

   A. They do not trust each other.

   B. They have become friends.

   C. They act like strangers.

   D. They know each other well.

(continued)

4. According to the story, Mr. Micawber is in debt. However, he calculates the cost of "putting bow-windows to the house, 'in case anything turned up.'" Why does he do this?

   A. because he does not realize the extent of his debt

   B. because he is very optimistic

   C. because he believes he should not have to pay bills

   D. because he expects to have work soon

5. Which social issue do the prisoners address with their petition?

   A. child labor

   B. overtime pay

   C. mandatory education

   D. the imprisonment of debtors

Lesson Checklist
Lessons 1–2

Check off the activities you complete with each lesson. Evaluate your accomplishments at the end of each lesson. Pay attention to teacher evaluations and comments.

Unit Objectives	Lesson 1 (Date:_____)	Lesson 2 (Date:_____)
STEP 1 **Phonemic Awareness and Phonics** • Say the sounds for the vowel phonograms: <u>aw</u> (/ ô / as in **saw**), <u>au</u> (/ ô / as in **pause**), <u>ew</u> (/ yo͞o / as in **chew**), <u>eu</u> (/ o͞o / as in **sleuth** and / o͞o / as in **neuron**). • Write the letters for the sounds / ô /, / yo͞o /, / o͞o /, and / o͞o / using vowel phonograms.	❏ Discover It: Sounds for <u>au</u> and <u>aw</u> ❏ Vowel Chart (T)	❏ Exercise 1: Listening for Sounds in Words: Sounds for <u>du</u> and <u>tu</u>
STEP 2 **Word Recognition and Spelling** • Read and spell multisyllable words. • Read and spell the **Essential Words:** *aunt, bought, brought, caught, source, view.* • Read and spell words with prefixes, suffixes, and roots.	❏ Exercise 1: Spelling Pretest 1 ❏ Memorize It	❏ Exercise 2: Write It: Essential Words ❏ Word Fluency 1
STEP 3 **Vocabulary and Morphology** • Identify synonyms. • Identify and define noun suffixes. • Use the meanings of prefixes, suffixes, and roots to define words.	❏ Unit Vocabulary ❏ Explore It (T) ❏ Write It: Personal Note	❏ Exercise 3: Choose It: Affixed Words ❏ Write It: Journal Entry
STEP 4 **Grammar and Usage** • Identify relative pronouns, participial phrases, and adjectival clauses. • Identify the present perfect tense. • Identify regular and irregular past participles. • Use a colon to introduce a list.	❏ Exercise 2: Identify It: Present Perfect Tense Verbs ❏ Exercise 3: Identify It: Pronouns	❏ Exercise 4: Identify It: Relative Pronouns ❏ Exercise 5: Identify It: Adjectival Clauses
STEP 5 **Listening and Reading Comprehension** • Interpret visual information. • Use context-based strategies to define words. • Identify setting and rising action. • Identify, understand, and answer questions that use different types of signal words.	❏ Independent Text: "A View of the Eye" ❏ Exercise 4: Phrase It ❏ Exercise 5: Use the Clues	❏ Passage Fluency 1 ❏ Exercise 6: Using Visuals: Diagrams
STEP 6 **Speaking and Writing** • Use visual and text information to answer questions. • Write responses using signal words. • Organize information in a graphic organizer for a narrative composition. • Write a narrative composition.	❏ Exercise 6: Rewrite It	❏ Exercise 7: Answer It
Self-Evaluation (5 is the highest) **Effort** = I produced my best work. **Participation** = I was actively involved in tasks. **Independence** = I worked on my own.	**Effort:** 1 2 3 4 5 **Participation:** 1 2 3 4 5 **Independence:** 1 2 3 4 5	**Effort:** 1 2 3 4 5 **Participation:** 1 2 3 4 5 **Independence:** 1 2 3 4 5
Teacher Evaluation	**Effort:** 1 2 3 4 5 **Participation:** 1 2 3 4 5 **Independence:** 1 2 3 4 5	**Effort:** 1 2 3 4 5 **Participation:** 1 2 3 4 5 **Independence:** 1 2 3 4 5

Lesson 3 (Date:_____)	Lesson 4 (Date:_____)	Lesson 5 (Date:_____)
❑ Discover It: Sounds for _eu_ and _ew_ ❑ Vowel Chart (T)	❑ Exercise 1: Listening for Sounds in Words: Sound-Spelling Patterns for Suffix -_al_	❑ Content Mastery: Sounds for _au_, _aw_, _eu_, and _ew_
❑ Exercise 1: Sort It: / o͞o / and / yo͞o / ❑ Divide It ❑ Word Fluency 2	❑ Make a Mnemonic ❑ Present It: Mnemonics for Confusing Word Pairs	❑ Content Mastery: Spelling Posttest 1 ❑ Present It: Mnemonics for Confusing Word Pairs
❑ Vocabulary Focus ❑ Use the Clues ❑ Expression of the Day	❑ Exercise 2: Match It: Affixed Words	❑ Exercise 1: Rewrite It: Affixed Words ❑ Exercise 2: Build It: Using Morphemes
❑ Identify It: Participles and Participial Phrases	❑ Exercise 3: Choose It: Present Perfect Tense Verbs ❑ Masterpiece Sentences: Stage 4	❑ Exercise 3: Rewrite It: Sentences
❑ Instructional Text: "My First View of Ellis Island" and "The New Colossus"	❑ Comprehend It ❑ Take Note: Details of a Setting	❑ Comprehend It
❑ Exercise 2: Answer It	❑ Spotlight on Setting ❑ Exercise 4: Write It: Plan a Descriptive Composition ❑ Challenge Text: "Ansel Adams: View Through a Lens"	❑ Write It: Descriptive Composition ❑ Revise It: Descriptive Composition ❑ Challenge Text: "Ansel Adams: View Through a Lens" ❑ Exercise 4: Challenge Writing: Describe Something Unforgettable
Effort: 1 2 3 4 5 **Participation:** 1 2 3 4 5 **Independence:** 1 2 3 4 5	**Effort:** 1 2 3 4 5 **Participation:** 1 2 3 4 5 **Independence:** 1 2 3 4 5	**Effort:** 1 2 3 4 5 **Participation:** 1 2 3 4 5 **Independence:** 1 2 3 4 5
Effort: 1 2 3 4 5 **Participation:** 1 2 3 4 5 **Independence:** 1 2 3 4 5	**Effort:** 1 2 3 4 5 **Participation:** 1 2 3 4 5 **Independence:** 1 2 3 4 5	**Effort:** 1 2 3 4 5 **Participation:** 1 2 3 4 5 **Independence:** 1 2 3 4 5

Check off the activities you complete with each lesson. Evaluate your accomplishments at the end of each lesson. Pay attention to teacher evaluations and comments.

Unit Objectives	Lesson 6 (Date:_____)	Lesson 7 (Date:_____)
STEP 1 — Phonemic Awareness and Phonics • Say the sounds for the vowel phonograms: <u>aw</u> (/ ô / as in **saw**), <u>au</u> (/ ô / as in **pause**), <u>ew</u> (/ yōō / as in **chew**), <u>eu</u> (/ ōō / as in **sleuth** and / ōō / as in **neuron**). • Write the letters for the sounds / ô /, / yōō /, / ōō /, and / ōō / using vowel phonograms.	❑ Content Mastery: Using Student Performance	❑ Exercise 1: Using a Dictionary
STEP 2 — Word Recognition and Spelling • Read and spell multisyllable words. • Read and spell the **Essential Words:** *aunt, bought, brought, caught, source, view.* • Read and spell words with prefixes, suffixes, and roots.	❑ Exercise 1: Spelling Pretest 2 ❑ Word Fluency 3	❑ Build It: Words With Suffixes ❑ Word Fluency 4
STEP 3 — Vocabulary and Morphology • Identify synonyms. • Identify and define noun suffixes. • Use the meanings of prefixes, suffixes, and roots to define words.	❑ Vocabulary Focus ❑ Use the Clues ❑ Expression of the Day	❑ Exercise 2: Add It: Prefixes ❑ Expression of the Day
STEP 4 — Grammar and Usage • Identify relative pronouns, participial phrases, and adjectival clauses. • Identify the present perfect tense. • Identify regular and irregular past participles. • Use a colon to introduce a list.	❑ Exercise 2: Identify It: Complex Sentences ❑ Exercise 3: Identify It: Confusing Words	❑ Identify It: Simple or Complex Sentences
STEP 5 — Listening and Reading Comprehension • Interpret visual information. • Use context-based strategies to define words. • Identify setting and rising action. • Identify, understand, and answer questions that use different types of signal words.	❑ Instructional Text: "Amigo Brothers" ❑ Comprehend It ❑ Map It: Plot Analysis (T)	❑ Comprehend It
STEP 6 — Speaking and Writing • Use visual and text information to answer questions. • Write responses using signal words. • Organize information in a graphic organizer for a narrative composition. • Write a narrative composition.	❑ Exercise 4: Write It: Shaping the Topic	❑ Map It: Plot Analysis (T)
Self-Evaluation (5 is the highest) **Effort** = I produced my best work. **Participation** = I was actively involved in tasks. **Independence** = I worked on my own.	**Effort:** 1 2 3 4 5 **Participation:** 1 2 3 4 5 **Independence:** 1 2 3 4 5	**Effort:** 1 2 3 4 5 **Participation:** 1 2 3 4 5 **Independence:** 1 2 3 4 5
Teacher Evaluation	**Effort:** 1 2 3 4 5 **Participation:** 1 2 3 4 5 **Independence:** 1 2 3 4 5	**Effort:** 1 2 3 4 5 **Participation:** 1 2 3 4 5 **Independence:** 1 2 3 4 5

Lesson 8 (Date:_____)	Lesson 9 (Date:_____)	Lesson 10 (Date:_____)
❏ Exercise 1: Listening for Word Parts: Prefixes and Suffixes		
❏ Exercise 2: Divide It: Morpheme Parts	❏ Discover It: Adding -ial and -al	❏ Content Mastery: Spelling Posttest 2
❏ Exercise 3: Replace It: Synonyms ❏ Explore It (T)	❏ Content Mastery: Word Relationships ❏ Content Mastery: Morphology	❏ Content Mastery: Using Student Performance ❏ Using a Dictionary: Word Origins ❏ Find It: Word Derivations ❏ Write a Mini-Dialog: Idioms
❏ Exercise 4: Identify It: Confusing Words ❏ Exercise 5: Diagram It: Sentences With Adjectival Clauses	❏ Content Mastery	❏ Content Mastery: Using Student Performance
❏ Comprehend It ❏ Take Note: Rising Action ❏ Map It: Plot Analysis (T)	❏ Instructional Text: "Amigo Brothers" ❏ Exercise 1: Answer It: Multiple Choice	❏ Revise It: Narrative Essay
❏ Exercise 6: Write It: Narrative Outline	❏ Write It: Narrative ❏ Challenge Text: "View Through a Window"	❏ Revise It: Narrative Essay ❏ Challenge Text: "View Through a Window"
Effort: 1 2 3 4 5 **Participation:** 1 2 3 4 5 **Independence:** 1 2 3 4 5	**Effort:** 1 2 3 4 5 **Participation:** 1 2 3 4 5 **Independence:** 1 2 3 4 5	**Effort:** 1 2 3 4 5 **Participation:** 1 2 3 4 5 **Independence:** 1 2 3 4 5
Effort: 1 2 3 4 5 **Participation:** 1 2 3 4 5 **Independence:** 1 2 3 4 5	**Effort:** 1 2 3 4 5 **Participation:** 1 2 3 4 5 **Independence:** 1 2 3 4 5	**Effort:** 1 2 3 4 5 **Participation:** 1 2 3 4 5 **Independence:** 1 2 3 4 5

Exercise 1 · Spelling Pretest 1

▶ Write the word your teacher repeats.

1. _____   6. _____   11. _____

2. _____   7. _____   12. _____

3. _____   8. _____   13. _____

4. _____   9. _____   14. _____

5. _____   10. _____   15. _____

Exercise 2 · Identify It: Present Perfect Tense Verbs

▶ Read each sentence.

▶ Identify and underline the verb that is in present perfect tense.

▶ Determine whether that verb phrase expresses an action occurring at an unspecified time in the past, or an action occurring in the past and continuing in the present.

▶ Check the correct box.

	Action Completed at an Unspecified Time	Continuing Action
1. The optician has dilated the patient's eyes.		
2. Humans have relied mainly on the sense of sight since the beginning of time.		
3. Since Rex lost his sight, he has adapted to a new world.		
4. Light rays reach the retina after muscles have adjusted the shape of the lens.		
5. The woman has taken photos since early this morning.		

Exercise 3 · Identify It: Pronouns

▶ Read each sentence.

▶ Identify the pronoun and underline it.

▶ Decide if the pronoun is a nominative, object, or possessive pronoun.

▶ Copy the pronoun into the correct column below.

	Nominative	Object	Possessive
1. Human beings have five senses to help them.			
2. Some rely more on their sense of sight than on the other senses.			
3. The rest of the family has good sight, but mine is poor.			
4. Everyone values the sense of sight.			
5. The sense of sight allows us to see the world.			
6. Sometimes we call the eye an eyeball.			
7. The retina receives light and converts it into nerve impulses.			
8. These nerve impulses are sent to the brain, and the brain converts them into images.			
9. You can imagine the eye as being a movie camera.			
10. Sight can be damaged, so be sure to protect yours.			

▶ Copy the indefinite pronouns on the line below.

_____

Unit 28 · Lesson 1

Exercise 4 · Phrase It

▸ Use the penciling strategy to "scoop" the phrases in each sentence.

▸ Read the sentences as you would speak them.

From "A View of the Eye"

Sometimes we call the eye an "eyeball." Your eye is a ball about one inch in diameter. Most of the ball is covered by a tough white bag. This is called the *sclera,* or the white of the eye. At the front of the ball is a hole that lets in light. This hole is called the *pupil.* It appears as a black dot in the middle of your eye. It isn't really colored black. Looking into the pupil is like looking through the door into a dark room. The pupil is black because there is no light inside the eye to make things visible.

Exercise 5 · Use the Clues

▶ Read the two sentences from **"A View of the Eye"** below.

▶ Reread the underlined word **iris**.

▶ Circle the pronoun **it**. Use **it** to identify words that define **iris**.

▶ Underline words that **it** refers back to.

▶ Draw an arrow connecting the word **iris** with the words that tell what it is.

▶ Look for the word **like** in the first sentence. Then draw a box around the thing that **iris** is compared to.

▶ Write a definition for **iris**. Then answer the questions.

> The colored ring around the pupil acts like a curtain. It is called the <u>iris</u>.

Define It:

iris: _____

What is an iris compared to?

_____

▶ How does this comparison help you understand the job that an iris does?

_____

_____

Exercise 6 · Rewrite It

▶ Read each of the following pairs of sentences.

▶ Look at the boldface noun or noun phrase in the second sentence.

▶ Look at the underlined phrase in the first sentence.

▶ Combine the sentences into a single sentence by placing the underlined phrase from the first sentence after the boldface noun or noun phrase in the second sentence.

> **Example:** Light is <u>reflected off the flower</u>. The **light** passes through the cornea.
> The light <u>reflected off the flower</u> passes through the cornea.

1. The smooth white material is <u>covering most of your eyeball</u>. The **smooth white material** is called the *sclera*.

   _____

   _____

2. Light is <u>focused onto the retina</u>. The **light** is changed into nerve impulses.

   _____

   _____

3. Nerve impulses are <u>sent to the brain</u>. The **nerve impulses** are developed into visual images.

   _____

   _____

4. Light is <u>reaching the retina</u>. The **light** is sent along to the brain.

   _____

   _____

5. Visual information is <u>collected by the brain</u>. The **visual information** is used so quickly that we are not aware of the process.

   _____

   _____

Exercise 1 · Listening for Sounds in Words: Sounds for _du_ and _tu_.

▶ Say each sound in the **Sound Bank** along with your teacher.

Sound Bank

/ cho͞o /	/ chə /	/ jo͞o /	/ jə /

▶ Say each word in the first column of the chart with your teacher.

▶ Identify the pronunciation of the underlined letters in each word.

▶ Label the first column with the sound for **du**.

▶ Read each word in the column with your teacher.

▶ Repeat the same process for the remaining columns.

▶ If you are unsure of the pronunciation of **du** or **tu** in any of the words in the chart, check a dictionary.

du =	**du** =	**tu** =	**tu** =
gra<u>du</u>ate	e<u>du</u>cate	sta<u>tu</u>e	cen<u>tu</u>ry
mo<u>du</u>le	pen<u>du</u>lum	punc<u>tu</u>ate	for<u>tu</u>nate
no<u>du</u>le	frau<u>du</u>lent	vir<u>tu</u>al	spa<u>tu</u>la

Unit 28 · Lesson 2

Exercise 2 · Write It: Essential Words

▸ Review the **Essential Words** in the **Word Bank**.

Word Bank

bought	caught	source	view	brought	aunt

▸ Put the words in alphabetical order and write them on the lines.

▸ Write one sentence for each **Essential Word**.

▸ Check that each sentence uses sentence signals—correct capitalization, commas, and end punctuation.

1. _____

    _____

2. _____

    _____

3. _____

    _____

4. _____

    _____

5. _____

    _____

6. _____

    _____

Exercise 3 · Choose It: Affixed Words

▸ Read each sentence.

▸ Choose the correct word to complete the sentence and write it in the blank.

▸ Circle each prefix and suffix, and underline the root or base word in the selected word.

▸ Write the word and its definition on the line. Use your **Morphemes for Meaning Cards** and a dictionary as resources.

1. In a cold winter, a car's radiator needs _____ to keep it functioning.

   a. antimatter   b. antifreeze   c. antitheft

   _____

   word   definition

2. A person's license is not _____ to another person.

   a. referable   b. preferable   c. transferable

   _____

   word   definition

3. The immigrant was able to _____ her passport for another five years.

   a. extend   b. pretend   c. contend

   _____

   word   definition

4. The father _____ to move the family to the United States.

   a. contended   b. intended   c. distended

   _____

   word   definition

5. After the long journey, the family's arrival in New York was very _____.

   a. promotional   b. institutional   c. emotional

   _____

   word   definition

Unit 28 · Lesson 2

Exercise 4 · Identify It: Relative Pronouns

▸ Read each sentence.

▸ Underline the independent clause.

▸ Identify the relative pronoun and circle it.

▸ Draw an arrow from the relative pronoun to its antecedent.

1. A person whose eyesight is good is very fortunate.

2. The iris, which surrounds the pupil, acts like a curtain.

3. Scientists who study the pupil are amazed by its complexity.

4. The eye's pupil is a hole that lets in light.

5. The school has appointed a person whom they think is competent.

Exercise 5 · Identify It: Adjectival Clauses

▸ Read each sentence.

▸ Identify the relative pronoun and circle it.

▸ Underline the adjectival clause.

1. Light is let into the eye by the pupil, which is at the front of the eyeball.

2. The iris controls the amount of light that enters the eye.

3. The woman, whose retina had become detached, had serious eye problems.

4. The student, who is going to be a doctor, has a vision difficulty.

5. The blind person was helped to cross the street by a passerby whom he asked for assistance.

Exercise 6 · Using Visuals: Diagrams

▶ Read the title of the diagram below and look at the picture.

▶ Read the sentences below the diagram. The sentences are not in the proper order.

▶ Write the number of each step in the process of seeing. Use information from **"A View of the Eye"** on *Student Text* page 149, as well as the numbers on the drawing, to help you.

How the Eye Sends a Picture to the Brain

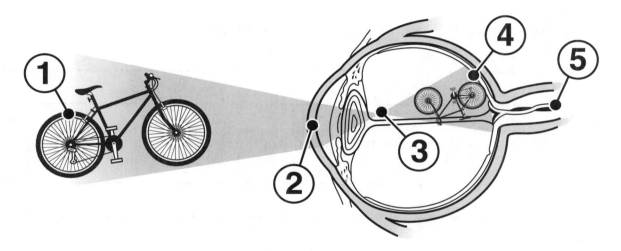

____ Light changes into nerve impulses that are sent to the brain through the optic nerve.

____ The eye views an image.

____ The retina reads the image upside down.

____ Light reflected off the image passes through the cornea.

____ The light rays cross as they go through the cornea.

Unit 28 · Lesson 2

Exercise 7 · Answer It

▶ Use information from the text and the diagram and caption in **"A View of the Eye"** to answer each of these questions. Write complete sentences.

1. Why does the pupil appear black?

_____

_____

2. What is the clear layer of skin covering the eye called?

_____

_____

3. What job do the lens and the cornea do together?

_____

_____

4. How are impulses sent to the brain?

_____

_____

5. Why are the images read by the retina upside down?

_____

_____

Exercise 1 · Sort It: / $\overline{oo}$ / and / $y\overline{oo}$ /

▶ Read each word in the **Word Bank**.

Word Bank

deuce	few	eulogy	pewter	grew
feud	neutron	view	jewel	new

▶ Identify the sound for **eu** or **ew** in the word.

▶ Write the word under the correct heading.

/ $\overline{oo}$ /	/ $y\overline{oo}$ /

Unit 28 · Lesson 3

Exercise 2 · Answer It

▶ Read each question carefully.

▶ Underline the signal word or words in each question.

▶ Write the answer in complete sentences.

1. Form a hypothesis about why Edward and his family decided to immigrate to the United States.

_____

_____

_____

2. Make an inference about what Edward thought the Statue of Liberty symbolized.

_____

_____

_____

3. Explain the significance of the target word **view** in this story.

_____

_____

_____

_____

_____

_____

_____

(continued)

Exercise 2 (continued) · Answer It

4. Paraphrase the last five lines of the poem "**The New Colossus**," starting with the phrase "Give me your tired, your poor."

_____

_____

_____

_____

5. Assess the significance of the message communicated in the poem. Keep in mind that the poem is inscribed on the Statue of Liberty.

_____

_____

_____

_____

_____

Exercise 1 · Listening for Sounds in Words: Sound-Spelling Patterns for Suffix -al

▶ Say each sound in the **Sound Bank** with your teacher.

Sound Bank

| / ch$\overline{oo}$ / | / sh / | / j$\overline{oo}$ / |

▶ Say each word in the first column with your teacher.

▶ Identify the pronunciation of the underlined letters.

▶ Label the column with the correct sound from the **Sound Bank**.

▶ Read the words in the column with your teacher.

▶ Repeat the same process for the remaining columns.
Hint: One of the sound patterns in the **Sound Bank** is used twice.

▶ If needed, use the pronunciation markings in a dictionary to identify the sound for the part of the word spelled <u>ci</u>, <u>ti</u>, <u>du</u>, or <u>tu</u>.

<u>ci</u> =	<u>ti</u> =	<u>du</u> =	<u>tu</u> =
offi<u>ci</u>al	par<u>ti</u>al	indivi<u>du</u>al	vir<u>tu</u>al
so<u>ci</u>al	residen<u>ti</u>al	gra<u>du</u>al	fac<u>tu</u>al
spe<u>ci</u>al	sequen<u>ti</u>al	resi<u>du</u>al	intellec<u>tu</u>al

Exercise 2 · Match It: Affixed Words

▶ Read each word.

▶ Match the word to its definition.

▶ Use your knowledge of prefixes, roots and base words, and suffixes, as well as your **Morphemes for Meaning Cards** and a dictionary, as resources.

▶ Answer the questions at the bottom.

Word	Definition
1. gradual	**a.** characterized by fact
2. malodorous	**b.** relating to an adverb
3. progress	**c.** having a bad odor
4. adverbial	**d.** progressing by regular degrees
5. factual	**e.** to step forward; movement toward a goal

▶ Circle the answer to each of the following questions:

1. What word means the same as **malodorous**?
   a. fresh   b. fragrant   c. smelly

2. What word means the opposite of **progress**?
   a. ingress   b. regress   c. digress

3. What word means the opposite of **factual**?
   a. real   b. imaginary   c. actual

4. Copy the words from the exercise above that have connectives.

_____

5. Explain the function of a connective.

_____

_____

_____

Exercise 3 · Choose It: Present Perfect Tense Verbs

▶ Read each sentence.

▶ Read the answer choices.

▶ Select the one that is in the present perfect tense and write it in the blank.
Note: More than one answer may sound correct, but only one is in the present perfect tense.

▶ Determine if the verb phrase expresses an action occurring at an unspecified time in the past, or an action occurring in the past and continuing in the present.

▶ Check the correct box.

1. I saw Ansel Adams' photos, which _____ in the museum since 1976.
   a. had hung   b. are hanging   c. have hung

2. Many people _____ much about photography by studying Adams' prints.
   a. have learned   b. has learned   c. having learned

3. My family _____ a print of the picture *Monolith* for a long time.
   a. have have   b. has had   c. had had

4. My friend _____ a new digital camera as a gift.
   a. had received   b. has received   c. having received

5. Adams' landscape images _____ many aspiring photographers.
   a. have influenced   b. has influenced   c. is influenced

	Unspecified Time in the Past	Started in the Past, Continuing in the Present
1.		
2.		
3.		
4.		
5.		

Exercise 4 · Write It: Plan a Descriptive Composition

▶ Use the activity below to plan how you will organize your ideas in your descriptive composition.

▶ Write the name of the place you want to describe on the blank.

▶ List concrete details (sights, sounds, and smells) in the boxes.

▶ Then list how you felt and what you did in this new place.

A View of: _____

What did you see?	
What did you hear?	
What did you smell?	

How did the place make you feel?	
What did you do there?	

Exercise 1 · Rewrite It: Affixed Words

▶ Read the words in the **Word Bank**.

Word Bank

factual	malfunctioning	partial	egress
antiseptic	graduation	adverbial	

▶ Read each sentence.

▶ Replace the underlined phrase in the sentence with a word from the **Word Bank**.

▶ Use your **Morphemes for Meaning Cards** and a dictionary as references as needed.

▶ Reread each sentence to check your work.

Sentence with underlined phrase:	Sentence with phrase changed to a single word:
1. The state of receiving a degree from high school is a very special occasion.	_____ from high school is a very special occasion.
2. The step out from the building was clearly marked.	The _____ from the building was clearly marked.
3. The accident was caused by badly functioning brakes.	The accident was caused by _____ brakes.
4. The student's report on immigration was characterized by facts.	The student's report on immigration was _____.
5. The relating to an adverb clause came after the independent clause.	The _____ clause came after the independent clause.

Exercise 2 · Build It: Using Morphemes

▸ Read the directions for each example.

▸ Use the given morphemes to build a word that matches the definition.

▸ Write the word on the line. Remember to assimilate the prefix and apply spelling rules when writing the word.

1. Use this set of morphemes to build a word meaning "the state of stretching out."

| in- | ex- | ten | -ing | -sion |

_____

2. Use this set of morphemes to build a word meaning "able to bear before."

| pro- | pre- | fer | -sion | -able |

_____

3. Use this set of morphemes to build a word meaning "bad practice."

| sub- | mal- | practice | -tion | -ed |

_____

4. Use this set of morphemes to build a word meaning "a state of stretching to."

| in- | ad- | ten | -ed | -tion |

_____

5. Use this set of morphemes to build a word meaning "characterized by stepping forward."

| con- | pro- | gress | -or | -ive |

_____

Exercise 3 · Rewrite It: Sentences

▸ Read the paragraph with your teacher.

▸ Underline each past tense verb that is written incorrectly and write the correct form above it.

▸ Revise each sentence as directed, using the **Masterpiece Sentence Cue Chart**. Remember that **Stage 4: Paint Your Subject** can be used to paint any noun.

▸ Proofread for spelling and punctuation, paying special attention to the past participles.

1. The stepfather buyed tickets for the family for America. 2. They catched the boat in Naples. 3. They arrived in Ellis Island. 4. They were excited. 5. They saw the Statue of Liberty.

(continued)

Exercise 3 (continued) · Rewrite It: Sentences

Item	Use these Masterpiece Sentence stages to expand each sentence.	Make this change.
1.	Stages 2, 4, and 5	Write an adjectival clause telling **which one** about the stepfather. Write an adverbial phrase telling **how** the stepfather bought the tickets. Improve the sentence by adding a descriptor for **family**.
2.	Stage 4	Write an adjectival clause telling **which one** about the boat.
3.	Stage 5	Vary the sentence pattern by not starting the sentence with a pronoun and verb.
4.	Stage 4 and Stage 5	Vary the sentence pattern by not starting the sentence with a pronoun and verb. Write an adjectival clause telling which one about the families.
5.	Stage 4 and Stage 5	Write a participial phrase describing the Statue of Liberty.

_____

_____

_____

_____

_____

_____

Unit 28 · Lesson 5

Exercise 4 · Challenge Writing: Describe Something Unforgettable

The Task: Write a three-paragraph descriptive narrative of something you saw that was unforgettable. Tell how you happened to see that amazing sight, and explain why you will never forget it.

First, talk with a small group of other students about the topic of your essay. Tell them about the amazing thing you saw. Listen to their experiences, too. Then complete items 1–3 below to help you plan the paragraphs in your description.

Descriptive Narrative Planning Guide

Use the space below each direction to plan your paragraphs. You do not need to use complete sentences.

1. **Introductory paragraph**.

   Tell what sight you will be describing: _____

   _____

   Tell how it was that you saw the amazing sight. (where you were, what you did; was it on a trip with your family?)

   When I saw it: _____

   Where I saw it: _____

   Events that led up to viewing the sight: _____

   _____

   _____

   _____

   _____

   (continued)

Exercise 4 (continued) · Challenge Writing: Describe Something Unforgettable

2. **Second paragraph**. List descriptive details. Use clear, precise sensory words.

What I saw: _____

_____

What I heard: _____

_____

What I felt:_____

_____

Ask yourself other questions about the sight. You might start with these:

• Did the sight change as I watched, like a sunset or sunrise?

• What mood or feelings did I experience as I watched?

_____

_____

_____

3. **Third paragraph**. List ideas for a conclusion. Tell why the sight and the experience were memorable and meaningful to you.

_____

_____

_____

_____

Exercise 1 · Spelling Pretest 1

▶ Write the word your teacher repeats.

1. _____   6. _____   11. _____

2. _____   7. _____   12. _____

3. _____   8. _____   13. _____

4. _____   9. _____   14. _____

5. _____   10. _____   15. _____

Exercise 2 · Identify It: Complex Sentences

▶ Read each sentence.

▶ Draw one line under the independent clause.

▶ Look to see if the sentence contains a dependent clause. If it does, look for and circle the subordinating conjunction or the relative pronoun. Draw two lines under the dependent clause that it introduces.

▶ Determine whether the sentence is a simple or complex sentence, and circle the correct answer.

1. The two boys had been friends for many, many years.
   a. simple sentence   b. complex sentence

2. Antonio, who had a long reach, was the better boxer.
   a. simple sentence   b. complex sentence

3. Felix had a muscular frame that made him the better slugger.
   a. simple sentence   b. complex sentence

4. Although they were friends, they were scheduled to fight each other in the tournament.
   a. simple sentence   b. complex sentence

5. The boys fought with enormous energy and great determination.
   a. simple sentence   b. complex sentence

Exercise 3 · Identify It: Confusing Words

▶ Read each sentence and the word choices below the sentence.

▶ Use what you know about the meaning and function of each word to choose the correct word.

▶ Refer to the *Student Text*, page 142, if you need help.

▶ Copy the correct word into the blank.

1. There was _____ time in the schedule this year for athletics.
   a. less   b. fewer

2. As he was leaving the house, the young boxer's mother told him to _____ his boxing gloves with him.
   a. bring   b. take

3. Later the boxer forgot to _____ his clothes home with him.
   a. bring   b. take

4. Of the ten boys, _____ than three were involved in boxing.
   a. less   b. fewer

5. The coach at the gym said to collect all the towels and _____ them to the laundromat.
   a. bring   b. take

Exercise 4 · Write It: Shaping the Topic

Topic 1

1. Make a list of suspenseful competitions you have been in. You can include sporting events, auditions, contests, and so on.

_____

_____

_____

_____

_____

2. Did any of the competitions you listed above end in a surprising or dramatic way? If so, write an X next to that event.

Topic 2

3. Make a list of tense or competitive situations that you have been in with friends.

_____

_____

_____

_____

_____

4. Do you think you can use rising action to describe the event? Would you feel comfortable sharing the event with others? If you answered yes to both these questions, write an X next to that topic.

(continued)

Exercise 4 (continued) · Write It: Shaping the Topic

Choose a Topic

5. Tell the ideas that are marked with an X to a partner. If you did not write an X next to any ideas, then ask your partner to help you brainstorm topics. Write the suggestions here.

_____

_____

_____

_____

_____

6. Based on the thinking you have done so far, what narrative event do you think you would most enjoy writing about?

_____

_____

_____

Unit 28 Lesson 7

Unit 28 · Lesson 7

Exercise 1 · Using a Dictionary

▸ Turn to the **Vocabulary** section in the back of the *Student Text*.

▸ Locate the first word and its pronunciation.

▸ Write the pronunciation for the word on the line next to the word.

▸ Use the markings to read the word aloud.

▸ Complete numbers 2–5 using the same process.

Word	Pronunciation
1. awe	_____
2. barrage	_____
3. pensively	_____
4. aesthetics	_____
5. intuitive	_____

▸ Use a classroom dictionary or www.yourdictionary.com to complete numbers 6–10.

6. leukemia	_____
7. eucalyptus	_____
8. naturalize	_____
9. fluctuate	_____
10. constituent	_____

194 Unit 28 • Lesson 7

Exercise 2 · Add It: Prefixes

▶ Read each word.

▶ Add a prefix to each word to create an antonym.

▶ Choose from these prefixes: **de-**, **un-**, **in-**, **mis-**, and **non-**.
   Note: Prefixes may be used more than once.

    1. hydrate: _____

    2. saturated: _____

    3. official: _____

    4. formal: _____

    5. fortune: _____

▶ Write a sentence with each antonym you wrote.

    1. _____

    2. _____

    3. _____

    4. _____

    5. _____

Exercise 1 · Listening for Word Parts: Prefixes and Suffixes

▸ Listen to each word your teacher says.

▸ Repeat the word.

▸ Mark **Yes** or **No** to tell if you hear a prefix.

▸ If **yes**, write the prefix you hear under the heading **Prefix**.

▸ Mark **Yes** or **No** to tell if you hear a suffix.

▸ If **yes**, write the suffix you hear under the heading **Suffix**.

	Prefixes			Suffixes		
	Do you hear a prefix in the word?		If **Yes**, write the prefix.	Do you hear a suffix in the word?		If **Yes**, write the suffix.
	Yes	No	Prefix	Yes	No	Suffix
1.						
2.						
3.						
4.						
5.						
6.						
7.						
8.						
9.						
10.						

(continued)

Exercise 1 (continued) · Listening for Word Parts: Prefixes and Suffixes

	Prefixes			Suffixes		
	Do you hear a prefix in the word?		If **Yes**, write the prefix.	Do you hear a suffix in the word?		If **Yes**, write the suffix.
	Yes	No	Prefix	Yes	No	Suffix
11.						
12.						
13.						
14.						
15.						

Exercise 2 · Divide It: Morpheme Parts

▸ Read each word.

▸ Break the word into its morpheme parts.

▸ Write these word parts in the blank. Be careful to spell each word part correctly. Place a plus sign (+) between word parts.

1. degrade = _____

2. antismoking = _____

3. contented = _____

4. centigrade = _____

5. preferable = _____

6. maladjustment = _____

7. hyperextend = _____

8. extensive = _____

9. intention = _____

10. congressional = _____

Exercise 3 · Replace It: Synonyms

▶ Read each sentence below, noting the underlined word.

▶ Look in the **Unit Vocabulary** box in the *Student Text*, page 137, to find a synonym for the underlined word.

▶ Write the synonym on the line.

1. I want to be there to <u>congratulate</u> them for their efforts.

   congratulate: _____

2. The car accident was my <u>responsibility</u>.

   responsibility: _____

3. <u>Inform</u> yourself by reading the newspaper.

   inform: _____

4. Put the <u>plate</u> in the dishwasher.

   plate: _____

5. Eating <u>uncooked</u> meat is not healthy.

   uncooked: _____

6. The wind speed can <u>change</u> during a storm.

   change: _____

7. Driving is still <u>novel</u> to many 18-year-olds.

   novel: _____

8. This is a <u>real</u> autograph of my favorite singer.

   real: _____

9. Stand under the <u>canopy</u> while I unlock the door.

   canopy: _____

10. The <u>gemstones</u> sparkled in the showcase.

    gemstones: _____

Unit 28 · Lesson 8

Exercise 4 · Identify It: Confusing Words

▸ Read each sentence and the word choices below the sentence.

▸ Use what you know about the meaning and function of each word to choose the correct word to complete the sentence.

▸ Copy the word into the blank.

▸ Read the completed sentence to check your answer.

1. The spectators _____ through the turnstiles to enter the arena.
   a. gone   b. went

2. The atmosphere in the arena was _____ intense than I thought it would be.
   a. less   b. fewer

3. My friends and I are going to _____ flags to decorate the arena when we go to the event.
   a. bring   b. take

4. Felix's mother asked him to _____ all his gear home after the fight.
   a. bring   b. take

5. After the bout the boxer _____ on the mat and rested.
   a. lay   b. lied

6. The boxer's punches came _____ bolts of lightning.
   a. as   b. like

7. There were fifty _____ people in attendance than expected.
   a. less   b. fewer

8. All their friends had _____ to see the fight.
   a. gone   b. went

9. This year the promoter had _____ money to spend on advertising the boxing competition.
   a. less   b. fewer

10. Felix knows he can punch harder _____ his friend.
    a. then   b. than

Exercise 5 · Diagram It: Sentences With Adjectival Clauses

▶ Do the first example with your teacher.

▶ Read each of the remaining sentences.

▶ Circle the relative pronoun.

▶ Draw an arrow from the relative pronoun to its antecedent.

▶ Draw two lines under the adjectival clause.

▶ Diagram the sentence.

1. Antonio glanced at Felix, who stared straight ahead.

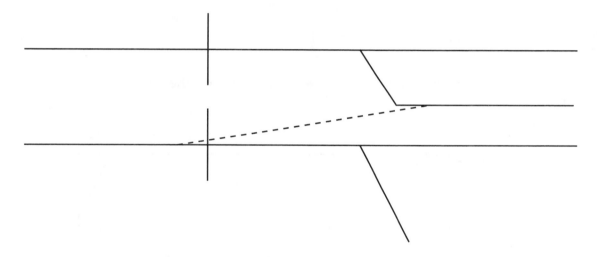

2. The boxer unleashed blows that flattened his opponent.

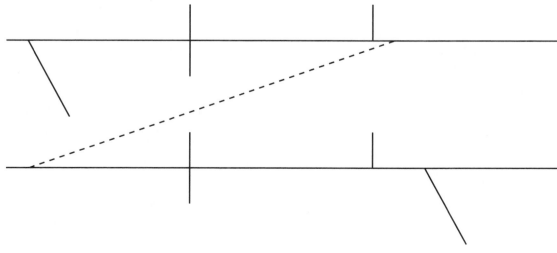

(continued)

Exercise 5 *(continued)* · Diagram It: Sentences With Adjectival Clauses

3. The crowd, which appreciated good sportsmanship, roared with approval.

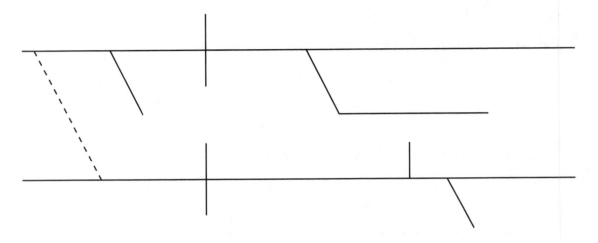

4. The champion, whose real name is unknown, left the arena.

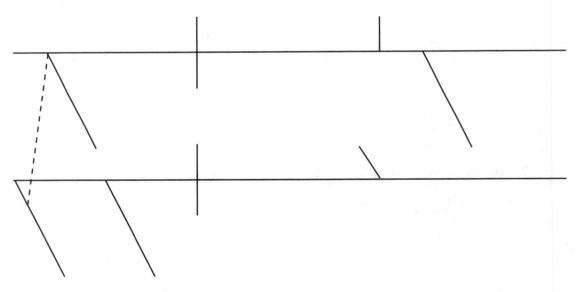

(continued)

5. The two boys, whom everyone now recognized, traded more blows.

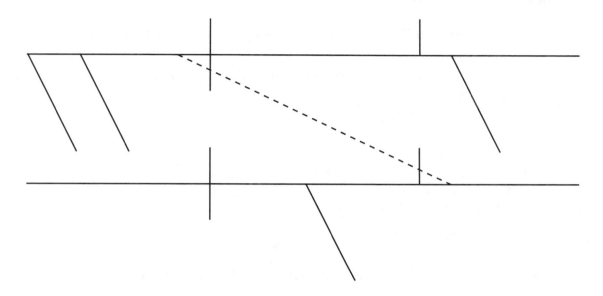

Exercise 6 · Write It: Narrative Outline

▶ Use the outline below to plan how you will organize your ideas in your narrative.

▶ List each main story event. Then, under each event, list key details that will make your story interesting to readers.

▶ Remember that your outline should include rising action and build to a climax.

Introduction: Initiating Event

Event that started the whole story:	

Second Paragraph: Rising Action

Another event:	
Detail:	
Detail:	
Detail:	

(continued)

Third Paragraph: Rising Action

Another event:	
Detail:	
Detail:	
Detail:	

Fourth Paragraph: Climax

Turning point, or most exciting moment:	
Detail:	
Detail:	
Detail:	

(continued)

Exercise 6 (continued) · Write It: Narrative Outline

Resolution/Conclusion

How things turned out:	

Exercise 1 · Answer It: Multiple Choice

▶ Read each question and its answer choices.

▶ Turn to **Text Connection 8, "Amigo Brothers,"** in the *Interactive Text,* pages C59–C72, if you need to check story information.

▶ Underline the correct answer.

▶ Discuss the answers with your teacher.

1. How are Felix and Antonio alike?

    A. They are both best at slugging.

    B. They have the same physical build.

    C. They both place boxing above everything else.

    D. They both love to win.

2. What is the climax of **"Amigo Brothers"**?

    A. when Antonio and Felix charge at each other

    B. when Antonio and Felix walk out of the ring

    C. when Felix starts yelling at Antonio

    D. when Felix decides to stay with his aunt

3. Which of the following statements best captures the message of **"Amigo Brothers"**?

    A. You should never fight a friend.

    B. Winning should come before friendship.

    C. A strong friendship can endure competition.

    D. Competition destroys friendships.

(continued)

Exercise 1 *(continued)* · Answer It: Multiple Choice

4. **"Amigo Brothers"** is an example of _____.

    A. a nonfiction narrative

    B. a fictional narrative

    C. an autobiographical narrative

    D. an informational text

5. What do you think most likely happened after the boxing match?

    A. Antonio and Felix continued to be close friends.

    B. Antonio and Felix slowly drifted apart.

    C. Antonio and Felix had a big argument.

    D. Antonio decided to give up boxing.

Check off the activities you complete with each lesson. Evaluate your accomplishments at the end of each lesson. Pay attention to teacher evaluations and comments.

Unit Objectives	Lesson 1 (Date:_____)	Lesson 2 (Date:_____)
STEP 1 — **Phonemic Awareness and Phonics** • Say the sounds for the phonograms: **all** and **al** (/ ô / as in **call** or **salt**), **alk** (/ ôk / as in **talk**), **wa** (/ wŏ / as in **swap** or / wô / as in **water**), **qua** (/ kwŏ / as in **quad** or / kwô / as in *quart*), **war** (/ wôr / as in **ward** or / wər / as in **backward**), and **wor** (/ wûr / as in **word**). • Write the letters for the sounds / ôl /, / ôk /, / wô /, / kwô /, / wôr /, / wûr /, and / wər / using phonograms.	❏ Discover It: Sounds for *wa* and *qua* ❏ Vowel Chart (T)	❏ Discover It: Sounds for *al*, *all*, and *alk* ❏ Vowel Chart (T)
STEP 2 — **Word Recognition and Spelling** • Read and spell multisyllable words. • Read and spell the **Essential Words:** *oh, straight, whole, whom, whose, wolf.* • Read words with prefixes, suffixes, and roots.	❏ Exercise 1: Spelling Pretest 1 ❏ Memorize It	❏ Exercise 1: Write It: Essential Words ❏ Word Fluency 1
STEP 3 — **Vocabulary and Morphology** • Identify multiple meanings for words. • Identify and define noun suffixes. • Use the meanings of prefixes, suffixes, and roots to define words.	❏ Unit Vocabulary ❏ Multiple Meaning Map (T) ❏ Write It: Journal Entry	❏ Exercise 2: Choose It: Affixed Words
STEP 4 — **Grammar and Usage** • Identify relative pronouns and adjectival clauses. • Identify participial phrases. • Identify the past perfect tense.	❏ Exercise 2: Identify It: Past Perfect Tense Verbs ❏ Exercise 3: Identify It: Pronouns	❏ Exercise 3: Identify It: Relative Pronouns and Adjectival Clauses ❏ Exercise 4: Identify It: Confusing Words
STEP 5 — **Listening and Reading Comprehension** • Interpret visual information. • Use context-based strategies to define words. • Identify imagery in poetry. • Identify features of persuasive writing. • Understand different types of signal words.	❏ Independent Text: "Advertisements: It's Your Call" ❏ Exercise 4: Phrase It ❏ Exercise 5: Use the Clues	❏ Passage Fluency 1 ❏ Exercise 5: Using Visuals: Commercial Transcripts and Print Ads
STEP 6 — **Speaking and Writing** • Use visual and text information to answer questions. • Write responses to sentences with signal words. • Organize information in a graphic organizer and write a persuasive composition.	❏ Exercise 6: Rewrite It	❏ Exercise 6: Answer It
Self-Evaluation (5 is the highest) **Effort** = I produced my best work. **Participation** = I was actively involved in tasks. **Independence** = I worked on my own.	Effort: 1 2 3 4 5 Participation: 1 2 3 4 5 Independence: 1 2 3 4 5	Effort: 1 2 3 4 5 Participation: 1 2 3 4 5 Independence: 1 2 3 4 5
Teacher Evaluation	Effort: 1 2 3 4 5 Participation: 1 2 3 4 5 Independence: 1 2 3 4 5	Effort: 1 2 3 4 5 Participation: 1 2 3 4 5 Independence: 1 2 3 4 5

Lesson 3 (Date:_____)	**Lesson 4** (Date:_____)	**Lesson 5** (Date:_____)
❑ Discover It: Sounds for _war_ and _wor_	❑ Exercise 1: Listening for Sounds in Words: Sound-Spelling Patterns	❑ Content Mastery: Variant Sounds for _a_
❑ Divide It ❑ Word Fluency 2	❑ Make a Mnemonic ❑ Present It: Mnemonics for Confusing Word Pairs	❑ Content Mastery: Spelling Posttest 1 ❑ Present It: Mnemonics for Confusing Word Pairs
❑ Vocabulary Focus ❑ Use the Clues ❑ Expression of the Day	❑ Exercise 2: Match It: Affixed Words	❑ Exercise 1: Rewrite It: Affixed Words ❑ Exercise 2: Build It: Using Morphemes
❑ Identify It: Pronouns	❑ Exercise 3: Identify It: Present Perfect Tense Verbs and Past Perfect Tense Verbs ❑ Masterpiece Sentences: Stage 4	❑ Exercise 3: Rewrite It: Sentences
❑ Instructional Text: "Cell Phones for Teens: A Good Call for Safety?"	❑ Take Note: Structure of a Persuasive Essay ❑ Map It: Persuasive Writing (T)	❑ Write It: Persuasive Essay (T)
❑ Exercise 1: Answer It	❑ Exercise 4: Write It: Shaping the Topic ❑ Map It: Persuasive Writing (T) ❑ Challenge Text: "For the Love of a Man"	❑ Revise It: Persuasive Essay ❑ Challenge Text: "For the Love of a Man" ❑ Exercise 4: Challenge Writing: Letter to the Editor
Effort: 1 2 3 4 5 **Participation:** 1 2 3 4 5 **Independence:** 1 2 3 4 5	**Effort:** 1 2 3 4 5 **Participation:** 1 2 3 4 5 **Independence:** 1 2 3 4 5	**Effort:** 1 2 3 4 5 **Participation:** 1 2 3 4 5 **Independence:** 1 2 3 4 5
Effort: 1 2 3 4 5 **Participation:** 1 2 3 4 5 **Independence:** 1 2 3 4 5	**Effort:** 1 2 3 4 5 **Participation:** 1 2 3 4 5 **Independence:** 1 2 3 4 5	**Effort:** 1 2 3 4 5 **Participation:** 1 2 3 4 5 **Independence:** 1 2 3 4 5

Check off the activities you complete with each lesson. Evaluate your accomplishments at the end of each lesson. Pay attention to teacher evaluations and comments.

Unit Objectives	Lesson 6 (Date:_____)	Lesson 7 (Date:_____)
STEP 1 — Phonemic Awareness and Phonics • Say the sounds for the phonograms: <u>all</u> and <u>al</u> (/ ô / as in **call** or **salt**), <u>alk</u> (/ ôk / as in **talk**), <u>wa</u> (/ wŏ / as in **swap** or / wô / as in **water**), <u>qua</u> (/ kwŏ / as in **quad** or / kwô / as in **quart**), <u>war</u> (/ wôr / as in **ward** or / wər / as in **backward**), and <u>wor</u> (/ wûr / as in **word**). • Write the letters for the sounds / ôl /, / ôk /, / wô /, / kwô /, / wôr /, / wûr /, and / wər / using phonograms.	❑ Content Mastery: Using Student Performance	❑ Exercise 1: Using a Dictionary
STEP 2 — Word Recognition and Spelling • Read and spell multisyllable words. • Read and spell the **Essential Words:** oh, straight, whole, whom, whose, wolf. • Read words with prefixes, suffixes, and roots.	❑ Exercise 1: Spelling Pretest 2 ❑ Word Fluency 3	❑ Build It: Words With Suffixes ❑ Word Fluency 4
STEP 3 — Vocabulary and Morphology • Identify multiple meanings for words. • Identify and define noun suffixes. • Use the meanings of prefixes, suffixes, and roots to define words.	❑ Vocabulary Focus ❑ Use the Clues ❑ Expression of the Day	❑ Vocabulary Focus ❑ Multiple Meaning Map (T) ❑ Expression of the Day
STEP 4 — Grammar and Usage • Identify relative pronouns and adjectival clauses. • Identify participial phrases. • Identify the past perfect tense.	❑ Exercise 2: Identify It: Sentence Structure ❑ Exercise 3: Punctuate It: Commas	❑ Exercise 2: Identify It: Confusing Words ❑ Identify It: Adjectives and Participial Phrases
STEP 5 — Listening and Reading Comprehension • Interpret visual information. • Use context-based strategies to define words. • Identify imagery in poetry. • Identify features of persuasive writing. • Understand different types of signal words.	❑ Instructional Text: "A Call to Poetry" ❑ Comprehend It ❑ Exercise 4: Take Note: Imagery Through Figurative Language	❑ Comprehend It ❑ Take Note: Imagery Through Figurative Language
STEP 6 — Speaking and Writing • Use visual and text information to answer questions. • Write responses to sentences with signal words. • Organize information in a graphic organizer and write a persuasive composition.	❑ Exercise 5: Write It: Shaping the Topic	❑ Exercise 3: Write It: Explore Your Topic
Self-Evaluation (5 is the highest) **Effort** = I produced my best work. **Participation** = I was actively involved in tasks. **Independence** = I worked on my own.	**Effort:** 1 2 3 4 5 **Participation:** 1 2 3 4 5 **Independence:** 1 2 3 4 5	**Effort:** 1 2 3 4 5 **Participation:** 1 2 3 4 5 **Independence:** 1 2 3 4 5
Teacher Evaluation	**Effort:** 1 2 3 4 5 **Participation:** 1 2 3 4 5 **Independence:** 1 2 3 4 5	**Effort:** 1 2 3 4 5 **Participation:** 1 2 3 4 5 **Independence:** 1 2 3 4 5

Lesson 8 (Date:_____)	Lesson 9 (Date:_____)	Lesson 10 (Date:_____)
❑ Exercise 1: Listening for Word Parts: Prefixes and Suffixes		
❑ Exercise 2: Build It: Words With Prefixes, Suffixes, and Roots	❑ Exercise 1: Identify It: Spelling Rules	❑ Content Mastery: Spelling Posttest 2
❑ Exercise 3: Fill In: Multiple Meanings	❑ Content Mastery: Multiple Meanings ❑ Content Mastery: Affixed Words	❑ Content Mastery: Using Student Performance ❑ Using a Dictionary: Word Origins ❑ Find It: Word Derivations ❑ Write a Mini-Dialog: Idioms
❑ Exercise 4: Punctuate It: Commas ❑ Exercise 5: Diagram It: Sentences With Adjectival Clauses (T)	❑ Content Mastery	❑ Content Mastery: Using Student Performance
❑ Comprehend It ❑ Exercise 6: Take Note: Imagery Through Figurative Language	❑ Instructional Text: "A Call to Poetry" ❑ Exercise 2: Answer It: Multiple Choice	❑ Revise It: Descriptive Paragraph
❑ Write It: Descriptive Paragraph Outline	❑ Write It: Descriptive Paragraph ❑ Challenge Text: "The Sounding of the Call"	❑ Revise It: Descriptive Paragraph ❑ Present It: Descriptive Paragraph ❑ Challenge Text: "The Sounding of the Call"
Effort: 1 2 3 4 5 **Participation:** 1 2 3 4 5 **Independence:** 1 2 3 4 5	**Effort:** 1 2 3 4 5 **Participation:** 1 2 3 4 5 **Independence:** 1 2 3 4 5	**Effort:** 1 2 3 4 5 **Participation:** 1 2 3 4 5 **Independence:** 1 2 3 4 5
Effort: 1 2 3 4 5 **Participation:** 1 2 3 4 5 **Independence:** 1 2 3 4 5	**Effort:** 1 2 3 4 5 **Participation:** 1 2 3 4 5 **Independence:** 1 2 3 4 5	**Effort:** 1 2 3 4 5 **Participation:** 1 2 3 4 5 **Independence:** 1 2 3 4 5

Lesson 1

Exercise 1 · Spelling Pretest 1

▶ Write the word your teacher repeats.

1. _____   6. _____   11. _____

2. _____   7. _____   12. _____

3. _____   8. _____   13. _____

4. _____   9. _____   14. _____

5. _____   10. _____   15. _____

Exercise 2 · Identify It: Past Perfect Tense Verbs

▶ Read each sentence.

▶ Identify the two verbs in the sentence and underline them.

▶ Determine which verb is in the past perfect tense and label it PPT.

▶ Write the order of the actions in the sentence on the line.

1. The cell phone company had offered a special price for July, so many families ordered phones.

   _____

   _____

2. The boy's parents had bought him a cell phone when he left for college.

   _____

   _____

3. Before she purchased her phone, my friend had read only one article about cell phones.

   _____

   _____

4. I had finished my homework early, so I made phone calls to several friends.

   _____

   _____

5. The soccer player had scored a goal a second before the whistle sounded.

   _____

   _____

Exercise 3 · Identify It: Pronouns

▸ Read each sentence.

▸ Identify the pronoun and underline it.

▸ Decide if the pronoun is a nominative, object, or possessive pronoun.

▸ Copy each of these pronouns into the correct column below.

▸ Copy the pronouns that are indefinite pronouns on the line below.

	Nominative	Object	Possessive
1. Ads try to convince us to buy products.			
2. Some are aimed directly at young people.			
3. A lot of pressure is put on them to buy items.			
4. Everyone must look at ads critically.			
5. Buyers must realize the decision to buy or not to buy is theirs.			
6. Grandma had a cell phone, and I had mine, too.			
7. Grandma called me right after school.			
8. We cannot use cell phones in some areas.			
9. Cell phones are helpful, so protect yours.			
10. You must remember to keep the phone's battery charged.			

▸ List the indefinite pronouns used in the above sentences on the line below.

_____

Exercise 4 · Phrase It

▸ Use the penciling strategy to "scoop" the phrases in each sentence.

▸ Read the sentences as you would speak them.

from "Advertisements: It's Your Call"

Advertising is often aimed at young people. Young people spend billions of dollars every year. They also influence how their parents spend money. It is important to look critically at ads that are aimed at you. While ads do inform you about products, they also try to persuade you to buy them. Advertisers try to make you think that buying their product will make you happy and improve your life. Of course, not many products will really do this.

Exercise 5 · Use the Clues

▶ Read the excerpt below.

▶ Reread the underlined word **medium**.

▶ Reread the entire sentence. The sentence says, "TV is another medium. . . ." This tells you that TV is one example of a medium. The sentence also tells you that other examples came before TV.

▶ Circle **TV**.

▶ Reread the sentences that precede the sentence in which this word appears. Circle two other examples of a **medium**.

▶ Write a definition for **medium** in this context. Then answer the question.

---

from "Advertisements: It's Your Call"

Ads come in many forms. One form is the print ad. Much space in magazines

and newspapers is used for ads. Print ads use pictures and words to persuade

readers to buy products and services. Other ads are broadcast on the radio.

Between songs, companies try to sell products and services. TV is another

<u>medium</u> filled with ads.

Define It:

medium: _____

The plural form of **medium** is **media**. Write four kinds of media listed in the text above.

_____

Exercise 6 · Rewrite It

▶ Read each of the following pairs of sentences.

▶ Look at the subordinating conjunctions listed in the box.

▶ Choose a subordinating conjunction from the box that makes clear the logical connection between the two sentences.

▶ Use that subordinating conjunction to combine the two sentences into a single sentence.

although	while	because	if	unless

Example: Ads provide some information about products. They also try to persuade you to buy those products.
While ads provide some information about products, they also try to persuade you to buy those products.

1. Young people spend billions of dollars every year. Advertising is often aimed at them.

   _____

   _____

   _____

2. Advertisers study the people who buy their products. They know a lot about what those people like to buy.

   _____

   _____

   _____

(continued)

Exercise 6 (continued) · Rewrite It

3. Consumers do not read ads carefully. They may spend too much money.

_____

_____

_____

4. Young people look at product information carefully. They may buy a bad product.

_____

_____

_____

5. Cell phone ads may include some price information. There may still be hidden costs.

_____

_____

_____

Exercise 1 · Write It: Essential Words

▶ Review the **Essential Words** in the **Word Bank**.

Word Bank

wolf	whole	straight	whom	whose	oh

▶ Put the words in alphabetical order and write them on the lines.

▶ Write one sentence for each **Essential Word**.

▶ Check that each sentence uses sentence signals—correct capitalization, commas, and end punctuation.

1. _____

   _____

2. _____

   _____

3. _____

   _____

4. _____

   _____

5. _____

   _____

6. _____

   _____

Unit 29 · Lesson 2

Exercise 2 · Choose It: Affixed Words

▸ Read each sentence.

▸ Choose the correct word to complete the sentence and write it in the blank.

▸ Circle each prefix and suffix, and underline the root or base word of the word chosen.

▸ Write the word and its definition on the line. Use your **Morphemes for Meaning Cards** and a dictionary as resources.

1. The town holds its _____ meetings in March and October.

   a. semiliquid   b. semiannual   c. semitone

   _____

   word   definition

2. The new _____ of a cell tower in the park was challenged by the neighbors.

   a. instruction   b. obstruction   c. construction

   _____

   word   definition

3. The phone call was _____ by constant static.

   a. disrupted   b. erupted   c. ruptured

   _____

   word   definition

4. Loud cheering _____ at the end of the concert.

   a. disrupted   b. erupted   c. corrupted

   _____

   word   definition

5. The _____ for obtaining a cell phone is very simple.

   a. rupture   b. puncture   c. procedure

   _____

   word   definition

Exercise 3 · Identify It: Relative Pronouns and Adjectival Clauses

▶ Read each sentence.

▶ Identify the relative pronoun and circle it.

▶ Identify the adjectival clause and underline it twice.

▶ Draw an arrow from the relative pronoun to its antecedent.

1. People who create advertisements study teenage behavior.

2. Some ads offer products that are overpriced.

3. Advertisers, who are paid to promote products, try to get people to remember the products they advertise.

4. The big advertisement on the sports page, which featured an athletic superstar, was very successful.

5. Athletes, whom teenagers respect, are paid large sums to appear in ads.

Exercise 4 · Identify It: Confusing Words

▸ Read each sentence and the word choices below the sentence.

▸ Use what you know about the meaning and function of each word to choose the correct word to complete the sentence.

▸ Refer to the *Student Text* if needed.

▸ Copy the correct word into the blank.

1. Most of the students _____ are in my class have cell phones.
    a. who   b. which

2. The new cell phones, _____ sounded so good in the ads, really were not worth the money.
    a. who   b. which

3. My parents have _____ given me a cell phone.
    a. all ready   b. already

4. The firefighter, _____ was standing outside the building, was talking on a cell phone.
    a. who   b. which

5. My bag is packed, and I am _____ to leave.
    a. all ready   b. already

Exercise 5 · Using Visuals: Commercial Transcripts and Print Ads

▸ Read the title of the table below.

▸ Read the sentences listed in the left column of the table.

▸ Use information presented in the print ad and the radio commercial transcript in the *Student Text*, pages 191–192, to complete the table. Write the information in the right-hand column of the table.

▸ If information listed in the left column of the table is not provided in the ad, write **???**.

Evaluating the IM Wireless Free Cell Phone Ad	
Product being advertised:	camera cell phone
Company selling the phone:	
Number to call for more information:	
Free times to call on nights and weekends:	
Cost of 2 phones after rebate:	$49.99 plus tax and fees
Cost of 2 phones before rebate:	
Amount of rebate:	$50
Special features of the phone:	
Requirements to use phone:	2-year service agreement
Cost of service agreement:	

Exercise 6 · Answer It

▶ Use information from the text and from the commercial transcript and print ad in **"Advertisements: It's Your Call"** to answer each of these questions. Write complete sentences.

1. Is the camera phone advertised in the ad really "free"? Why or why not?

_____

_____

_____

_____

2. The print ad says that the price of the phone is $49.99 plus taxes and fees. Does the ad explain what fees will be charged? Why do you think this information is not made clear in the ad?

_____

_____

_____

_____

3. What is the catch to the "free" calls on nights and weekends?

_____

_____

_____

_____

(continued)

Exercise 6 (continued) · Answer It

4. How many times does the word **free** appear in the commercial transcript? How many times does it appear in the print ad? Why might the advertisers want the word **free** to appear more than once in their ads?

_____

_____

_____

_____

5. Advertisers create ads that are targeted or directed at particular groups of consumers, such as teens, parents with young children, or the elderly. What group do you think is being targeted in the radio commercial? Do you think this same group is being targeted in the print ad? Why or why not?

_____

_____

_____

_____

Exercise 1 · Answer It

▸ Underline the signal word in the question.

▸ Write the answer in complete sentences.

1. Identify the author's main reason for why kids should have cell phones.

_____

_____

_____

_____

_____

2. Outline the main points the author makes to support her view that kids should have cell phones.

_____

_____

_____

_____

_____

3. Critique the author's point that cell phones will make young people safer.

_____

_____

_____

_____

_____

(continued)

Exercise 1 *(continued)* · **Answer It**

4. Explain the generalization that the author is making about phone companies when she writes, "Instead of just targeting young people with eye-popping features and flashy advertising campaigns, they should work to make safety-first cell phones available and affordable for all families."

_____

_____

_____

_____

_____

5. In the third paragraph of the essay, the author gives several reasons why parents might not want their children to have cell phones. Make an inference about why the author takes parents' concerns into account in her essay.

_____

_____

_____

_____

_____

Exercise 1 · Listening for Sounds in Words: Sound-Spelling Patterns

▸ Say each sound in the **Sound Bank** with your teacher.

Sound Bank

/ wŏ /	/ kwŏ /	/ ôl /	/ ôk /	/ wôr /	/ wûr /

▸ Say each word in the first column with your teacher.

▸ Identify the pronunciation of the underlined letters.

▸ Label the column with the correct sound from the **Sound Bank**.

▸ Repeat the same process for the remaining columns.

▸ If needed, use the pronunciation markings in a dictionary or www.yourdictionary.com to identify the sound-spelling patterns.

<u>al</u>, <u>all</u> =	<u>alk</u> =	<u>wa</u> =	<u>qua</u> =	<u>war</u> =	<u>wor</u> =
<u>al</u>ways	b<u>alk</u>	s<u>wa</u>n	<u>qua</u>lify	a<u>war</u>d	net<u>wor</u>k
<u>al</u>ready	crossw<u>alk</u>	<u>wa</u>nder	squ<u>a</u>nder	re<u>war</u>d	<u>wor</u>thwhile
inst<u>all</u>ment	st<u>alk</u>	stop<u>wa</u>tch	q<u>ua</u>ntum	<u>war</u>rant	<u>wor</u>ry

▸ Practice reading the word lists above with a partner.

Exercise 2 · Match It: Affixed Words

▶ Read each word.

▶ Match the word to its definition from word parts. Use your knowledge of prefixes, roots and suffixes, your **Morphemes for Meaning Cards**, and a dictionary as resources.

▶ Answer the questions at the bottom.

Word	Definition from Word Parts
1. rupture	**a.** the act of sending in
2. sustenance	**b.** state of being put together
3. pertinence	**c.** state of holding from below
4. admittance	**d.** state of holding thoroughly
5. composure	**e.** process of breaking

▶ Circle the answer to each of the following questions:

1. If the Latin root **volens** means "wishing," what does **malevolence** mean?
a. state of wishing good will   b. state of wishing bad will   c. state of being happy

2. What word means the opposite of **antisocial**?
a. unfriendly   b. unsocial   c. social

3. What word means "half of a circle"?
a. demicircle   b. semicircle   c. seminal

4. What word means the opposite of **obstruction**?
a. stoppage   b. blockage   c. assistance

5. What word means the same as **disrupt**?
a. break   b. fix   c. mend

Exercise 3 · Identify It: Present Perfect Tense Verbs and Past Perfect Tense Verbs

▸ Read each sentence.

▸ Identify the verb in the perfect tense and underline it.

▸ Determine whether the verb phrase is in the present perfect tense, or the past perfect tense.

▸ Circle the correct answer.

1. Cell phones have become extremely popular with young people.
   a. present perfect tense   b. past perfect tense

2. I had written the phone number on a piece of paper, but then I lost it.
   a. present perfect tense   b. past perfect tense

3. My family has had a family cell phone service for some time now.
   a. present perfect tense   b. past perfect tense

4. The advertisers had signed a contract with the young star before he became famous.
   a. present perfect tense   b. past perfect tense

5. The lost boy had been alone until rescuers found him.
   a. present perfect tense   b. past perfect tense

Exercise 4 · Write It: Shaping the Topic

▶ Use the activity below to generate ideas to support the following position:

Position: Kids should not be allowed to have cell phones.

Who is your audience?

_____

What is your purpose for writing?

_____

Reasons to Support Your Position

1. Make a list of reasons why it is not a good idea for kids to own cell phones.

_____

_____

_____

2. Look at the reasons you listed in 1 above. Which is the strongest? Put an X next to the strongest reason.

Anticipated Objections

3. List at least one reason why some people may feel it is a good idea for kids to have cell phones. (You may use a reason that the author of "**Cell Phones for Teens: A Good Call for Safety?**" gave in her essay.)

_____

_____

4. What could you say to convince people that this is **not** a good reason to buy a cell phone for a kid? Write your idea here.

_____

Exercise 1 · Rewrite It: Affixed Words

▶ Read the words in the **Word Bank**.

Word Bank

submitted	tenure	semitones
credence	corrupted	admittance

▶ Read each sentence.

▶ Replace the underlined phrase in the sentence with a word from the **Word Bank** which makes sense.

▶ Use your **Morphemes for Meaning Cards** and a dictionary as references as needed.

▶ Reread each sentence to check your work.

Sentence With Underlined Phrase:	Sentence With Phrase Changed to a Single Word:
1. The code for the cell phones was all <u>broken together</u>.	The code for the cell phones was all _____.
2. <u>The state of holding office</u> is granted to teachers who have demonstrated excellence.	_____ is granted to teachers who have demonstrated excellence.
3. It is not possible to give <u>a state of believing</u> to all advertisements we hear and see.	It is not possible to give _____ to all advertisements we hear and see.
4. The music scale was made up of whole tones and <u>half tones</u>.	The music scale was made up of whole tones and _____.
5. The student <u>sent under</u> an application for a cell phone.	The student _____ an application for a cell phone.

Exercise 2 · Build It: Using Morphemes

▶ Read the directions for each example.

▶ Build a word with the given morphemes that matches the definition.

▶ Write the word on the line. Remember to assimilate the prefix if required and apply any spelling rules, and remember tense when building verbs

1. Use this set of morphemes to build a word meaning "state of breaking apart."

in-	dis-	rupt	-ing	-sion

_____

2. Use this set of morphemes to build a word meaning "built against."

pro-	ob-	struct	-sion	-ed

_____

3. Use this set of morphemes to build a word meaning "state of bearing in."

in-	con-	fer	-ence	-ure

_____

4. Use this set of morphemes to build a word meaning "a state of taking to."

in-	ad-	cept	-tion	-ance

_____

5. Use this set of morphemes to build a word meaning "process of throwing together."

con-	pro-	ject	-ure	-ence

_____

Exercise 3 · Rewrite It: Sentences

▸ Read the paragraph with your teacher.

▸ Underline any past tense verb form that is used incorrectly and write the correct form above it.

▸ Revise each sentence as directed using the **Masterpiece Sentence Cue Chart**. Remember that **Stage 4: Paint Your Subject** can be used to paint any noun.

▸ Proofread for spelling and punctuation, paying special attention to the past participles.

---

1. The boy had an accident. 2. He lied on the side of the road. 3. A person called his parents for him. 4. They comed and got him. 5. They later got him a cell phone.

(continued)

Exercise 3 (continued) · Rewrite It: Sentences

Item	Use these Masterpiece Sentence stages to expand each sentence.	Make this change.
1.	Stage 4	Write an adjectival clause telling **which one** about the boy.
2.	Stage 4	Write a participial phrase describing how he lay
3.	Stage 2 and Stage 4	Write an adjectival clause telling **which one** about the driver. Write a compound predicate to make the actions clearer.
4.	Stage 2, Stage 4 and Stage 5	Write a participial phrase to describe the parents. Add an adverb to modify the verb. Use a different word for **got**. Vary the sentence structure by not starting the sentence with a pronoun and verb.
5.	Stage 4 and Stage 5	Avoid repetition of the pronoun **they** by replacing it with the noun it stands for. Write an adjectival clause describing the cell phone. Use a different word for **got**.

_____

_____

_____

_____

_____

_____

_____

Exercise 4 · Challenge Writing: Letter to the Editor

The Task: Use the **Guidelines for Writing a Business Letter** and your completed **Map It: Persuasive Writing** template to help you write a letter to the editor. In your letter, support one of the following positions:

- Flashing billboards should (or should not) be restricted in certain areas.

- After-school sports programs should (or should not) be paid for by the community.

Guidelines for Writing a Business Letter

- Use formal language. (For example, do not use contractions, such as **isn't**. Write **is not**.)

- Say enough to explain your points, but do not say more than you need to be clear.

- Be polite and friendly.

- Check your spelling, grammar, and punctuation.

Exercise 1 · Spelling Pretest 2

▶ Write the word your teacher repeats.

1. _____   6. _____   11. _____

2. _____   7. _____   12. _____

3. _____   8. _____   13. _____

4. _____   9. _____   14. _____

5. _____   10. _____   15. _____

Exercise 2 · Identify It: Sentence Structure

▶ Read each sentence.

▶ Draw a line under each independent clause.

▶ Look to see if the sentence contains a dependent clause. If it does, look for and circle the subordinating conjunction or the relative pronoun. Then draw two lines under the dependent clause that the circled word introduces.

▶ Determine if the sentence is a simple, compound, or complex sentence and circle the correct answer.

1. Naomi Shihab Nye wrote "Postscript", and Luis J. Rodriguez wrote "The Calling."
a. simple   b. compound   c. complex

2. Rodriguez writes of a boy waiting for his calling.
a. simple   b. compound   c. complex

3. Nye writes of a person whose words were hurtful.
a. simple   b. compound   c. complex

4. In bear country, silence that swiftly flows between the juniper trees surrounds a person.
a. simple   b. compound   c. complex

5. Everyone has a calling, but only some hear it.
a. simple   b. compound   c. complex

Exercise 3 · Punctuate It: Commas

▶ Read each sentence.

▶ Place commas where needed.

▶ Identify the reason for the commas and circle the correct answer.

▶ Answer the question below.

1. The publishing company is moving to 10 Read Street Bookville Arizona next month.
   a. series   b. date   c. address   d. nonessential dependent clause

2. The poem which we read in class really appealed to me.
   a. series   b. date   c. address   d. nonessential dependent clause

3. The poem spoke of damp earth massive sounds winter sun and ice shadows.
   a. series   b. date   c. address   d. nonessential dependent clause

4. The poetry book was published on May 6 2005 and quickly sold out.
   a. series   b. date   c. address   d. nonessential dependent clause

5. Leslie Marmon Silko who is a poet wrote about nature.
   a. series   b. date   c. address   d. nonessential dependent clause

▶ Name the type of dependent clause used in both of the complex sentences above, and tell what introduces these clauses.

_____

_____

Exercise 4 · Identify It: Figurative Language

▸ Use the chart below to take notes on figurative language (metaphors, similes, personification, and symbols) used in the three poems in **"A Call to Poetry."**

"Postscript"			
Line	Thing Being Described	What It Is Compared to or What It Represents	Type of Figurative Language

(continued)

Exercise 4 *(continued)* · **Identify It: Figurative Language**

	"The Calling"		
Line	Thing Being Described	What It Is Compared to or What It Represents	Type of Figurative Language

(continued)

Exercise 4 (continued) · Identify It: Figurative Language

"Story from Bear Country"			
Line	Thing Being Described	What It Is Compared to or What It Represents	Type of Figurative Language

Exercise 5 · Write It: Shaping the Topic

▶ You have been given the following writing prompt:
Write a descriptive paragraph about a familiar activity. Describe the activity in detail and include at least one metaphor or simile comparing that activity to something else.

▶ Use this activity to help you narrow the topic to something you would like to write about.

1. List 3–4 activities that you are very familiar with. You might include

   • things you do every day or very often (for example: reading, cooking, watching TV)

   • things you most enjoy doing (for example: drawing, playing basketball, singing)

   _____

   _____

   _____

   _____

2. Look at your list of activities and ask yourself the following questions:

   • Which topic do I feel really strongly about?

   • Which topic can I describe in great detail?

   • Which topic do I have an original perspective on, that is, a point of view that might be new or unusual?

3. Circle the topic that you would most like to write about.

Exercise 1 · Using a Dictionary

▶ Turn to the **Vocabulary** section in the back of the *Student Text*.

▶ Find the word **clamor** and its pronunciation.

▶ Write the diacritical markings for that word on the line in item 1 below.

▶ Use the markings to read the word aloud.

▶ Complete numbers 2–5 using the same process.

Word	Pronunciation
1. clamor	_____
2. languished	_____
3. primordial	_____
4. scenario	_____
5. writhe	_____

▶ Use a classroom dictionary or www.yourdictionary.com to complete numbers 6–10.

6. architecture	_____
7. fluorescence	_____
8. forfeiture	_____
9. picture	_____
10. pitcher	_____

Exercise 2 · Identify It: Confusing Words

▶ Read each sentence and the word choices below the sentence.

▶ Use what you know about the meaning and function of each word to choose the correct word to complete the sentence.

▶ Refer to the *Student Text* page 184, if needed.

▶ Copy the word into the blank.

▶ Read the completed sentence to check your answer.

1. The students _____ were absent missed a great presentation.
   a. who   b. which

2. The equipment was _____ for the soccer match.
   a. all ready   b. already

3. Our class has _____ had its final exams.
   a. all ready   b. already

4. I prefer poems _____ make me think.
   a. who   b. which

5. My parents, _____ enjoy poetry, gave me a book of poems.
   a. who   b. which

6. This poem has a stronger rhythm _____ that poem.
   a. then   b. than

7. On Saturdays I like to _____ on a mat in the sun and read.
   a. lay   b. lie

8. There are _____ cars on the highway during the weekend.
   a. less   b. fewer

9. All the family had _____ to a movie, so there was no one home when the delivery person arrived.
   a. gone   b. went

10. The teacher told us to _____ all our belongings with us when we left class.
   a. bring   b. take

Exercise 3 · Write It: Explore Your Topic

▶ Use this activity to begin exploring the topic you chose in Exercise 5 of Lesson 6, **Write It: Shaping a Topic**.

Activity: _____

sights		
sounds		
smells		
taste		
touch, things you feel		

Exercise 1 · Listening for Word Parts: Prefixes and Suffixes

▶ Listen to each word your teacher says.

▶ Repeat the word.

▶ Mark **Yes** or **No** to tell if you hear a prefix.

▶ If **yes**, write the prefix you hear under the heading **Prefix**.

▶ Mark **Yes** or **No** to tell if you hear a suffix.

▶ If **yes**, write the suffix you hear under the heading **Suffix**.

	Prefixes				Suffixes		
	Do you hear a prefix on the word?		If **Yes**, write the prefix.		Do you hear a suffix on the word?		If **Yes**, write the suffix.
	Yes	No	Prefix		Yes	No	Suffix
1.							
2.							
3.							
4.							
5.							
6.							
7.							
8.							
9.							
10.							

(continued)

Exercise 1 (continued) · Listening for Word Parts: Prefixes and Suffixes

Prefixes			Suffixes		
Do you hear a prefix in the word?		If **Yes**, write the prefix.	Do you hear a suffix in the word?		If **Yes**, write the suffix.
Yes	No	Prefix	Yes	No	Suffix
11.					
12.					
13.					
14.					
15.					

Exercise 2 · Build It: Words With Prefixes, Suffixes, and Roots

▶ Read the word parts in each table.

▶ Combine word parts to build as many words as you can. (To build some words, you may use three word parts.)

▶ Record the words on the lines below the table.

▶ Check a dictionary to verify that the words you write are real words.

1.

de-	in-	struct	-ure

_____   _____   _____   _____

2.

ab-	bank-	rupt	-ure

_____   _____   _____   _____

3.

in-	de-	struct	-tion

_____   _____   _____   _____

4.

semi-	month	week	-ly

_____   _____   _____   _____

5.

inter	e	rupt	-tion

_____   _____   _____   _____

Exercise 3 · Fill In: Multiple Meanings

▶ Read the words in the **Word Bank**.

Word Bank

stall	swarm	swallow	world	call

▶ Read each sentence.

▶ Fill in the blank with a word from the **Word Bank** that makes sense. (You will use each word twice.)

1. A _____ has pointed wings and a forked tail.

2. I'm afraid my car will _____ in heavy traffic.

3. The cow will remain in its _____ all night.

4. A _____ of bees left the hive to start a new colony.

5. That insult was hard to _____ .

6. A _____ of passengers headed toward the gate at the airport.

7. Please _____ me when it's time to leave.

8. Internships are available all over the _____ .

9. The animal _____ includes creatures of all sizes and shapes.

10. A duck _____ makes a loud quacking sound.

Exercise 4 · Punctuate It: Commas

▸ Read each sentence.

▸ Place commas where needed.

▸ Identify the reason for the commas and circle the correct answer.

▸ Answer the question below.

1. March 22 2006 was the last time our team won the championship.
   a. series   b. date   c. address   d. nonessential dependent clause

2. Poetry can evoke many images feelings and emotions in its readers.
   a. series   b. date   c. address   d. nonessential dependent clause

3. The student read his original poem which was about adolescence.
   a. series   b. date   c. address   d. nonessential dependent clause

4. Applications for the scholarship were sent to Ideal Learning 200 Brown Road Utica NY 13502.
   a. series   b. date   c. address   d. nonessential dependent clause

5. The new coach whose record is amazing will start at the school in the fall.
   a. series   b. date   c. address   d. nonessential dependent clause

▸ Name the type of dependent clause used in both of the complex sentences above, and tell what introduces these clauses.

_____

_____

Exercise 5 · Diagram It: Sentences With Adjectival Clauses

▸ Read each sentence.

▸ Circle the relative pronoun.

▸ Draw an arrow from the relative pronoun to its antecedent.

▸ Draw two lines under the adjectival clause.

▸ Diagram the sentence.

1. My English class, which meets during first period, is studying Shakespeare.

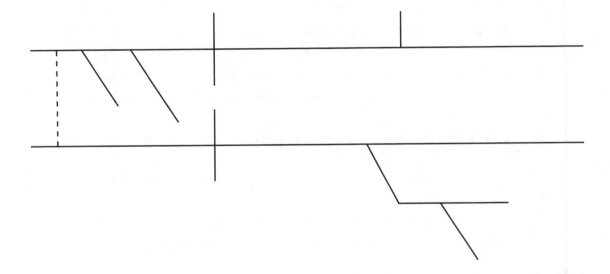

2. The poems had a message that the student understood.

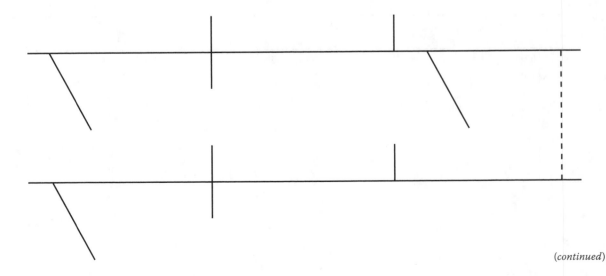

(continued)

Exercise 5 (continued) · Diagram It: Sentences With Adjectival Clauses

3. Nye writes about a person whose words were hurtful.

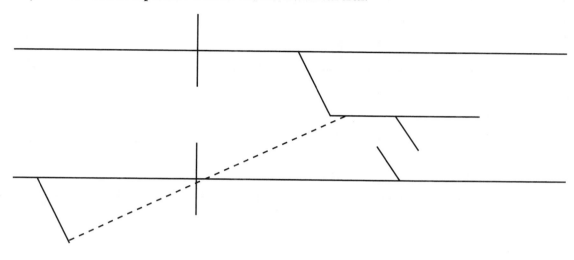

4. The poem, which spoke of the future, appealed to me.

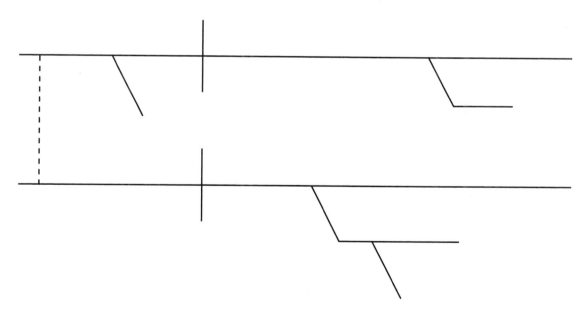

(continued)

Exercise 5 (continued) · Diagram It: Sentences With Adjectival Clauses

5. Leslie Marmon Silko, who is a poet, has written about nature.

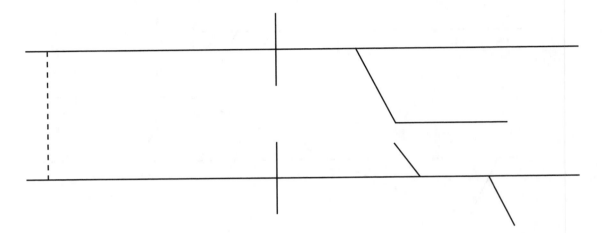

Exercise 1 • Identify It: Spelling Rules

▶ Read each numbered word.

▶ Write its base word and suffix in the next two columns.

▶ Check each box that identifies the spelling rule used to add the word ending.

	Base Word	Suffix	Advanced Doubling Rule	Drop It	No Rule
Example 1: literature					
Example 2: occurrence					
1. exposure					
2. departure					
3. admittance					
4. confidence					
5. insurance					
6. competence					
7. excellence					
8. annoyance					
9. guidance					
10. composure					

Unit 29 · Lesson 9

Exercise 2 · Answer It: Multiple Choice

▸ Read each question and its answer choices.

▸ Turn to **Text Connection 10**, "**A Call to Poetry**," in the *Interactive Text*, pages C76–C83, if you need to check story information.

▸ Underline the correct answer.

1. The line **without a single word flying from my mouth** from "**Postscript**" is an example of

   A. a simile

   B. a metaphor

   C. personification

   D. a symbol

2. The line **The calling came to me** from "**The Calling**" is an example of

   A. a simile

   B. a metaphor

   C. personification

   D. a symbol

3. The speaker in "**The Calling**" might best be described as

   A. regretful over being a writer

   B. happy about not being a photographer

   C. angry about being called to war

   D. thankful to have been called to do important work

(continued)

Exercise 2 (continued) · Answer It: Multiple Choice

4. Read the following lines from "**Story from Bear Country**":
   their beauty will overcome your memory
   like winter sun
   melting ice shadow from snow

   In these lines, beauty is compared to winter sun through the use of _____.

   A. a simile

   B. a metaphor

   C. personification

   D. a symbol

5. Read the following lines from "**Story from Bear Country**":
   and you will remain with them
   locked forever inside yourself

   What do these lines suggest that the self or body is being compared to?

   A. a bear

   B. a forest

   C. a cage

   D. a mountain

Check off the activities you complete with each lesson. Evaluate your accomplishments at the end of each lesson. Pay attention to teacher evaluations and comments.

Unit Objectives	Lesson 1 (Date:_____)	Lesson 2 (Date:_____)
STEP 1 **Phonemic Awareness and Phonics** • Say the sounds for the letter combinations: <u>ch</u> (/ k / as in *chord*), <u>que</u> (/ k / as in *oblique*), <u>ph</u> (/ f / as in *phone*), <u>gh</u> (/ f / as in *enough*), and <u>sc</u> (/ s / as in *science*). • Write the various letters or letter combinations for the sounds / k /, / f /, and / s /.	❑ Discover It: Sounds for *ch*, *que*, *ph*, *gh*, and *sc*	❑ Exercise 1: Review: Sounds for *ch* and *que*
STEP 2 **Word Recognition and Spelling** • Read and spell multisyllable words. • Read and spell the **Essential Words** *behalf, bouquet, broad, mountain, sew, shepherd.* • Read and spell words with prefixes, suffixes, and roots.	❑ Exercise 1: Spelling Pretest 1 ❑ Memorize It	❑ Exercise 2: Write It: Essential Words ❑ Word Fluency 1
STEP 3 **Vocabulary and Morphology** • Identify and define noun and adjective suffixes. • Use the meanings of prefixes, suffixes, and roots to define words.	❑ Unit Vocabulary ❑ Explore It (T) ❑ Write It: Journal Entry	❑ Exercise 3: Combine It: Prefix Plus Root
STEP 4 **Grammar and Usage** • Identify relative pronouns and subordinating conjunctions. • Identify adjectival clauses and adverbial clauses. • Identify the perfect tenses. • Identify basic sentence patterns: simple, compound, and complex.	❑ Exercise 2: Identify It: Future Perfect Tense Verbs ❑ Exercise 3: Identify It: Subordinating Conjunctions and Relative Pronouns	❑ Exercise 4: Identify It: Adverbial Clauses and Adjectival Clauses ❑ Exercise 5: Identify It: Confusing Words
STEP 5 **Listening and Reading Comprehension** • Interpret visual information. • Use context-based strategies to define words. • Identify elements of plot. • Identify, understand, and answer questions that use different types of signal words.	❑ Independent Text: "The Eighteenth Camel" ❑ Exercise 4: Phrase It ❑ Exercise 5: Use the Clues	❑ Passage Fluency 1 ❑ Exercise 6: Using Visuals: Mathematical Calculations and Symbols
STEP 6 **Speaking and Writing** • Use visual and text information to answer questions. • Write responses using signal words. • Organize information for a plot summary. • Write a response to literature composition.	❑ Exercise 6: Rewrite It	❑ Exercise 7: Answer It
Self-Evaluation (5 is the highest) **Effort** = I produced my best work. **Participation** = I was actively involved in tasks. **Independence** = I worked on my own.	**Effort:** 1 2 3 4 5 **Participation:** 1 2 3 4 5 **Independence:** 1 2 3 4 5	**Effort:** 1 2 3 4 5 **Participation:** 1 2 3 4 5 **Independence:** 1 2 3 4 5
Teacher Evaluation	**Effort:** 1 2 3 4 5 **Participation:** 1 2 3 4 5 **Independence:** 1 2 3 4 5	**Effort:** 1 2 3 4 5 **Participation:** 1 2 3 4 5 **Independence:** 1 2 3 4 5

Lesson 3 (Date:_____)	Lesson 4 (Date:_____)	Lesson 5 (Date:_____)
❑ Exercise 1: Review: Sounds for _ph_, _gh_, and _sc_ ❑ Exercise 2: Present It: Letter Sounds, Position-Spelling Patterns, and Sound-Spelling Patterns	❑ Present It: Letter Sounds, Position-Spelling Patterns, and Sound-Spelling Patterns	❑ Present It: Letter-Sounds, Position-Spelling Patterns, and Sound-Spelling Patterns
❑ Divide It ❑ Word Fluency 2	❑ Make a Mnemonic ❑ Present It: Mnemonics for Confusing Word Pairs and Triplets	❑ Content Mastery: Spelling Posttest 1 ❑ Present It: Mnemonics for Confusing Word Pairs
❑ Vocabulary Focus ❑ Use the Clues ❑ Expression of the Day	❑ Vocabulary Focus ❑ Use the Clues	❑ Exercise 1: Identify It: Functions of Suffixes
❑ Identify It: Simple, Compound, or Complex Sentences	❑ Exercise 1: Identify It: Perfect Tense Verbs ❑ Masterpiece Sentences: Stage 4	❑ Exercise 2: Rewrite It: Sentences
❑ Instructional Text: "The Pig: An Individual Dilemma" ❑ Comprehend It	❑ Instructional Text: "The Pig: An Individual Dilemma" ❑ Comprehend It	❑ Instructional Text: "The Pig: An Individual Dilemma" ❑ Exercise 3: Answer It: Multiple Choice
❑ Exercise 3: Answer It	❑ Answer It ❑ Challenge Text: "A Remarkable Individual"	❑ Map It: Plot Analysis (T) ❑ Challenge Text: "A Remarkable Individual" ❑ Exercise 4: Challenge Writing: Writing an Interview
Effort: 1 2 3 4 5 **Participation:** 1 2 3 4 5 **Independence:** 1 2 3 4 5	**Effort:** 1 2 3 4 5 **Participation:** 1 2 3 4 5 **Independence:** 1 2 3 4 5	**Effort:** 1 2 3 4 5 **Participation:** 1 2 3 4 5 **Independence:** 1 2 3 4 5
Effort: 1 2 3 4 5 **Participation:** 1 2 3 4 5 **Independence:** 1 2 3 4 5	**Effort:** 1 2 3 4 5 **Participation:** 1 2 3 4 5 **Independence:** 1 2 3 4 5	**Effort:** 1 2 3 4 5 **Participation:** 1 2 3 4 5 **Independence:** 1 2 3 4 5

Check off the activities you complete with each lesson. Evaluate your accomplishments at the end of each lesson. Pay attention to teacher evaluations and comments.

Unit Objectives	Lesson 6 (Date:_____)	Lesson 7 (Date:_____)
STEP 1 **Phonemic Awareness and Phonics** • Say the sounds for the letter combinations: ch (/ k / as in *chord*), que (/ k / as in *oblique*), ph (/ f / as in *phone*), gh (/ f / as in *enough*), and sc (/ s / as in *science*). • Write the various letters or letter combinations for the sounds / k /, / f /, and / s /.	❑ Present It: Letter Sounds, Position-Spelling Patterns, and Sound-Spelling Patterns	❑ Exercise 1: Using a Dictionary
STEP 2 **Word Recognition and Spelling** • Read and spell multisyllable words. • Read and spell the **Essential Words** *behalf, bouquet, broad, mountain, sew, shepherd.* • Read and spell words with prefixes, suffixes, and roots.	❑ Exercise 1: Spelling Pretest 2 ❑ Word Fluency 3	❑ Exercise 2: Fill In: Confusing Words ❑ Word Fluency 4
STEP 3 **Vocabulary and Morphology** • Identify and define noun and adjective suffixes. • Use the meaning of prefixes, suffixes, and roots to define words.	❑ Exercise 2: Match It: Affixed Words ❑ Expression of the Day	❑ Expression of the Day
STEP 4 **Grammar and Usage** • Identify relative pronouns and subordinating conjonctions. • Identify adjectival clauses and adverbial clauses. • Identify the perfect tenses. • Identify basic sentence patterns: simple, compound, and complex.	❑ Exercise 3: Identify It: Sentence Structure ❑ Exercise 4: Punctuate It: Commas, Colons, and Semicolons	❑ Identify It: Simple, Compound, or Complex Sentence
STEP 5 **Listening and Reading Comprehension** • Interpret visual information. • Use context-based strategies to define words. • Identify elements of plot. • Identify, understand, and answer questions that use different types of signal words.	❑ Map It: Plot Analysis (T)	❑ Exercise 3: Responding to Literature
STEP 6 **Speaking and Writing** • Use visual and text information to answer questions. • Write responses using signal words. • Organize information for a plot summary. • Write a response to literature composition.	❑ Challenge Text: "A Remarkable Individual, Part II"	❑ Write It: Response to Literature ❑ Challenge Text: "A Remarkable Individual, Part II"
Self-Evaluation (5 is the highest) **Effort** = I produced my best work. **Participation** = I was actively involved in tasks. **Independence** = I worked on my own.	**Effort:** 1 2 3 4 5 **Participation:** 1 2 3 4 5 **Independence:** 1 2 3 4 5	**Effort:** 1 2 3 4 5 **Participation:** 1 2 3 4 5 **Independence:** 1 2 3 4 5
Teacher Evaluation	**Effort:** 1 2 3 4 5 **Participation:** 1 2 3 4 5 **Independence:** 1 2 3 4 5	**Effort:** 1 2 3 4 5 **Participation:** 1 2 3 4 5 **Independence:** 1 2 3 4 5

Lesson 8 (Date:_____)	Lesson 9 (Date:_____)	Lesson 10 (Date:_____)
❑ Exercise 1: Listening for Word Parts: Prefixes and Suffixes		❑ Summative Test: Phonemic Awareness and Phonics
❑ Progress Indicators: Test of Silent Word Reading Fluency (TOSWRF)	❑ Progress Indicators: Spelling Inventory	❑ Content Mastery: Spelling Posttest 2
❑ Present It: Loan Words from African and Middle Eastern Languages ❑ Explore It (T)		❑ Summative Test: Vocabulary and Morphology
❑ Exercise 2: Diagram It: Sentences With Adjectival Clauses (T)	❑ Exercise 1: Punctuate It: Commas, Colons, and Semicolons ❑ Exercise 2: Identify It: Confusing Words	❑ Summative Test: Grammar and Usage
❑ Revise It: Response to Literature		❑ Progress Indicator: Degrees of Reading Power (DRP)
❑ Revise It: Response to Literature	❑ Summative Test: Composition	
Effort: 1 2 3 4 5 **Participation:** 1 2 3 4 5 **Independence:** 1 2 3 4 5	**Effort:** 1 2 3 4 5 **Participation:** 1 2 3 4 5 **Independence:** 1 2 3 4 5	**Effort:** 1 2 3 4 5 **Participation:** 1 2 3 4 5 **Independence:** 1 2 3 4 5
Effort: 1 2 3 4 5 **Participation:** 1 2 3 4 5 **Independence:** 1 2 3 4 5	**Effort:** 1 2 3 4 5 **Participation:** 1 2 3 4 5 **Independence:** 1 2 3 4 5	**Effort:** 1 2 3 4 5 **Participation:** 1 2 3 4 5 **Independence:** 1 2 3 4 5

Exercise 1 · Spelling Pretest 1

▶ Write the word your teacher repeats.

1. _____   6. _____   11. _____

2. _____   7. _____   12. _____

3. _____   8. _____   13. _____

4. _____   9. _____   14. _____

5. _____   10. _____   15. _____

Exercise 2 · Identify It: Future Perfect Tense Verbs

▸ Read each sentence.

▸ Identify the two verbs in the sentence and underline them.

▸ Determine which verb is in the future perfect tense and label it FPT.

▸ Write the order of the actions in the sentence on the line provided.

1. Once the camels are unloaded, the family will have brought all their belongings to the new camp.

_____

_____

2. When the problem is solved, the brothers will have learned some math.

_____

_____

3. The wise woman will have given the brothers a gift that resolves their argument.

_____

_____

4. By the time the father dies, he will have given the brothers many gifts.

_____

_____

5. When the woman leaves with her camel, each will have received his correct share.

_____

_____

Exercise 3 · Identify It: Subordinating Conjunctions and Relative Pronouns

▸ Read each sentence.

▸ Identify and circle the subordinating conjunction or the relative pronoun.

▸ Copy the word into the correct column.

	Subordinating Conjunction	Relative Pronoun
1. The father, who was a wealthy Bedouin, left his sons seventeen camels.		
2. The sons argued because they could not divide the camels between them.		
3. The sons continued to argue until a wealthy woman offered a solution.		
4. The woman offered a camel, which belonged to her herd.		
5. Finally the brothers settled the argument that threatened to destroy their family.		

Exercise 4 · Phrase It

▸ Use the penciling strategy to "scoop" the phrases in each sentence.

▸ Read the sentences as you would speak them.

based on "The Eighteenth Camel"

In olden times, camels served as vehicles. They furnished transportation for many peoples of the Arabian deserts. The beasts served in other ways, too. Camels were valued for their milk, meat, and skins. The beasts had great importance in the desert economy. A Bedouin measured his wealth by the number of camels he owned.

Unit 30 · Lesson 1

Exercise 5 · Use the Clues

▶ Read the excerpt below.

▶ Reread the underlined word **distressed**.

▶ Reread the entire sentence.

▶ Underline the participial phrase **distressed by the fighting**. Circle the pronoun that this phrase modifies.

▶ Then look at the rest of the sentence and the sentence that follows. Ask yourself, "How did the woman probably feel about the fighting?"

▶ Write a definition for **distressed** in the context of this selection.

---

from "The Eighteenth Camel"

Now, in the area lived a wealthy Arabian woman. <u>Distressed</u> by the fighting,

she offered the brothers one of her own camels. She hoped it would help to

settle the dispute.

Define It:

distressed: _____

Exercise 6 · Rewrite It

▸ Read each of the following pairs of sentences.

▸ Look at the subordinating conjunctions listed in the **Word Bank**.

Word Bank

although	while	because	if	unless

▸ Choose a subordinating conjunction from the **Word Bank** that makes clear the logical connection between the two sentences. Does it make most sense to show a contrast, a reason, or a condition?

▸ Use that subordinating conjunction to combine the two sentences into a single sentence.

> **Example:** You like solving puzzles. You will enjoy reading "**The Eighteenth Camel.**"
> **If** you like solving puzzles, you will enjoy reading "**The Eighteenth Camel.**"

1. The three brothers could not see how to share the seventeen camels fairly. They became angry with one another.

   _____

   _____

   _____

2. Someone looked for a peaceful solution. The brothers might never have made peace.

   _____

   _____

   _____

3. The situation seemed impossible to solve. There was a peaceful solution.

   _____

   _____

   _____

(continued)

Exercise 6 *(continued)* · Rewrite It

4. The Arabian woman was distressed by the fighting. She offered the brothers one of her own camels.

_____

_____

_____

5. The woman had not offered her camel. The problem may not have been resolved.

_____

_____

_____

Exercise 1 · Review: Sounds for *ch* and *que*

▶ Repeat each word in the **ch** column as your teacher says it.

▶ Practice reading the list with a partner.

▶ Repeat the process with the words in the **que** column.

ch = / k /	que = / k /
ar<u>ch</u>itect	baro<u>que</u>
<u>ch</u>emical	cli<u>que</u>
me<u>ch</u>anic	criti<u>que</u>
s<u>ch</u>edule	grotes<u>que</u>
s<u>ch</u>olar	mysti<u>que</u>
stoma<u>ch</u>	opa<u>que</u>

Exercise 2 · Write It: Essential Words

▶ Review the **Essential Words** in the **Word Bank**.

Word Bank

mountain	shepherd	bouquet	behalf	sew	broad

▶ Put the words in alphabetical order and write them on the lines.

▶ Write one sentence for each **Essential Word**.

▶ Check that each sentence uses sentence signals—correct capitalization, commas, and end punctuation.

1. _____

_____

2. _____

_____

3. _____

_____

4. _____

_____

5. _____

_____

6. _____

_____

Exercise 3 · Combine It: Prefix Plus Root

▶ Read each prefix and root.

▶ Underline the last letter of the prefix.

▶ Underline the first letter of the root and write it on the line.

▶ Decide if the last letter of the prefix should change to the first letter of the root.

▶ Combine the prefix and root and write the whole word on the line.

	Prefix	Root or Base Word	1st Letter of Root or Base Word	Whole Word
1.	sub-	+ ply		
2.	ad-	+ fect		
3.	ob-	+ pose		
4.	ad-	+ set		
5.	ad-	+ pend		
6.	ob-	+ press		
7.	ad-	+ cede		
8.	sub-	+ cess		
9.	ob-	+ fer		
10.	ad-	+ nul		

Unit 30 · Lesson 2

Exercise 4 · Identify It: Adverbial Clauses and Adjectival Clauses

▶ Read each sentence.

▶ Identify and circle the subordinating conjunction or relative pronoun

▶ Identify the dependent clause and draw two lines under it.

▶ Determine whether the dependent clause is adverbial or adjectival.

▶ Circle the correct answer.

1. The brothers could not solve their problem until the wise woman helped them.
   a. adverbial clause   b. adjectival clause

2. Sometimes a difficult situation needs a person who will act as a catalyst.
   a. adverbial clause   b. adjectival clause

3. Camels had great importance in the desert because they provided food and transportation.
   a. adverbial clause   b. adjectival clause

4. Camels, which can travel long distances without water, can carry very heavy loads.
   a. adverbial clause   b. adjectival clause

5. Today, there are still camel herds that roam the deserts.
   a. adverbial clause   b. adjectival clause

Exercise 5 · Identify It: Confusing Words

▸ Read each sentence and the word choices below the sentence.

▸ Use what you know about the meaning and function of each word to choose the correct word to complete the sentence.

▸ Refer to the *Student Text,* page 224, if needed.

▸ Copy the correct word into the blank.

1. If _____ late for class, you will get a detention slip.
   a. your   b. you're

2. The brothers argued about _____ inheritance.
   a. there   b. their   c. they're

3. Unless my friends get here soon, _____ going to miss the game.
   a. there   b. their   c. they're

4. Remember to check _____ answers before handing in your test.
   a. your   b. you're

5. The journey to get _____ will be very challenging.
   a. there   b. their   c. they're

Unit 30 · Lesson 2

Exercise 6 · Using Visuals: Mathematical Calculations and Symbols

▸ Read the information in the table below.

▸ Look carefully at the mathematical calculations and the symbols.

▸ Use information presented in the table to retell the story of the "The Eighteenth Camel." Explain how many camels the wealthy Bedouin left for each son. Then explain why the three sons had trouble dividing up the camels fairly.

---

17 Camels

The first son would get half of the camels.	$\frac{1}{2} \times 17 = \frac{17}{2} = 8\frac{1}{2}$	
The second son would get a third of the camels.	$\frac{1}{3} \times 17 = \frac{17}{3} = 5\frac{2}{3}$	
The third son would get one ninth of the camels.	$\frac{1}{9} \times 17 = \frac{17}{9} = 1\frac{8}{9}$	

Total = **16 $\frac{1}{18}$**

$8\frac{1}{2} = 8\frac{9}{18}$
$5\frac{2}{3} = 5\frac{12}{18}$
$1\frac{8}{9} = 1\frac{16}{18}$

$14\frac{37}{18} = 16\frac{1}{18}$

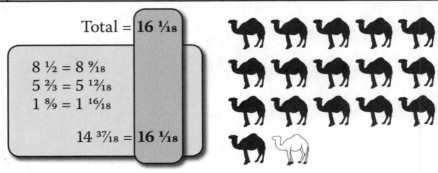

Exercise 7 · Answer It

▶ Use information from the "**The Eighteenth Camel**" in the *Student Text*, pages 230–231, and from the mathematical equations and symbols shown on page 276 of the *Interactive Text* to answer each of these questions. Write complete sentences.

1. When there were 17 camels, how many camels did each son get?

_____

_____

_____

2. Why did the three sons have trouble dividing up the 17 camels fairly?

_____

_____

_____

3. If it had been possible to divide up the 17 camels, would all the brothers' shares have totaled 17 camels? If not, what would the total have been?

_____

_____

4. Once there were 18 camels to divide, how many camels did each son get?

_____

_____

_____

5. How did the woman help the sons by giving them one more camel?

_____

_____

_____

_____

Exercise 1 · Review: Sounds for *ph*, *gh*, and *sc*

▸ Repeat each word in the **ph** column as your teacher says it.

▸ Practice reading the list with a partner.

▸ Repeat the process with the words in the **gh** and **sc** columns.

ph = / f /	gh = / f /	sc = / s /
bibliography	enough	adolescence
biography	roughen	discipline
elephant	roughage	muscle
nephew	roughneck	scene
telegraph	slough	scent
triumph	toughen	scientists

Exercise 2 · Present It: Letter Sounds, Position-Spelling Patterns, and Sound-Spelling Patterns

▸ Discuss these basic presentation skills with your teacher:

- ❑ Good projection
- ❑ Expression: appropriate change of tone, volume, rate of speaking, and pauses
- ❑ Academic English: correct pronunciation of words and correct sentence structure
- ❑ Appropriate facial expression
- ❑ Good eye contact
- ❑ Appropriate gestures
- ❑ Appropriate posture

▸ Practice using these skills when making formal presentations.

Exercise 3 · Answer It

▶ Underline the signal word in the question.

▶ Write the answer in complete sentences.

1. List some key details that describe the main character, Kibuka.

_____

_____

_____

_____

_____

_____

_____

2. Contrast how Kibuka felt about keeping the young piglet with how he felt about having a full-grown pig.

_____

_____

_____

_____

_____

_____

_____

_____

_____

(continued)

3. As the story progresses, Kibuka begins to experience conflict as a result of keeping the pig. After reading lines 167–171, stop and predict what may happen next in the story to resolve the problem for Kibuka. Base your prediction on what has already happened in the story, as well as what you might logically expect as a reader.

_____

_____

_____

_____

_____

4. Explain why you think Kibuka allowed Musisi to haul the pig off to Ggombolola Headquarters so that a butcher could carve the pig up.

_____

_____

_____

_____

_____

5. Think about how Kibuka felt about his retirement at the beginning of the story. Infer how the experience of having the pig might have changed how Kibuka viewed retirement.

_____

_____

_____

_____

_____

Exercise 1 · Identify It: Perfect Tense Verbs

▸ Read each sentence.

▸ Identify the verb that is in the present perfect tense, past perfect tense, or future perfect tense. Draw a line under it.

▸ Copy the verb into the correct column.

1. Kibuka had worked for many years before he retired.

2. His grandson has brought him a pig as a gift.

3. The pig has thrived because Kibuka looks after it well.

4. By next week, the pig will have eaten all the food Kibuka has in the house.

5. Many of the neighbors will have enjoyed a feast of cooked pig by the time Yosefu returns.

	Present Perfect Tense	Past Perfect Tense	Future Perfect Tense
1.			
2.			
3.			
4.			
5.			

Exercise 1 · Identify It: Functions of Suffixes

▶ Read each root or base word and suffix pair.

▶ Complete the third column in the chart by combining the root or base word and suffix.

▶ Determine the part of speech and write it in the fourth column in the chart.

▶ Use your **Morphemes for Meaning Cards** and a dictionary as needed.

	Root/Base Word	Suffix	Root/Base Word + Suffix	Part of Speech
1.	vis	ible		
2.	human	ity		
3.	hero	ic		
4.	fact	ual		
5.	accept	ance		

Exercise 2 · Rewrite It: Sentences

▶ Read the paragraph below with your teacher.

▶ Underline any past tense verb that is used incorrectly and write the correct form above it.

▶ Revise each sentence as directed using the **Masterpiece Sentence Cue Chart**. Remember that **Stage 4: Paint Your Subject** can be used to paint any noun.

▶ Proofread for spelling and punctuation, paying special attention to the past participles.

---

1. Kibuka found retirement lonely. 2. His grandson brung him a pig.

3. He raised the pig. 4. The pig growed enormous. 5. Kibuka put the pig on

a leash.

Item	Use these Masterpiece Sentence stages to expand each sentence.	Make this change.
1.	Stage 4	Write an adjectival clause telling **which one** about Kibuka.
2.	Stage 4 and Stage 5	Write an adjectival clause telling **which one** about the pig. Add an adjective to describe the pig. Use the word from the text to replace **pig**.
3.	Stage 5	Use the grandfather's name instead of **he** to be more specific. Add an independent clause to form a compound sentence.
4.	Stage 4	Write an adverbial clause telling **why** the pig grew.
5.	Stage 4	Write an adverbial clause telling **why** Kibuka put the pig on a leash.

_____

_____

_____

_____

_____

Unit 30 · Lesson 5

Exercise 3 · Answer It: Multiple Choice

▸ Read each question and its answer choices.

▸ Turn to **Text Connections 11 and 12, "The Pig: An Individual Dilemma, Parts I and II,"** in the *Interactive Text*, pages C84–C95, if you need to check story information.

▸ Underline the correct answer.

▸ Discuss the answers with your teacher.

1. At the beginning of the story, Kibuka can best be described as

    A. angry and blaming

    B. bored and self-pitying

    C. confused and irritated

    D. peaceful and accepting

2. At the end of the story, Kibuka can best be described as

    A. angry and blaming

    B. bored and self-pitying

    C. confused and irritated

    D. peaceful and accepting

3. Why did Kibuka's grandson bring Kibuka the piglet?

    A. He wanted to give his grandfather a retirement gift.

    B. He thought the piglet would make an excellent meal for his grandfather.

    C. He tried to give the piglet to Kibuka's friend Yosefu, but Yosefu was away from home.

    D. He knew that his grandfather was lonely and needed a friend.

(continued)

4. Which of the following made the pig more of a burden?

    A. Its snoring kept Kibuka up until dawn.

    B. It would regularly fall into the Kalasanda stream.

    C. It required a great deal of food.

    D. All of the above

5. Which of the following events represents the major turning point of the story?

    A. Kibuka returns from work at the Ggombolola Headquarters.

    B. Kibuka tethers the pig to a tree so that he can get to sleep.

    C. The pig is killed by a motorcyclist.

    D. Kibuka has lunch with his friend Yosefu.

Unit 30 • Lesson 5

Exercise 4 • Challenge Writing: Writing an Interview

▶ Below is an excerpt of an interview with a man who served in the U.S. Army during World War II.

▶ Read the excerpt. Then complete items 1–4 to plan your own interview questions for Erik Weihenmayer.

Memories of War: An Interview with Col. Lowell Aitken

Q: What was it like to be in battle?

A: You were always afraid, but when you got busy you didn't have time to worry. When you're 18, you don't think anything can happen to you.

Q: What are some of your memories of being in battle?

A: In the Philippines, my battalion went behind enemy lines to rescue prisoners being held in the Los Banos International Camp. We crossed a large lake and attacked the camp at the same time the 11th Airborne Division dropped paratroopers. We took the camp and freed the prisoners.

---

1. List some things that you already know about Erik Weihenmayer.

   _____

   _____

   _____

   _____

(continued)

Exercise 4 (continued) · Challenge Writing: Writing an Interview

2. Based on what you already know about Mr. Weihenmayer, list some things that you want to know more about.

_____

_____

_____

_____

3. List some other things that you and your readers would enjoy learning about him.

_____

_____

_____

_____

4. Use the information that you listed in 1–3 above to write four questions for Mr. Weihenmayer on a separate sheet of paper.

Exercise 1 · Spelling Pretest 2

▶ Write the word your teacher repeats.

1. _____   6. _____   11. _____

2. _____   7. _____   12. _____

3. _____   8. _____   13. _____

4. _____   9. _____   14. _____

5. _____   10. _____   15. _____

Exercise 2 · Match It: Affixed Words

▶ Read each word.

▶ Match the word to the definition constructed from its morphemes. Use your **Morpehemes for Meaning Cards** and a dictionary to help you.

▶ Answer the questions at the bottom.

1. aggressive	**a.** to hold together badly
2. postponement	**b.** thrown against
3. malcontent	**c.** characterized by stepping toward
4. objected	**d.** state of folding under
5. supplication	**e.** state of placing after

▶ Circle the answers to the following questions:

1. What word means the opposite of **malcontent**?
a. malevolent   b. content   c. discontent

2. What does the root in **supplication** mean?
a. hold   b. told   c. fold

3. What does the prefix in the word **postponement** mean?
a. after   b. before   c. never

▶ Write the answers to the following questions:

1. Copy the words that have assimilated prefixes.

_____

2. What does the suffix in the word **aggressive** mean?

_____

Exercise 3 · Identify It: Sentence Structure

▶ Read each sentence.

▶ Underline the independent clause once.

▶ Look for and circle the subordinating conjunction or relative pronoun. Underline twice the dependent clause that it introduces.

▶ Determine if the sentence is a simple, compound, or complex sentence and circle the correct answer.

1. Kibuka, who lived alone, loved the little piglet.
   a. simple   b. compound   c. complex

2. The pig slept on Kibuka's bed, and it kept him awake with its loud snoring.
   a. simple   b. compound   c. complex

3. The neighbors brought their food scraps over for the pig.
   a. simple   b. compound   c. complex

4. Kibuka's grandson gave Kibuka a pig, which became his best friend.
   a. simple   b. compound   c. complex

5. There was scarcely a mark on the pig, but its head lay at a strange angle.
   a. simple   b. compound   c. complex

Exercise 4 · Punctuate It: Commas, Colons, and Semicolons

▸ Read each sentence.

▸ Place one or more commas, a colon, or a semicolon where needed.

▸ Circle the reason for using that punctuation.

1. Early in the morning, on Tuesday May 1 2006 the ceremony began.
   a. series   b. nonessential dependent clause   c. date

2. The piglet which grew to be a large pig was hit by a motorcycle.
   a. two independent clauses   b. nonessential dependent clause   c. address

3. The pig was butchered the meat was divided among Kibuka's neighbors.
   a. two independent clauses   b. nonessential dependent clause   c. address

4. When Kibuka worked for the government, he did the following filing telephoning and ordering.
   a. two independent clauses   b. series   c. nonessential dependent clause

5. The government offices were at Ggombolola Headquarters 200 Main Street Ggombolola.
   a. two independent clauses   b. nonessential dependent clause   c. address

Exercise 1 · Using a Dictionary

▸ Turn to the **Vocabulary** section (dictionary) of the *Student Text*.

▸ Locate the first word and its pronunciation.

▸ Write the pronunciation for the word on the line next to the word.

▸ Use the markings to read the word aloud.

▸ Complete numbers 2–5 using the same process.

Word	Pronunciation
1. derision	_____
2. foliage	_____
3. perpetual	_____
4. stoic	_____
5. treachery	_____

▸ Use a classroom dictionary or www.yourdictionary.com to complete numbers 6–10.

Word	Pronunciation
6. ascetic	_____
7. cholesterol	_____
8. hierarchy	_____
9. metaphor	_____
10. phenomenon	_____

Exercise 2 · Fill In: Confusing Words

▶ Read each sentence.

▶ Consider the spellings and the meanings of the confusing words in parentheses.

▶ Fill in the blank with the correct answer.

▶ Use a dictionary as a resource.

1. I kept my money _____ in one clip; I had $22.00 _____.
   (altogether, all together)

2. _____ going to tell me _____ money this is?
   (who's, whose)

3. They will _____ all forms of payment _____ checks.
   (accept, except)

4. I want to eat this _____ of pie in _____.
   (peace, piece)

5. _____, when are you going to feed the _____?
   (sow, sew, so)

6. I need thirty-_____ dollars on the _____ of July

   _____ tickets.
   (forth, for, four, fourth)

7. It's easy to _____ _____ change.
   (loose, lose)

8. _____ you help me bring in _____ for the fire?
   (would, wood)

9. I took a _____ of the _____ for our school paper.
   (pitcher, picture)

10. Let's _____ to make sure the puppy's _____ are okay.
    (pause, paws)

Exercise 3 · Responding to Literature

▶ When writers respond to literature, they summarize all or part of a text and then analyze or evaluate it. When writers respond to fictional literature, often they express an opinion about the characters, the plot, or the ideas or messages of the story.

▶ Read items 1–4 below. Discuss each item with a partner. Take turns expressing your opinions. Use specific details from **"The Pig: An Individual Dilemma"** to support your judgments.

1. Was Kibuka an interesting character? Why or why not?

2. Was Kibuka's behavior at the end of the story reasonable or unreasonable? Why do you think so?

3. How did you feel about the ending of the story? Would you change it? If so, how would you change it? Why?

4. Tell what you liked and disliked about the story. Then tell whether or not you would recommend the story to someone else, and why.

Exercise 1 · Listening for Word Parts: Prefixes and Suffixes

▶ Listen to each word your teacher says.

▶ Repeat the word.

▶ Mark **Yes** or **No** to tell if you hear a prefix.

▶ If **yes**, write the prefix you hear under the heading **prefix**.

▶ Mark **Yes** or **No** to tell if you hear a suffix.

▶ If **yes**, write the suffix you hear under the heading **suffix**.

	Prefixes			Suffixes		
	Do you hear a prefix on the word?		If **Yes**, write the prefix.	Do you hear a suffix on the word?		If **Yes**, write the suffix.
	Yes	No	Prefix	Yes	No	Suffix
1.						
2.						
3.						
4.						
5.						
6.						
7.						
8.						
9.						
10.						

(continued)

Unit 30 · Lesson 8

Exercise 1 (continued) · Listening for Word Parts: Prefixes and Suffixes

	Prefixes			Suffixes		
	Do you hear a prefix in the word?		If **Yes**, write the prefix.	Do you hear a suffix in the word?		If **Yes**, write the suffix.
	Yes	No	Prefix	Yes	No	Suffix
11.						
12.						
13.						
14.						
15.						

Exercise 2 · Diagram It: Sentences With Adjectival Clauses

▶ Read each sentence.

▶ Circle the relative pronoun.

▶ Draw an arrow from the relative pronoun to its antecedent.

▶ Draw two lines under the adjectival clause.

▶ Diagram the sentence.

1. Kibuka, whose feet hurt, rested beside the path.

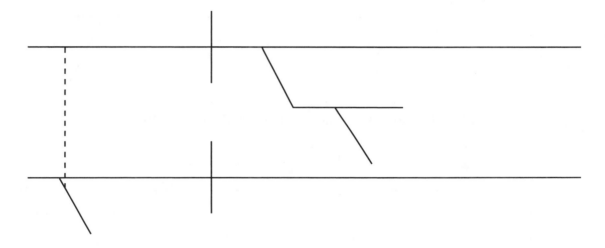

2. The old man put the pig, which enjoyed a walk, on a leash.

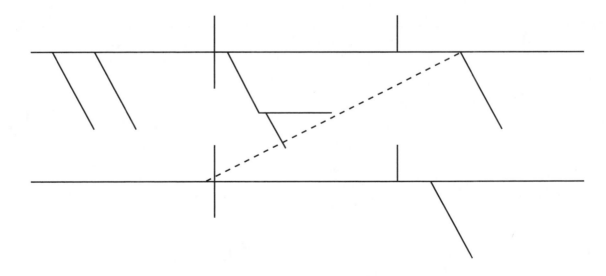

(continued)

Exercise 2 *(continued)* · **Diagram It: Sentences With Adjectival Clauses**

3. The motorcycle that hit the pig was totaled in the accident.

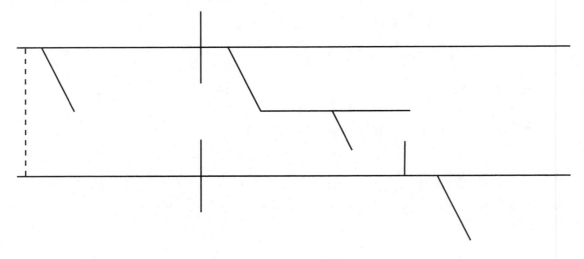

4. Nantando, who did not see the accident, made up colorful details.

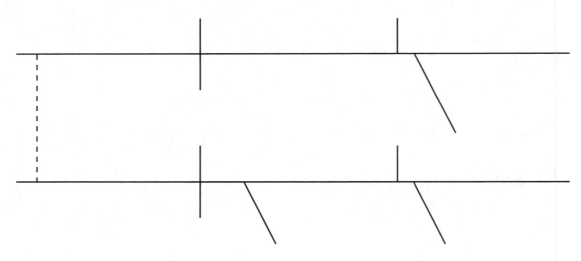

(continued)

5. Kibuka shared the pork with any neighbor who wanted some.

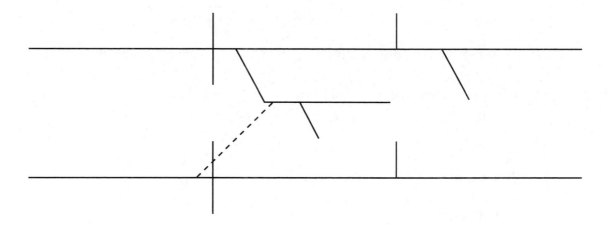

Exercise 1 · Punctuate It: Commas, Colons, and Semicolons

▶ Read each sentence.

▶ Place one or more commas, a colon, or a semicolon where needed.

▶ Circle the reason for the punctuation.

1. The accident occurred at 715 p.m.

    a. series   b. compound sentence   c. time

2. Dear Sir or Madame
Please find enclosed a check for ten dollars.

    a. two independent   b. business letter greeting   c. address
       clauses

3. The villagers received their share of the pork they cooked it immediately.

    a. two independent   b. nonessential dependent   c. address
       clauses   clause

4. Kibuka walked from his house through the village along the path and beside the river.

    a. two independent   b. series   c. nonessential dependent
       clauses   clause

5. Kibuka whom villagers respected now lived alone.

    a. two independent   b. nonessential dependent   c. address
       clauses   clause

Exercise 2 · Identify It: Confusing Words

▶ Read each sentence and the word choices below the sentence.

▶ Use what you know about the meaning and function of each word to choose the correct word to complete the sentence.

▶ Refer to the *Student Text*, page 224, for help.

▶ Copy the correct word into the blank.

1. Please take _____ share of the meat.
   a. your   b. you're

2. In the village _____ cooking the pork.
   a. there   b. their   c. they're

3. The villagers prepare _____ favorite meals.
   a. there   b. their   c. they're

4. The pig was hit right _____.
   a. there   b. their   c. they're

5. If _____ riding a motorcycle, please be careful.
   a. your   b. you're

Text Connections

Circle Poems Take Many Forms

1 *A poem begins with a lump in the throat, a home-sickness or a love-sickness. It is a reaching-out toward expression; an effort to find fulfillment. A complete poem is one where the emotion has found its thought and the thought has found the*
5 *words.* Robert Frost, 20th century poet

What Is Poetry?

Poetry is a special kind of literature. A poem uses words sparingly [1] and imaginatively. Most poems are meant to be read out loud because the language of poetry combines the
10 qualities of speech and song.

> ### Use the Clues A:
> - Read lines 7–10.
> - Use meaning signals and context clues to answer the question in the bold heading, **What Is Poetry?**
> - Circle the meaning signal.
> - Highlight the context clues that helped you define **poetry**.
>
> _____
>
> _____
>
> _____
>
> _____

Poetry often includes six major elements: thought, form, imagery, melody, meter, and mood. In this unit, we will be learning about two elements: thought and form. The thought is the sum of the poet's ideas. One element of a poem's
15 thought is its theme. A poem's theme may be stated as a universal truth, a truth that is not limited by time and space.

_____

[1] **sparingly:** in a limited manner

Comprehend It

Answer the questions below in the space provided.

1. What does Robert Frost think is the purpose of a poem?

_____

_____

_____

2. Why is the sense of hearing important to poetry?

_____

_____

_____

_____

_____

_____

_____

(continued)

Text Connection 1 (continued)

Comprehend It

3. Circle the punctuation marks in "Outwitted" that the poet uses to help establish the meter, or rhythm, in the poem. Which line in the poem has two pauses?

_____

_____

4. Who or what helps the speaker "take in" the person who excluded him?

_____

_____

5. What initial consonant does the poet repeat in the third and fourth lines to add rhythm and music to the poem?

_____

_____

Poems come in many different forms as well. Let's look at two major forms of poetry: closed form and open form, or free verse. Closed form poetry is written in specific patterns,
20 often with regular rhythm, line lengths, and line groupings called stanzas. Open form poetry does not use regular rhythmic patterns, has varying line lengths, and has no set line groups or stanzas.

Use the Clues B:

- Read lines 17–23.
- Use meaning signals and context clues to define the phrase **closed form**.
- Circle the meaning signal.
- Highlight the context clues that helped you define **closed form**.

_____

_____

_____

_____

Closed Form

25   Our first experience of poetry is often nursery rhymes and songs, so we usually think that poetry rhymes. Rhyming poetry is one kind of poetry; it repeats the same or similar sounds of words in a defined pattern. For example, in the poem below, the word "out" rhymes with "flout." Read the
30 poem out loud. What other two words rhyme in the poem?

Outwitted
by Edwin Markham
He drew a circle that shut me <u>out</u>—
Heretic, a rebel, a thing to flout².
35 But Love and I had the wit to win:
We drew a circle that took him in!

_____

² **flout:** to mock; make fun of

(continued)

Text Connection 1 (continued)

What are the thought and theme of this poem? What makes "Outwitted" a closed form poem?

Haiku—A Closed Form

40 The haiku poetry form originated in Japan. A haiku consists of three lines with 5, 7, and 5 syllables respectively. Because there is a limit to the number of syllables in each line and the number of lines, it is considered a closed form. Even though haiku poems are very short, they are intended to convey[3] profound[4] emotion and insight. Read the poems 45 out loud. Count the number of syllables in each line.

From **Haiku: This Other World**
by Richard Wright

#745
In the summer lake,
50 The moon gives a long shiver,
Then swells round again.

#716
With mouth gaping[5] wide,
Swallowing strings of wild geese—
55 Hungry autumn moon.

Identify It: Adjectives

What adjective describes **shiver**? _____

What adjective describes **geese**? _____

---

[3] **convey:** to express; carry

[4] **profound:** intellectually deep; insightful

[5] **gaping:** opening wide

Comprehend It

6. What do you think might have happened to make the image of the moon in the lake look like it was shivering?

_____

_____

_____

_____

_____

_____

7. How might the moon look like it was swallowing geese?

_____

_____

_____

_____

_____

_____

8. Draw a box around the words in each haiku that show the poet is describing a full or near full moon.

(continued)

A haiku is often about an individual experience with the environment that transcends every day experience. Read the haiku poems out loud again. What are the thoughts or themes being expressed in these haiku poems?

60 **Open Form or Free Verse**

Another form of poetry is called free verse or open form. Free verse does not have regular rhyme. Free verse uses the natural rhythm of language to emphasize the thought and theme. Free verse is a form preferred by many modern and

65 contemporary poets.

> ### Use the Clues C:
>
> - Read lines 62–66.
> - Use meaning signals and context clues to define the phrase **open form**.
> - Circle the meaning signal.
> - Highlight the context clues that helped you define **open form**.
>
> _____
>
> _____
>
> _____
>
> _____
>
> _____

(continued)

Text Connection 1 (continued)

Read the following poem out loud. Describe the poem's thought and theme.

The Life of a Man Is a Circle
by Black Elk, Lakota Sioux
70 The life of a man is a circle
From childhood to childhood,
And so it is in everything
Where power moves.

Our teepees were round like the nests
75 Of the birds, and these were always set
In a circle, the nation's hoop,
A nest of many nests,
Where the Great Spirit meant for us to hatch our children.

Identify It: Prepositional Phrases and Predicate Adjectives

1. What prepositional phrase modifies **life**? _____

2. What predicate adjective describes **teepees**? _____

3. What prepositional phrase modifies **nests**? _____

Comprehend It

9. How is the line "From childhood to childhood" related to the idea of a circle?

_____

_____

_____

_____

_____

10. What does the speaker compare the Lakota Sioux to in the second part of the poem?

_____

11. Draw a slash after each word in the poem where punctuation indicates you should pause. Then read the poem aloud again.

(continued)

Text Connection 1 (continued)

Comprehend It

12. What two words rhyme in the poem?

_____

_____

13. Mark where you should begin to read the poem with an X. Why should you begin at that point?

_____

_____

_____

_____

_____

_____

Concrete Form—An Open Form

80   Concrete poetry is a unique kind of poetry. The concrete poem uses a visual image to create its meaning. Concrete poems often have few words. The way the words are

85   arranged on the page is as important to the meaning of the poem as what the words say. Read the following

90   poem out loud. What is the thought or theme of the poem when it is read out loud?

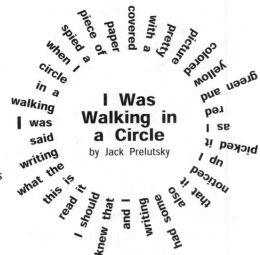

I Was Walking in a Circle
by Jack Prelutsky

Hearing a concrete poem read out loud may not give the

95   listener the whole experience or appreciation of the poem. A reader must see the poem on the page to understand the poem. Read the poem again. What is the theme or thought of the poem when it is typed in a circle on the page? What makes this poem an open form poem?

Circles in Nature

1 **Experimental Poetry**

Another open form is experimental poetry. This form "experiments" or tries something new with language. Experimental poetry has lots of variations [1], but

5 experimental poems have one thing in common. They try not to sound or look like closed form poetry. Read the poem below. What do you think is experimental about this poem?

Use the Clues A:

- Read lines 1–6.
- Use meaning signals to define the phrase **experimental poetry**.
- Circle the meaning signal.
- Highlight the context clues that helped you define **experimental poetry**.

_____

_____

_____

_____

_____

---

[1] **variations:** types; kinds

(continued)

Unit 25

Text Connection 2 (continued)

Take Note

Answer the questions below in the space provided.

1. Draw a circle around the part of the poem that is in parentheses. What is the focus of this part?

_____

_____

_____

_____

2. Write down two phrases from the poem that create unusual, playful images.

_____

_____

_____

_____

3. Put an X next to the parts of the poem with unusual line or word spacing. What effect do you think this spacing has?

_____

_____

_____

_____

who knows if the moon's

by E.E. Cummings*

10   who knows if the moon's
     a balloon,coming out of a key ^{2} city
     in the sky—filled with pretty people?
     (and if you and i should

     get into it, if they
15   should take me and take you into their balloon,
     why then
     we'd go up higher with all the pretty people

     than houses and steeples and clouds:
     go sailing
20   away and away sailing into a keen
     city which nobody's ever visited, where

     always
          it's
               Spring) and   everyone's
25   in love and flowers pick themselves

The modern poet E.E. Cummings (1894–1962) was famous for writing experimental poetry. Why do you think that Cummings refers to himself as "i" instead of "I" in the poem?

---

*You may see this poet's name typed in the following ways: e.e. cummings or e e cummings. However, scholars now believe that his preference was E.E. Cummings.

^{2} **keen:** splendid; fine

(continued)

30   Barbara Juster Esbensen's poem "circles" combines open form (free verse) and concrete form. It is another example of experimental poetry. What main thoughts does the poet share in this poem? Does the way the words appear on the page enhance³ the meaning of this poem?

35 **circles**
    by Barbara Juster Esbensen
                    Did you see? Did you
                            see
            the rainbow-scaled fish
40   arch into the air
                        and fall?

                    Did you see
            those perfect circles?
        Those hoops of water and light?
45   They fit together   one
                    inside another

                Wider and wider
                    they grow
                            out
50   and
            out
        and   out
            from the quick splash
                    to the shore

55 Circles
    set in wood— concentric⁴
    a round calendar
    Its widening rings grow slowly
    out

60   and out

    _____

        ³ **enhance:** to improve; add to
        ⁴ **concentric:** having a common center

Take Note

4. What event is described in the first three stanzas of this poem?

_____

_____

_____

_____

_____

5. Identify something in this section of the poem that shows its concrete form.

_____

_____

_____

_____

_____

_____

_____

6. What is this stanza of the poem about?

_____

_____

_____

(continued)

Text Connection 2 (continued)

Take Note

7. How does the poet connect the tree trunk to the ripples in the previous section of the poem?

_____

_____

_____

_____

8. These next two stanzas are about the circle formed by musk oxen when they try to protect themselves from wolves. What two things does the poet use to help describe the circle of musk oxen?

_____

_____

_____

9. What makes the circles in which the fawn hides?

_____

10. Look back through the poem up to this point. What does the poet do to show where one topic ends and another topic begins?

_____

_____

_____

_____

and   out
from the old tree's
earliest day
to the shore of
65 now

                        A circle
                is the shape of
            safety where wolf
                        shadows
70   prowl in the far north
                            where
    musk oxen stand — spokes
            of a dark muscular
                        wheel

75   Their massive [5] heads
        point in every direction
        a watchful compass-rose
            set in the snow

Deep in the forest
80 curled in its grassy
bed
the fawn
lies
dappled with circles
85 lies
hidden under
medallions of sunlight
and woodland gloom
almost invisible

_____

[5] **massive:** huge; great

90   Think of a circle   think
                of our planet
                     Earth
               solid globe
      spinning   holding us
95   holding
oceans and forests and drifting
                   deserts
    in the blackness of space

           Think of the sun
100   our blazing disk   our
                daystar
and the planet spinning from
       day into night and
                return
105   Think of all that light
     washing over us
flowing into starlit dark—
a whirling cycle of days
          and nights

110 A circle
  is the shape of sleep
  In hollow places
  deep under winter snow
  small animals dream   Their toes
115 are tucked up
  their tails curl down
  and around

  Heavy circular bears
  breathe
120 the slow sleep of cold
  nights and days

Take Note

11. What do the two stanzas that begin with **Think of** have in common?

_____

_____

_____

_____

12. Circle the two nouns the poet uses in place of the word **sun**.

13. This last section of the poem is about sleep. What sleeping creatures are mentioned?

_____

_____

(continued)

Text Connection 2 (continued)

Take Note

14. What do you think the last line of the poem means?

_____

_____

_____

_____

Sleep draws a soft line around you
curled and folded
in the arc ⁶ of an arm
125 holding the nighttime book

At the foot of the bed
the orange and white cat
has wound herself tight
and the circles of the moon coming in
130   fits her shape exactly!

Echoes for the eye!

Identify It: Adjectives in Poetry

Reread lines 37–131.

Find the adjectives that describe these nouns in the poem "circles."

_____ fish

_____ calendar

_____ wheel

_____ compass-rose

_____ cycle

⁶ **arc:** a curved line

The House on Mango Street
by Sandra Cisneros

1   *You remember periods in your own childhood, periods*
that affected you in different ways. As you read these segments
from Sandra Cisneros' The House on Mango Street, think
about the storyteller's childhood experiences, and see if you
5   *can relate to any of them. Have you ever had to <u>move</u>? What's*
it like to move into a new neighborhood? How does moving
into a new neighborhood translate to moving into a new
passage of your life?

Use the Clues A:

- Read lines 1–8.

- Reread the underlined word, **move**.

- Check the box that best defines the underlined word.
  What does the word **move** mean in this context?

  ❏ dance

  ❏ relocate

  ❏ make progress

- What clues did you use to choose this answer?

  _____

  _____

The House on Mango Street

10   We didn't always live on Mango Street. Before that we
lived on Loomis on the third floor, and before that we lived
on Keeler. Before Keeler it was Paulina, and before that I can't
remember. But what I remember most is moving a lot. Each
time it seemed there'd be one more of us. By the time we got
15   to Mango Street we were six—Mama, Papa, Carlos, Kiki, my
sister Nenny and me.

(continued)

Text Connection 3 (continued)

Take Note

As you review the **"The House on Mango Street,"** you should:

1. Underline information about the real house on Mango Street.

2. Circle information about the family's dream house.

The house on Mango Street is ours, and we don't have to pay rent to anybody, or share the yard with the people downstairs, or be careful not to make too much noise, and
20 there isn't a landlord banging on the ceiling with a broom. But even so, it's not the house we'd thought we'd get.

We had to leave the <u>flat</u> on Loomis quick. The water pipes broke and the landlord wouldn't fix them because the house was too old. We had to leave fast. We were using the
25 washroom next door and carrying water over in empty milk gallons. That's why Mama and Papa looked for a house, and that's why we moved into the house on Mango Street, far away, on the other side of town.

Use the Clues B:

- Read lines 22–28.
- Reread the underlined word, **flat**.
- Check the box that best defines the underlined word. What does the word **flat** mean in this context?
  - ❏ deflated
  - ❏ level
  - ❏ apartment on one floor
- What clues did you use to choose this answer?

  _____

  _____

They always told us that one day we would move into
30 a house, a real house that would be ours for always so we wouldn't have to move each year. And our house would have running water and pipes that worked. And inside it would have real stairs, not hallway stairs, but stairs inside like the houses on TV. And we'd have a basement and at least three
35 washrooms so when we took a bath we wouldn't have to tell everybody. Our house would be white with trees around it, a great big yard and grass growing without a fence. This was

(continued)

the house Papa talked about when he held a lottery ticket and
this was the house Mama dreamed up in the stories she told
40 us before we went to bed.

   But the house on Mango Street is not the way they told it
at all. It's small and red with tight steps in front and windows
so small you'd think they were holding their breath. Bricks
are crumbling in places, and the front door is so swollen you
45 have to push hard to get in. There is no front yard, only four
little elms the city planted by the curb. Out back is a small
garage for the car we don't own yet and a small yard that looks
smaller between the two buildings on either side. There are
stairs in our house, but they're ordinary hallway stairs, and
50 the house has only one washroom. Everybody has to share a
bedroom—Mama and Papa, Carlos and Kiki, me and Nenny.

   Once when we were living on Loomis, a nun from
my school passed by and saw me playing out front. The
laundromat downstairs had been boarded up because it had
55 been robbed two days before and the owner had painted on
the wood YES WE'RE OPEN so as not to <u>lose</u> business.

Use the Clues C:

- Read lines 52–56.

- Reread the underlined word, **lose**.

- Check the box that best defines the underlined word.
  What does the word **lose** mean in this context?

  ❏ decrease

  ❏ move

  ❏ misplace

- What clues did you use to choose this answer?

  _____

  _____

Where do you live? she asked.
There, I said pointing up to the third floor.
You live *there*?

(continued)

Text Connection 3 (continued)

60 *There.* I had to look to where she pointed—the third floor, the paint peeling, wooden bars Papa had nailed on the windows so we wouldn't fall out. You live *there*? The way she said it made me feel like nothing. *There.* I lived *there.* I nodded.

65   I knew then I had to have a house. A real house. One I could point to. But this isn't it. The house on Mango Street isn't it. For the time being, Mama says. Temporary [1], says Papa. But I know how those things go.

Boys & Girls

70   The boys and the girls live in separate worlds. The boys in their universe and we in ours. My brothers for example. They've got plenty to say to me and Nenny inside the house. But outside they can't be seen talking to girls. Carlos and Kiki are each other's best friend . . . not ours.

75   Nenny is too young to be my friend. She's just my sister and that was not my fault. You don't pick your sisters, you just get them and sometimes they come like Nenny.

    She can't play with those Vargas kids or she'll turn out just like them. And since she comes right after me, she is my

80 responsibility.

    Someday I will have a best friend all my own. One I can tell my secrets to. One who will understand my jokes without my having to explain them. Until then I am a red balloon, a balloon tied to an anchor.

---

[1] **temporary:** for a limited time; short-term

(continued)

85 **Laughter**

Nenny and I don't look like sisters . . . not right away. Not the way you can tell with Rachel and Lucy who have the same fat popsicle lips like everybody else in their family. But me and Nenny, we are more alike than you would know. Our

90 laughter for example. Not the shy ice cream bells' giggle of Rachel and Lucy's family, but all of a sudden and surprised like a pile of dishes breaking. And other things I can't explain.

One day we were passing a house that looked, in my

95 mind, like houses I had seen in Mexico. I don't know why. There was nothing about the house that looked exactly like the houses I remembered. I'm not even sure why I thought it, but it seemed to feel right.

Look at that house, I said, it looks like Mexico.

100 Rachel and Lucy look at me like I'm crazy, but before they can let out a laugh, Nenny says: Yes, that's Mexico all right. That's what I was thinking exactly.

Meme Ortiz

Meme Ortiz moved into Cathy's house after her family

105 moved away. His name isn't really Meme. His name is Juan. But when we asked him what his name was he said Meme, and that's what everybody calls him except his mother.

Meme has a dog with gray eyes, a sheepdog with two names, one in English and one in Spanish. 1 The dog is big,

110 like a man dressed in a dog suit, and runs the same way its owner does, clumsy and wild with the limbs <u>flopping all over the place</u> like untied shoes.

(continued)

Cathy's father built the house Meme moved into. It is wooden. Inside the floors slant. Some rooms uphill. Some
115 down. And there are no closets. 2 Out front there are twenty-one steps, all lopsided [2] and jutting like crooked teeth (made that way on purpose, Cathy said, so the rain will slide off), and when Meme's mama calls from the doorway, Meme goes scrambling up the twenty-one wooden stairs
120 with the dog with two names scrambling after him.

Around the back is a yard, mostly dirt, and a greasy bunch of boards that used to be a garage. But what you remember most is this tree, huge, with fat arms and mighty families of squirrels in the higher branches. All around, the
125 neighborhood of roofs, black-tarred and A-framed, and in their gutters, the balls that never came back down to earth. 3 Down at the base of the tree, the dog with two names barks into the empty air, and there at the end of the block, looking smaller still, our house with its feet tucked under
130 like a cat.

This is the tree we chose for the First Annual Tarzan Jumping Contest. Meme won. And broke both arms.

Bums in the Attic

I want a house on a hill like the ones with the gardens
135 where Papa works. We go on Sundays, Papa's day off. I used to go. I don't anymore. You don't like to go out with us, Papa says. Getting too old? Getting too stuck-up, says Nenny. 4 I don't tell them I am ashamed [3]—all of us staring out the window like the hungry. I am tired of looking at what we
140 can't have. When we win the lottery . . . Mama begins, and then I stop listening.

People who live on hills sleep so close to the stars they forget those of us who live too much on earth. They don't look down at all except to be content to live on hills. They
145 have nothing to do with last week's garbage or fear of rats. Night comes. Nothing wakes them but the wind.

---

[2] **lopsided:** sagging; leaning to one side

[3] **ashamed:** embarrassed

(continued)

One day I'll own my own house, but I won't forget who
I am or where I came from. 5 <u>Passing</u> bums will ask, Can I
come in? I'll offer them the attic [4], ask them to stay, because I
150 know how it is to be without a house.

Some days after dinner, guests and I will sit in front of a
fire. Floorboards will squeak upstairs. The attic grumble.

Rats? they'll ask.

Bums, I'll say, and I'll be happy.

Identify It: Participles and Participial Phrases.

Read each numbered sentence. Look at the underlined phrase in it.

Check the correct column to indicate whether the participle in the phrase is acting alone as an adjective (**A**), or is part of a participial phrase (**PP**).

Write the noun or pronoun that is being described on the line.

	A	PP	
1.	❑	❑	_____
2.	❑	❑	_____
3.	❑	❑	_____
4.	❑	❑	_____
5.	❑	❑	_____

155 **A Smart Cookie**

I could've been somebody, you know? my mother says and
sighs. She has lived in this city her whole life. She can speak
two languages. She can sing an opera. She knows how to fix
a TV. But she doesn't know which subway train to take to get
160 downtown. I hold her hand very tight while we wait for the
right train to arrive.

She used to draw when she had time. Now she draws with
a needle and thread, little knotted rosebuds, tulips made
of silk thread. Someday she would like to go to the ballet.
165 Someday she would like to see a play. She borrows opera

---

[4] **attic:** space under the roof of a house

(continued)

records from the public library and sings with velvety lungs powerful as morning glories.

Today while cooking oatmeal she is Madame Butterfly until she sighs and points the wooden spoon at me. I could've
170 been somebody, you know? Esperanza, you go to school. Study hard. That Madame Butterfly was a fool. She stirs the oatmeal. Look at my *comadres.* She means Izaura whose husband left and Yolanda whose husband is dead. Got to take care all your own, she says shaking her head.
175 Then out of nowhere:

Shame is a bad thing, you know. It keeps you down. You want to know why I quit school? Because I didn't have nice clothes. No clothes, but I had brains.

Yup, she says disgusted, stirring again. I was a smart
180 cookie then.

Alicia & I Talking on Edna's Steps

I like Alicia because once she gave me a little leather purse with the word GUADALAJARA stitched on it, which is home for Alicia, and one day she will go back there. But today
185 she is listening to my sadness because I don't have a house.

You live right here, 4006 Mango, Alicia says and points to the house I am ashamed of.

No, this isn't my house I say and shake my head as if shaking could undo the year I've lived here. I don't belong. I don't ever
190 want to come from here. You have a home, Alicia, and one day you'll go there, to a town you remember, but me I never had a house, not even a photograph . . . only one I dream of.

No, Alicia says. Like it or not you are Mango Street, and one day you'll come back too.
195 Not me. Not until somebody makes it better.

Who's going to do it? The mayor?

And the thought of the mayor coming to Mango Street makes me laugh out loud.

Who's going to do it? Not the mayor.

(continued)

200 **A House of My Own**

Not a flat. Not an apartment in back. Not a man's house. Not a daddy's. A house all my own. With my porch [5] and my pillow, my pretty purple petunias. My books and my stories. My two shoes waiting beside the bed. Nobody to shake a
205 stick at. Nobody's garbage to pick up after.

Only a house quiet as snow, a space for myself to go, clean as paper before the poem.

Mango Says Goodbye Sometimes

I like to tell stories. I tell them inside my head. I tell them
210 after the mailman says, Here's your mail. Here's your mail he said.

I make a story for my life, for each step my brown shoe takes. I say, "And so she trudged up the wooden stairs, her sad brown shoes taking her to the house she never liked."
215 I like to tell stories. I am going to tell you a story about a girl who didn't want to belong.

We didn't always live on Mango Street. Before that we lived on Loomis on the third floor, and before that we lived on Keeler. Before Keeler it was Paulina, but what I remember
220 most is Mango Street, sad red house, the house I belong but do not belong to.

I put it down on paper and then the ghost does not ache [6] so much. I write it down and Mango says goodbye sometimes. She does not hold me with both arms. She sets
225 me free.

One day I will pack my bags of books and paper. One day I will say goodbye to Mango. I am too strong for her to keep me here forever. One day I will go away.

Friends and neighbors will say, What happened to that
230 Esperanza? Where did she go with all those books and paper? Why did she march so far away?

They will not know I have gone away to come back. For the ones I left behind. For the ones who cannot out.

From *The House on Mango Street* by Sandra Cisneros

---

[5] **porch:** a covered structure outside the entrance to a house

[6] **ache:** a dull, lasting pain

Comprehend It

Write a short summary of **"A House of My Own."**

_____

_____

_____

Why do you think Esperanza would come back to her neighborhood?

_____

_____

_____

_____

_____

_____

Rules of the Game
by Amy Tan

1   *Like Sandra Cisneros'* The House on Mango Street, *Amy Tan's "Rules of the Game," an excerpt from* The Joy Luck Club, *deals with childhood memories that involve movement.*

5   *In addition to being highly respected for their writing abilities, both writers are famous for their focus and keen insights into their own cultures. Sandra Cisneros writes about Latino culture; Amy Tan writes about Chinese Americans.*

     As you read these selections, think about what the word "movement" means in each selection. What did it mean in

10   The House on Mango Street? *Does "movement" have more than one layer of meaning?*

Section 1

     I was six when my mother taught me the art of invisible strength. It was a strategy for winning arguments, respect from others, and eventually, though neither of us knew it at

15   the time, chess games.

     "<u>Bite back your tongue</u>," scolded my mother when I cried loudly, yanking her hand toward the store that sold bags of salted plums.

(continued)

Use the Clues A:

- Read lines 16–18.

- Reread the underlined idiom **bite back your tongue**.

- Check the box that best defines the underlined phrase. What does the idiom **bite back your tongue** mean in this context?

  ❑ eat

  ❑ stop crying or talking

  ❑ sticking out your tongue

- What clues did you use to help you choose this answer?

  _____

  _____

Take Note

Summarize information about the setting below.

_____

_____

_____

_____

_____

_____

_____

_____

At home, she said, "Wise guy, he not go against wind. In
20 Chinese we say, Come from South, blow with wind—poom!—
North will follow. Strongest wind cannot be seen."

The next week I bit back my tongue as we entered the
store with the forbidden candies. When my mother finished
her shopping, she quietly plucked a small bag of plums from
25 the rack and put it on the counter with the rest of the items.

My mother imparted her daily truths so she could help
my older brothers and me rise above our circumstances. We
lived in San Francisco's Chinatown. Like most of the other
Chinese children who played in the back alleys of restaurants
30 and curio shops, I didn't think we were poor. My bowl was
always full, three five-course meals every day, beginning with
a soup full of mysterious things I didn't want to know the
names of.

(continued)

Unit 26

Take Note

Summarize information about the setting below.

_____

_____

_____

_____

_____

_____

_____

_____

Use the Clues B:

- Read lines 26–33.

- Reread the underlined idiom **rise above our circumstances**.

- Check the box that best defines the underlined phrase. What does the phrase **rise above our circumstances** mean in this context?

  ❑ stand up

  ❑ have a better life

  ❑ eat well

- What clues did you use to help you choose this answer?

  _____

  _____

We lived on Waverly Place, in a warm, clean, two-
35 bedroom flat that sat above a small Chinese bakery
specializing in steamed pastries and dim sum. In the early
morning, when the alley was still quiet, I could smell
fragrant red beans as they were cooked down to a pasty
sweetness. By daybreak, our flat was heavy with the odor of
40 fried sesame balls and sweet curried chicken crescents. From
my bed, I would listen as my father got ready for work, then
lock the door behind him, one-two-three clicks.

At the end of our two-block alley was a small sandlot
playground with swings and slides well-shined down the
45 middle with use. The play area was bordered by wood-slat
benches where old-country people sat cracking roasted
watermelon seeds with their golden teeth and scattering the
husks to an impatient gathering of gurgling pigeons. The
best playground, however, was the dark alley itself. It was
50 crammed with daily mysteries and adventures. My brothers
and I would peer into the medicinal herb shop, watching old
Li dole out onto a stiff sheet of white paper the right amount
of insect shells, saffron-colored seeds, and pungent leaves for

(continued)

Text Connection 4 (continued)

his ailing customers. It was said that he once cured a woman
55 dying of an ancestral curse that had eluded the best of
American doctors. Next to the pharmacy was a printer who
specialized in gold-embossed wedding invitations and festive
red banners.

Farther down the street was Ping Yuen Fish Market. The
60 front window displayed a tank crowded with doomed fish
and turtles struggling to gain footing on the slimy green-
tiled sides. A hand-written sign informed tourists, "Within
this store, is all for food, not for pet." Inside, the butchers
with their bloodstained white smocks deftly gutted the fish
65 while customers cried out their orders and shouted, "Give me
your freshest," to which the butchers always protested, "All
are freshest." On less crowded market days, we would inspect
the crates of live frogs and crabs which we were warned
not to poke, boxes of dried cuttlefish, and row upon row of
70 iced prawns, squid, and slippery fish. The sanddabs made
me shiver each time; their eyes lay on one flattened side and
reminded me of my mother's story of a careless girl who ran
into a crowded street and was crushed by a cab. "Was smash
flat," reported my mother.

75 At the corner of the alley was Hong Sing's, a four-table
café with a recessed stairwell in front that led to a door
marked "Tradesmen." My brothers and I believed the bad
people emerged from this door at night. Tourists never went
to Hong Sing's, since the menu was printed only in Chinese.
80 A Caucasian man with a big camera once posed me and my
playmates in front of the restaurant. He had us move to the
side of the picture window so the photo would capture the
roasted duck with its head dangling from a juice-covered
rope. After he took the picture, I told him he should go
85 into Hong Sing's and eat dinner. When he smiled and asked
me what they served, I shouted, "Guts and duck's feet and
octopus gizzards!" Then I ran off with my friends, shrieking
with laughter as we scampered across the alley and hid in
the entryway grotto of the China Gem Company, my heart
90 pounding with hope that he would chase us.

Take Note

Summarize information about
the setting below.

_____

_____

_____

_____

_____

_____

_____

_____

(continued)

Unit 26

Comprehend It

How did Waverly get her name?

_____

_____

_____

Describe Waverly's mother.

_____

_____

_____

Describe Waverly's motivation for asking her mother about Chinese torture.

_____

_____

_____

_____

My mother named me after the street we lived on: Waverly Place Jong, my official name for important American documents. But my family called me Meimei, "Little Sister." I was the youngest, the only daughter. Each morning before
95 school, my mother would twist and yank on my thick black hair until she had formed two tightly wound pigtails. One day, as she struggled to weave a hard-toothed comb through my disobedient hair, I had a sly thought.

I asked her, "Ma, what is Chinese torture?" My mother
100 shook her head. A bobby pin was wedged between her lips. She wetted her palm and smoothed the hair above my ear, then pushed the pin in so that it nicked sharply against my scalp.

"Who say this word?" she asked without a trace of knowing how wicked I was being. I shrugged my shoulders
105 and said, "Some boy in my class said Chinese people do Chinese torture."

"Chinese people do many things," she said simply. "Chinese people do business, do medicine, do painting. Not lazy like American people. We do torture. Best torture."
110 My older brother Vincent was the one who actually got the chess set. We had gone to the annual Christmas party held at the First Chinese Baptist Church at the end of the alley. The missionary ladies had put together a Santa bag of gifts donated by members of another church. None of the
115 gifts had names on them. There were separate sacks for boys and girls of different ages.

One of the Chinese parishioners had donned a Santa Claus costume with a stiff paper beard with cotton balls glued to it. I think the only children who thought he was the
120 real thing were too young to know that Santa Claus was not Chinese. When my turn came up, the Santa man asked me how old I was. I thought it was a trick question; I was seven according to the American formula and eight by the Chinese calendar. I said I was born on March 17, 1951. That seemed to
125 satisfy him. He then solemnly asked me if I had been a very, very good girl this year and did I obey my parents. I knew the only answer to that. I nodded back with equal solemnity.

Having watched the other children opening their gifts, I already knew that the big gifts were not necessarily the nicest

(continued)

130 ones. One girl my age got a large coloring book of biblical characters, while a less greedy girl who selected a smaller box received a glass vial of lavender toilet water. The sound of the box was also important. A ten-year-old boy had chosen a box that jangled when he shook it. It was a tin globe of the

135 world with a slit for inserting money. He must have thought it was full of dimes and nickels, because when he saw that it had just ten pennies, his face fell with such undisguised disappointment that his mother slapped the side of his head and led him out of the church hall, apologizing to the crowd

140 for her son who had such bad manners he couldn't appreciate such a fine gift.

As I peered into the sack, I quickly fingered the remaining presents, testing their weight, imagining what they contained. I chose a heavy, compact one that was

145 wrapped in shiny silver foil and a red satin ribbon. It was a twelve-pack of Life Savers and I spent the rest of the party arranging and rearranging the candy tubes in the order of my favorites. My brother Winston chose wisely as well. His present turned out to be a box of intricate plastic parts; the

150 instructions on the box proclaimed that when they were properly assembled he would have an authentic miniature replica of a World War II submarine.

Vincent got the chess set, which would have been a very decent present to get at a church Christmas party, except it

155 was obviously used and, as we discovered later, it was missing a black pawn and a white knight. My mother graciously thanked the unknown benefactor [1], saying, "Too good. Cost too much." At which point, an old lady with fine white, wispy hair nodded toward our family and said with a whistling

160 whisper, "Merry, merry Christmas."

When we got home, my mother told Vincent to throw the chess set away. "She not want it. We not want it," she said, tossing her head stiffly to the side with a tight, proud smile. My brothers have deaf ears. They were already lining up the chess

165 pieces and reading from the dog-eared instruction book.

---

[1] **benefactor:** a donor; person who gives something to another

(*continued*)

Section 2

I watched Vincent and Winston play during Christmas week. The chess board seemed to hold elaborate secrets waiting to be untangled. The chessmen were more powerful than Old Li's magic herbs that cured ancestral curses.
170 And my brothers wore such serious faces that I was sure something was at stake that was greater than avoiding the tradesmen's door to Hong Sing's.

"Let me! Let me!" I begged between games when one brother or the other would sit back with a deep sigh of
175 relief and victory, the other annoyed, unable to let go of the outcome. Vincent at first refused to let me play, but when I offered my Life Savers as replacements for the buttons that filled in for the missing pieces, he relented. He chose the flavors: wild cherry for the black pawn and peppermint for
180 the white knight. Winner could eat both.

As our mother sprinkled flour and rolled out small doughy circles for the steamed dumplings that would be our dinner that night, Vincent explained the rules, pointing to each piece. "You have sixteen pieces and so do I. One king
185 and queen, two bishops, two knights, two castles, and eight pawns. The pawns can only move forward one step, except on the first move. Then they can move two. But they can only take men by moving crossways like this, except in the beginning, when you can move ahead and take another pawn."
190 "Why?" I asked as I moved my pawn. "Why can't they move more steps?"

"Because they're pawns," he said.

"But why do they go crossways to take other men. Why aren't there any women and children?"
195 "Why is the sky blue? Why must you always ask stupid questions?" asked Vincent. "This is a game. These are the rules. I didn't make them up. See. Here. In the book." He jabbed a page with a pawn in his hand. "Pawn. P-A-W-N. Pawn. Read it yourself."
200 My mother patted the flour off her hands. "Let me see book," she said quietly. She scanned the pages quickly, not

(continued)

reading the foreign English symbols, seeming to search deliberately for nothing in particular.

"This American rules," she concluded at last. "Every time
205 people come out from foreign country, must know rules. You not know, judge say, Too bad, go back. They not telling you why so you can use their way go forward. They say, Don't know why, you find out yourself. But they knowing all the time. Better you take it, find out why yourself." She tossed her
210 head back with a satisfied smile.

I found out about all the whys later. I read the rules and looked up all the big words in a dictionary. I borrowed books from the Chinatown library. I studied each chess piece, trying to absorb the power it contained.

215 I learned about opening moves and why it's important to control the center early on; the shortest distance between two points is straight down the middle. I learned about the middle game and why tactics [2] between two adversaries [3] are like clashing ideas; the one who plays better has the
220 clearest plans for both attacking and getting out of traps. I learned why it is essential in the endgame to have foresight, a mathematical understanding of all possible moves, and patience; all weaknesses and advantages become evident to a strong adversary and are obscured to a tiring opponent. I
225 discovered that for the whole game one must gather invisible strengths and see the endgame before the game begins.

I also found out why I should never reveal "why" to others. A little knowledge withheld is a great advantage one should store for future use. That is the power of chess. It is a
230 game of secrets in which one must show and never tell.

I loved the secrets I found within the sixty-four black and white squares. I carefully drew a handmade chessboard and pinned it to the wall next to my bed, where at night I would stare for hours at imaginary battles. Soon I no longer lost any
235 games or Life Savers, but I lost my adversaries. Winston and Vincent decided they were more interested in roaming the streets after school in their Hopalong Cassidy cowboy hats.

---

[2] **tactics:** plans; strategies

[3] **adversaries:** opponents; foes

(continued)

On a cold spring afternoon, while walking home from
school, I detoured through the playground at the end of our
240 alley. I saw a group of old men, two seated across a folding
table playing a game of chess, others smoking pipes, eating
peanuts, and watching. I ran home and grabbed Vincent's
chess set, which was bound in a cardboard box with rubber
bands. I also carefully selected two prized rolls of Life Savers.
245 I came back to the park and approached a man who was
observing the game.

"Want to play?" I asked him. His face widened with
surprise and he grinned as he looked at the box under my arm.

"Little sister, been a long time since I play with dolls," he
250 said, smiling benevolently. I quickly put the box down next to
him on the bench and displayed my retort [4].

Lau Po, as he allowed me to call him, turned out to
be a much better player than my brothers. I lost many
games and many Life Savers. But over the weeks, with each
255 diminishing roll of candies, I added new secrets. Lau Po gave
me the names. The Double Attack from the East and West
Shores. Throwing Stones on the Drowning Man. The Sudden
Meeting of the Clan. The Surprise from the Sleeping Guard.
The Humble Servant Who Kills the King. Sand in the Eyes of
260 Advancing Forces. A Double Killing Without Blood.

There were also the fine points of chess etiquette. 1 Keep
captured men in neat rows, as well-tended prisoners. Never
announce "Check" with vanity, lest someone with an unseen
sword slit your throat. 2 Never hurl pieces into the sandbox
265 after you have lost a game, because then you must find them
again, by yourself, after apologizing to all around you. By the
end of the summer, Lau Po had taught me all he knew, and I
had become a better chess player.

A small weekend crowd of Chinese people and tourists
270 would gather as I played and defeated my opponents one
by one. 3 My mother would join the crowds during these
outdoor exhibition games. 4 She sat proudly on the bench,
telling my admirers with proper Chinese humility [5], "Is luck."

---

[4] **retort:** a quick reply or answer

[5] **humility:** meekness; modesty

(continued)

Text Connection 4 (continued)

5 A man who watched me play <u>in the park</u> suggested
275 that my mother allow me to play in local chess tournaments.
My mother smiled graciously, an answer that meant nothing.
I desperately wanted to go, but I bit back my tongue. I knew
she would not let me play among strangers. So as we walked
home I said in a small voice that I didn't want to play in the
280 local tournament. They would have American rules. If I lost,
I would bring shame on my family.

Identify It: Adverbs, Adverbial Phrases, and Adverbial Clauses

Read each numbered sentence on the previous page.

Decide if the underlined words contain an adverb (Adv.), adverbial phrase (Adv. Phrase), or an adverbial clause (Adv. Clause).

Check the column below.

	Adv.	Adv. Phrase	Adv. Clause
1.	❏	❏	❏
2.	❏	❏	❏
3.	❏	❏	❏
4.	❏	❏	❏
5.	❏	❏	❏

"Is shame you fall down nobody push you," said my
mother.

During my first tournament, my mother sat with me in
285 the front row as I waited for my turn. I frequently bounced
my legs to unstick them from the cold metal seat of the
folding chair. When my name was called, I leapt up. My
mother unwrapped something in her lap. It was her *chang*, a
small tablet of red jade which held the sun's fire. "Is luck," she

Comprehend It

How does Waverly convince her mother to let her play in a tournament?

_____

_____

_____

_____

_____

_____

_____

(continued)

Text Connection 4 (continued)

Comprehend It

Describe Waverly's mother's feelings about Waverly's success in chess.

_____

_____

_____

290 whispered, and tucked it into my dress pocket. I turned to my opponent, a fifteen-year-old boy from Oakland. He looked at me, wrinkling his nose.

As I began to play, the boy disappeared, the color ran out of the room, and I saw only my white pieces and his black
295 ones waiting on the other side. A light wind began blowing past my ears. It whispered secrets only I could hear.

"Blow from the South," it murmured. "The wind leaves no trail." I saw a clear path, the traps to avoid. The crowd rustled. "Shhh! Shhh!" said the corners of the room The wind
300 blew stronger. "Throw sand from the East to distract him." The knight came forward ready for the sacrifice. The wind hissed, louder and louder. "Blow, blow, blow. He cannot see. He is blind now. Make him lean away from the wind so he is easier to knock down."

305 "Check," I said, as the wind roared with laughter. The wind died down to little puffs, my own breath.

My mother placed my first trophy next to a new plastic chess set that the neighborhood Tao society had given to me. As she wiped each piece with a soft cloth, she said, "Next
310 time win more, lose less."

"Ma, it's not how many pieces you lost," I said. "Sometimes you need to lose pieces to get ahead."

"Better to lose less, see if you really need."

At the next tournament, I won again, but it was my
315 mother who wore the triumphant [6] grin.

"Lose eight piece this time. Last time was eleven. What I tell you? Better off lose less!" I was annoyed, but I couldn't say anything.

---

[6] **triumphant:** victorious; conquering

(continued)

320   I attended more tournaments, each one farther away from home. I won all games, in all divisions. The Chinese bakery downstairs from our flat displayed my growing collection of trophies in its window, amidst the dust-covered cakes that were never picked up. The day after I won an important regional tournament, the window encased a

325 fresh sheet cake with whipped-cream frosting and red script saying, "Congratulations, Waverly Jong, Chinatown Chess Champion." Soon after that, a flower shop, headstone engraver, and funeral parlor offered to sponsor me in national tournaments. That's when my mother decided I no

330 longer had to do the dishes. Winston and Vincent had to do my chores.

    "Why does she get to play and we do all the work," complained Vincent.

    "Is new American rules," said my mother. "Meimei play,

335 squeeze all her brains out for win chess. You play, worth squeeze towel."

    By my ninth birthday, I was a national chess champion. I was still some 429 points away from grand-master status, but I was touted as the Great American Hope, a child prodigy

340 and a girl to boot. They ran a photo of me in *Life* magazine next to a quote in which Bobby Fischer said, "There will never be a woman grand master." "Your move, Bobby," said the caption.

Comprehend It

Write a short summary of lines 166-366.

_____

_____

_____

_____

(continued)

The day they took the magazine picture I wore neatly
345 plaited braids clipped with plastic barrettes trimmed with
rhinestones. I was playing in a large high school auditorium
that echoed with phlegmy coughs and the squeaky rubber
knobs of chair legs sliding across freshly waxed wooden
floors. Seated across from me was an American man, about
350 the same age of Lau Po, maybe fifty. I remember that his
sweaty brow seemed to weep at my every move. He wore a
dark, malodorous suit. One of his pockets was stuffed with
a great white kerchief on which he wiped his palm before
sweeping his hand over the chosen chess piece with great
355 flourish.

In my crisp pink-and-white dress with scratchy lace at
the neck, one of two my mother had sewn for these special
occasions, I would clasp my hands under my chin, the
delicate points of my elbows poised lightly on the table in
360 the manner my mother had shown me for posing for the
press. I would swing my patent leather shoes back and forth
like an impatient child riding on a school bus. Then I would
pause, suck in my lips, twirl my chosen piece in midair as if
undecided, and then firmly plant it in its new threatening
365 place, with a triumphant smile thrown back at my opponent
for good measure.

Section 3

I no longer played in the alley of Waverly Place. I never
visited the playground where the pigeons and old men
gathered. I went to school, then directly home to learn new
370 chess secrets, cleverly concealed advantages, more escape
routes.

But I found it difficult to concentrate at home. My mother
had a habit of standing over me while I plotted out my
games. I think she thought of herself as my protective ally.
375 Her lips would be sealed tight, and after each move I made, a
soft "Hmmmmph" would escape from her nose.

"Ma, I can't practice when you stand there like that," I
said one day. She retreated to the kitchen and made loud
noises with the pots and pans. When the crashing stopped, I

(continued)

380 could see out of the corner of my eye that she was standing in the doorway. "Hmmmph!" Only this one sound came out of her tight throat.

My parents made many concessions to allow me to practice. One time I complained that the bedroom I shared
385 was so noisy that I couldn't think. Thereafter, my brothers slept in a bed in the living room facing the street. I said I couldn't finish my rice; my head didn't work right when my stomach was too full. I left the table with half-finished bowls and nobody complained. But there was one duty I couldn't
390 avoid. I had to accompany my mother on Saturday market days when I had no tournament to play. My mother would proudly walk with me, visiting many shops, buying very little. "This my daughter Wave-ly Jong," she said to whoever looked her way.

395 One day, after we left a shop I said under my breath, "I wish you wouldn't do that, telling everybody I'm your daughter." My mother stopped walking. Crowds of people with heavy bags pushed past us on the sidewalk, bumping into first one shoulder, then another.

400 "Aiii-ya. So shame be with mother?" She grasped my hand even tighter as she glared at me.

I looked down. "It's not that, it's just so obvious. It's just so embarrassing."

"Embarrass you be my daughter?" Her voice was cracking
405 with anger.

"That's not what I meant. That's not what I said."

"What you say?"

I knew it was a mistake to say anything more, but I heard my voice speaking. "Why do you have to use me to show
410 off? If you want to show off, then why don't you learn to play chess."

My mother's eyes turned into dangerous black slits. She had no words for me, just sharp silence.

I felt the wind rushing around my hot ears. I jerked
415 my hand out of my mother's tight grasp and spun around, knocking into an old woman. Her bag of groceries spilled to the ground.

(continued)

Text Connection 4 (continued)

Comprehend It

Explain how tension between Waverly and her mother builds.

_____

_____

_____

_____

_____

_____

"Aii-ya! Stupid girl!" my mother and the woman cried. Oranges and tin cans careened down the sidewalk. As my
420 mother stopped to help the old woman pick up the escaping food, I took off.

I raced down the street, dashing between people, not looking back as my mother screamed shrilly, "Meimei! Meimei!" I fled down an alley, past dark curtained shops
425 and merchants washing the grime off their windows. I sped into the sunlight, into a large street crowded with tourists examining trinkets and souvenirs. I ducked into another dark alley, down another street, up another alley. I ran until it hurt and I realized I had nowhere to go, that I was not running
430 from anything. The alleys contained no escape routes.

My breath came out like angry smoke. It was cold. I sat down on an upturned plastic pail next to a stack of empty boxes, cupping my chin with my hands, thinking hard. I imagined my mother, first walking briskly down one street or
435 another looking for me, then giving up and returning home to await my arrival. After two hours, I stood up on creaking legs and slowly walked home.

The alley was quiet and I could see the yellow lights shining from our flat like two tiger's eyes in the night. I
440 climbed the sixteen steps to the door, advancing quickly up each so as not to make any warning sounds. I turned the knob; the door was locked. I heard a chair moving, quick steps, the locks turning—click! click! click!—and then the door opened.

445 "About time you got home," said Vincent. "Boy, are you in trouble."

He slid back to the dinner table. On a platter were the remains of a large fish, its fleshy head still connected to

(continued)

bones swimming upstream in vain escape. Standing there
450 waiting for my punishment, I heard my mother speak in a
dry voice.

"We not concerning this girl. This girl not have
concerning for us."

Nobody looked at me. Bone chopsticks clinked against
455 the insides of bowls being emptied into hungry mouths.

I walked into my room, closed the door, and lay down on
my bed. The room was dark, the ceiling filled with shadows
from the dinnertime lights of neighboring flats.

In my head, I saw a chessboard with sixty-four black and
460 white squares. Opposite me was my opponent, two angry
black slits. She wore a triumphant smile. "Strongest wind
cannot be seen," she said.

Her black men advanced across the plane, slowly
marching to each successive level as a single unit. My white
465 pieces screamed as they scurried and fell off the board one by
one. As her men drew closer to my edge, I felt myself growing
light. I rose up into the air and flew out the window. Higher
and higher, above the alley, over the tops of tiled roofs, where
I was gathered up by the wind and pushed up towards the
470 night sky until everything below me disappeared and I was
alone.

I closed my eyes and pondered my next move.

"The Rules of the Game," from *The Joy Luck Club* by Amy Tan

Comprehend It

What does the narrator
compare to a game of chess?

_____

_____

David Copperfield

by Charles Dickens

Who Was Charles Dickens?

1   Charles Dickens (1812–1870) remains one of the most beloved storytellers in the English language. Initially, his stories appeared in newspapers, as serials, and people eagerly awaited chapters—much as people watch serials on television
5   today.

Charles Dickens addressed social issues that other writers avoided. His work set the stage for enormous social reform in England and around the world. Dickens' stories were written to promote social reform in many different
10   areas. This chapter of *David Copperfield* addresses two major social issues: child labor and the imprisonment of debtors.

In the 1800s, child labor was not uncommon in England and other places in the world. Debtors' prisons were full of people who were there simply because they couldn't pay their
15   bills. Eventually, both of these social issues were addressed through reform laws. The stories of Charles Dickens influenced social reform in England and around the world.

Those who have studied the life of Charles Dickens also realize that *David Copperfield* is an autobiographical novel.
20   It is fiction, but it has much of its basis in fact. The novel's story is told in the first person. It includes characters based on people in Dickens' life. In the chapter that follows, David Copperfield meets Mr. Micawber, an optimistic man with a large family, who is constantly plagued by debt collectors.
25   The second social issue of this book—that of imprisoning people who were in debt—begins here. Interestingly, authorities agree that the character of Mr. Micawber is based on Charles Dickens' father. A tragic experience occurred

(continued)

when Charles was 12 years old. His father was imprisoned
30 for debt, and Charles was sent to work in a factory to support
the family. This is essential in knowing and understanding
the passionate urgency of Dickens' efforts toward social
reform through his writing.

Summary of *David Copperfield*: Chapters 1–10

    In the first ten chapters, the reader learns that David
35 *Copperfield's father died before he was born. An only child,*
David lived with his mother and Peggotty, a housemaid who
cared for both David and his mother. David's mother married
a cruel man named Mr. Murdstone, who moved into the
Copperfields' home with his sister. Together, they stamped out
40 *all the joy in the home. When Chapter 11 opens, David is ten*
years old. His mother has just died, and the Murdstones have
fired Peggotty. They have removed David from school and sent
him off to London, to work in their factory, cleaning bottles.
Here, he first meets Mr. Micawber, with whom he will live for
45 *a time.*

Comprehend It

Reread the last two paragraphs. Identify the events in Charles Dickens' life that are similar to things that happen in the story about David Copperfield.

_____

_____

_____

_____

_____

_____

_____

_____

_____

(continued)

Unit 27

Text Connection 5 (continued)

Take Note

Reread the first paragraph. Underline words that describe the location and the appearance of the warehouse where David works. Then write a brief description of the warehouse, using your own words.

_____

_____

_____

_____

_____

_____

_____

_____

Section 1
Chapter 11: I begin life on my own account, and don't like it

Murdstone and Grinby's warehouse was at the waterside. It was down in Blackfriars. Modern improvements have altered the place; but it was the last house at the bottom of a narrow street, curving down hill to the river, with some
50 stairs at the end, where people took boat. It was a crazy old house with a <u>wharf</u> of its own, <u>abutting</u> on the water when the tide was in, and on the mud when the tide was out, and literally <u>overrun</u> with rats. Its panelled rooms, discoloured[1] with the dirt and smoke of a hundred years, I dare say; its
55 decaying floors and staircase; the squeaking and scuffling of the old grey rats down in the <u>cellars</u>; and the dirt and rottenness of the place; are things, not of many years ago, in my mind, but of the present instant. They are all before me, just as they were in the evil hour when I went among them for
60 the first time, with my <u>trembling</u> hand in Mr. Quinion's. . . .

Use the Clues:

- Read lines 46–60.
- Reread the underlined words: **wharf**, **abutting**, **overrun**, **cellars**, and **trembling**.
- Think about their meaning using context clues.
- Match each word with its synonym.
- Use a dictionary for help if needed.

1. cellars	a. pier
2. wharf	b. shaking
3. abutting	c. touching
4. overrun	d. basements
5. trembling	e. infested

_____

[1] **discoloured:** changed or spoiled in color; stained

(continued)

Text Connection 5 (continued)

There were three or four of us, counting me. My working place was established in a corner of the warehouse, where Mr. Quinion could see me, when he chose to stand up on the bottom rail of his stool in the counting-house, and look
65 at me through a window above the desk. Hither, on the first morning of my so auspiciously[2] beginning life on my own account, the oldest of the regular boys was summoned to show me my business. His name was Mick Walker, and he wore a ragged apron and a paper cap. He informed me that
70 his father was a bargeman, and walked, in a black velvet head-dress, in the Lord Mayor's Show. He also informed me that our principal associate would be another boy whom he introduced by the—to me—extraordinary name of Mealy Potatoes. . . .
75 No words can express the secret agony[3] of my soul as I sunk into this companionship. The deep remembrance of the sense I had, of being utterly without hope now; of the shame I felt in my position; of the misery it was to my young heart to believe that day by day what I had learned, and thought, and
80 delighted in, and raised my fancy and my emulation up by, would pass away from me, little by little, never to be brought back any more; cannot be written. As often as Mick Walker went away in the course of that forenoon, I mingled my tears with the water in which I was washing the bottles; and
85 sobbed as if there were a flaw in my own breast, and it were in danger of bursting.

The counting-house clock was at half past twelve, and there was general preparation for going to dinner, when Mr. Quinion tapped at the counting-house window, and
90 beckoned to me to go in. I went in, and found there a stoutish, middle-aged person, in a brown surtout[a] and black tights and shoes, with no more hair upon his head (which

Comprehend It

Reread lines 75–86. How does David feel abut working at the warehouse?

_____

_____

_____

_____

_____

_____

_____

Take Note

• Reread the description of Mr. Micawber in lines 90–99.

• Underline words and phrases that describe what he looks like.

• Review the meanings of the footnoted words.

• Then draw a quick cartoon or sketch of what Mr. Micawber looks like.

---

[2] **auspiciously:** favorably

[3] **agony:** a great pain

[a] **surtout:** a man's overcoat

(continued)

Comprehend It

Why do you think that David is impressed by the fact that Mr. Micawber seems **genteel**?

_____

_____

_____

_____

_____

_____

_____

_____

Comprehend It

Look up the definition of **lodgings** at the bottom of the page. Then write it here:

_____

_____

_____

Why is David going to be a lodger with Mr. Micawber? Who wrote to Mr. Micawber about renting David a room?

_____

_____

_____

_____

_____

_____

_____

_____

was a large one, and very shining) than there is upon an egg, and with a very extensive face, which he turned full upon
95   me. His clothes were shabby [4], but he had an imposing shirt-collar on. He carried a jaunty sort of a stick, with a large pair of rusty tassels to it; and a quizzing-glass [b] hung outside his coat,—for ornament, I afterwards found, as he very seldom looked through it, and couldn't see anything when he did.
100   "This," said Mr. Quinion, in allusion to myself, "is he."
   "This," said the stranger, with a certain condescending roll in his voice, and a certain indescribable air of doing something genteel [5], which impressed me very much, "is Master Copperfield. I hope I see you well, sir?"
105   I said I was very well, and hoped he was. I was sufficiently ill at ease, Heaven knows; but it was not in my nature to complain much at that time of my life, so I said I was very well, and hoped he was.
   "I am," said the stranger, "thank Heaven, quite well. I have
110 received a letter from Mr. Murdstone, in which he mentions that he would desire me to receive into an apartment in the rear of my house, which is at present unoccupied—and is, in short, to be let as a—in short," said the stranger, with a smile and in a burst of confidence, "as a bedroom—the
115 young beginner whom I have now the pleasure to—" and the stranger waved his hand, and settled his chin in his shirt-collar.
   "This is Mr. Micawber," said Mr. Quinion to me.
   "Ahem!" said the stranger, "that is my name."
120   "Mr. Micawber," said Mr. Quinion, "is known to Mr. Murdstone. He takes orders for us on commission, when he can get any. He has been written to by Mr. Murdstone, on the subject of your lodgings [c], and he will receive you as a lodger."

---

[4] **shabby:** worn; threadbare

[5] **genteel:** politeness traditionally associated with wealth and education

[b] **quizzing-glass:** a single eyeglass used to examine people or objects

[c] **lodgings:** furnished rooms for rent in a person's home

(continued)

"My address," said Mr. Micawber, "is Windsor Terrace,
125 City Road. I—in short," said Mr. Micawber, with the same
genteel air, and in another burst of confidence—"I live there."

I made him a bow.

"Under the impression," said Mr. Micawber, "that
your peregrinations in this metropolis have not as yet
130 been extensive, and that you might have some difficulty
in penetrating the arcana of the Modern Babylon in the
direction of the City Road, —in short," said Mr. Micawber, in
another burst of confidence, "that you might lose yourself—I
shall be happy to call this evening, and install you in the
135 knowledge of the nearest way."

I thanked him with all my heart, for it was friendly in him
to offer to take that trouble.

"At what hour," said Mr. Micawber, "shall I—"

"At about eight," said Mr. Quinion.

140 "At about eight," said Mr. Micawber. "I beg to wish you
good day, Mr. Quinion. I will intrude no longer."

1 So he put on his hat, and went out with his cane under
his arm: very upright, and <u>humming</u> a tune when he was
clear of the counting-house.

Section 2

145 2 At the <u>appointed</u> time in the evening, Mr. Micawber
reappeared. I washed my hands and face, to do the greater
honour to his gentility, and we walked to our house, as
I suppose I must now call it, together; Mr. Micawber
impressing the name of streets, and the shapes of corner
150 houses upon me, as we went along, that I might find my way
back, easily, in the morning.

3 My room was at the top of the house, at the back: a
close chamber; <u>stencilled</u> all over with an ornament, which
my young imagination represented as a blue muffin; and very
155 scantily furnished.

Comprehend It

Mr. Micawber's speech on lines 128–135 is very formal, and he uses many words to make his point. But his point is simple. What is he offering David, and why?

_____

_____

_____

_____

_____

Comprehend It

In line 138, Mr. Micawber starts to ask a question but does not finish it. What do you think he was going to ask?

"At what hour shall I

_____

_____

What can you infer from the fact that Mr. Quinion tells Mr. Micawber to come at eight o'clock?

_____

_____

(continued)

Text Connection 5 (continued)

Comprehend It

"Blood cannot be obtained from a stone" is an old saying. Why does Mrs. Micawber mention that when she is talking about Mr. Micawber?

_____

_____

_____

_____

_____

_____

Comprehend It

How does Mr. Micawber react when creditors shout up at his house?

First, _____

_____

_____.

Then, _____

_____

_____.

Which do you think best describes Mr. Micawber's attitude towards his debt?

_____ very realistic

_____ too optimistic

"I never thought," said Mrs. Micawber, when she came up, twin and all, to show me the apartment, and sat down to take breath, "before I was married, when I lived with papa and mama, that I should ever find it necessary to take a lodger.
160 But Mr. Micawber being in difficulties, all considerations of private feeling must give way."

I said: "Yes, ma'am."

"If Mr. Micawber's creditors will not give him time," said Mrs. Micawber, "they must take the consequences; and the
165 sooner they bring it to an issue the better. Blood cannot be obtained from a stone, neither can anything on account be obtained at present (not to mention law expenses) from Mr. Micawber."

The only visitors I ever saw, or heard of, were creditors.
170 They used to come at all hours, and some of them were quite ferocious. One dirty-faced man, I think he was a boot-maker, used to edge himself into the passage as early as seven o'clock in the morning, and call up the stairs to Mr. Micawber—"Come! You ain't out yet, you know. Pay us, will you? Don't
175 hide, you know; that's mean. I wouldn't be mean if I was you. Pay us, will you? You just pay us, d'ye hear? Come!"
4 Receiving no answer to these taunts, he would mount in his wrath to the words 'swindlers' and 'robbers'; and these being ineffectual too, would sometimes go to the extremity
180 of crossing the street, and roaring up at the windows of the second floor, where he knew Mr. Micawber was. At these times, Mr. Micawber would be transported with grief and mortification [6], even to the length (as I was once made aware by a scream from his wife) of making motions at himself
185 with a razor; but within half-an-hour afterwards, he would polish up his shoes with extraordinary pains, and go out, humming a tune with a greater air of gentility than ever. Mrs. Micawber was quite as elastic. 5 I have known her to be thrown into fainting fits by the king's taxes at

---

[6] **mortification:** shame; embarrassment

(continued)

190 three o'clock, and to eat lamb chops, breaded, and drink warm ale (paid for with two tea-spoons that had gone to the pawnbroker's) at four. . . .

Identify It: Participles and Participial Phrases

Read each numbered sentence.

Check the correct column to indicate whether the underlined word is a participle acting like an adjective (P), or is a participle introducing a participial phrase (PP).

Write the noun that is being described on the line.

	P	PP	
1.	❏	❏	_____
2.	❏	❏	_____
3.	❏	❏	_____
4.	❏	❏	_____
5.	❏	❏	_____

Take Note

Reread the last paragraph. Underline the text that tells how Mrs. Micawber's attitude is similar to that of her husband.

Text Connection 6

Comprehend It

Summarize David's life during this period of time.

_____

_____

_____

_____

_____

_____

_____

_____

_____

Comprehend It

David says he was too young and childish to take good care of himself. What example does he give to show this?

_____

_____

_____

_____

_____

_____

David Copperfield

by Charles Dickens

Section 1

1　In this house, and with this family, I passed my <u>leisure</u> time. My own <u>exclusive</u> breakfast of a penny loaf[a] and a pennyworth of milk, I provided myself. I kept another small loaf, and a <u>modicum</u> of cheese, on a particular shelf of a
5　particular cupboard, to make my supper on when I came back at night. This made a <u>hole</u> in the six or seven shillings[b], I know well; and I was out at the warehouse all day, and had to support myself on that money all the week. From Monday morning until Saturday night, I had no advice, no <u>counsel</u>, no
10　encouragement, no consolation [1], no assistance, no support, of any kind, from anyone, that I can call to mind, as I hope to go to heaven!

Use the Clues:

- Read lines 1–12.
- Reread the underlined words: **leisure**, **exclusive**, **modicum**, **hole**, and **counsel**.
- Think about their meaning using context clues.
- Match each word with its synonym.
- Use a dictionary for help if needed.

1. leisure   a. bit

2. exclusive   b. private

3. modicum   c. guidance

4. hole   d. deficit

5. counsel   e. extra

　　I was so young and childish, and so little qualified—how could I be otherwise?—to undertake the whole charge of my
15　own existence, that often, in going to Murdstone and Grinby's,

---

[1] **consolation:** comfort; reassurance

[a] **penny loaf:** a small loaf of bread bought for a penny

[b] **shillings:** coins in Great Britain worth one twentieth of a pound

(continued)

of a morning, I could not resist the stale pastry put out for sale at half-price at the pastrycooks' doors, and spent in that the money I should have kept for my dinner. Then, I went without my dinner, or bought a roll or a slice of pudding. . . .

20   We had half-an-hour, I think, for tea. When I had money enough, I used to get half-a-pint of ready-made coffee and a slice of bread and butter. When I had none, I used to look at a venison shop in Fleet Street; or I have strolled, at such a time, as far as Covent Garden Market, and stared at the pineapples.

25 I was fond of wandering about the Adelphi, because it was a mysterious place, with those dark arches. I see myself emerging one evening from some of these arches, on a little public-house close to the river, with an open space before it, where some coal-heavers were dancing; to look at whom I sat

30 down upon a bench. I wonder what they thought of me! . . .

I know I do not exaggerate, unconsciously and unintentionally, the scantiness of my resources or the difficulties of my life. I know that if a shilling were given me by Mr. Quinion at any time, I spent it in a dinner or a tea. I

35 know that I worked, from morning until night, with common men and boys, a shabby child. I know that I lounged about the streets, insufficiently and unsatisfactorily fed. I know that, but for the mercy of God, I might easily have been, for any care that was taken of me, a little robber or a little vagabond. . . .

40   My rescue from this kind of existence I considered quite hopeless, and abandoned, as such, altogether. I am solemnly convinced that I never for one hour was reconciled [2] to it, or was otherwise than miserably unhappy; but I bore [3] it; and even to Peggotty, partly for the love of her and partly for

45 shame, never in any letter (though many passed between us) revealed the truth.

Mr. Micawber's difficulties were an addition to the distressed state of my mind. In my forlorn state I became quite attached to the family, and used to walk about, busy

50 with Mrs. Micawber's calculations of ways and means,

---

[2] **reconciled:** prepared to accept; adjusted to something difficult

[3] **bore:** endured with tolerance and patience

(continued)

Comprehend It

How does David feel about his future?

_____

_____

_____

_____

_____

Text Connection 6 (continued)

Comprehend It

How do Mr. and Mrs. Micawber feel about their situation? How do you know?

_____

_____

_____

_____

_____

_____

_____

_____

_____

_____

Comprehend It

What does Mrs. Micawber mean when she tells David that "Mr. Micawber's difficulties are coming to a crisis"?

_____

_____

_____

and heavy with the weight of Mr. Micawber's debts. On a Saturday night, which was my grand treat—partly because it was a great thing to walk home with six or seven shillings in my pocket, looking into the shops and thinking what such a
55 sum would buy, and partly because I went home early—Mrs. Micawber would make the most heart-rending confidences to me; also on a Sunday morning, when I mixed the portion of tea or coffee I had bought over-night, in a little shaving-pot, and sat late at my breakfast. It was nothing at all unusual
60 for Mr. Micawber to sob violently at the beginning of one of these Saturday night conversations, and sing about jack's delight being his lovely Nan, towards the end of it. I have known him come home to supper with a flood of tears, and a declaration that nothing was now left but a jail; and go to bed making a
65 calculation of the expense of putting bow-windows[c] to the house, "in case anything turned up," which was his favourite expression. And Mrs. Micawber was just the same.

A curious equality of friendship, originating, I suppose, in our respective circumstances, sprung up between me and
70 these people, notwithstanding the ludicrous disparity [4] in our years. But I never allowed myself to be prevailed upon to accept any invitation to eat and drink with them out of their stock (knowing that they got on badly with the butcher and baker, and had often not too much for themselves), until Mrs.
75 Micawber took me into her entire confidence. This she did one evening as follows:

"Master Copperfield," said Mrs. Micawber, "I make no stranger of you, and therefore do not hesitate to say that Mr. Micawber's difficulties are coming to a crisis."
80 It made me very miserable to hear it, and I looked at Mrs. Micawber's red eyes with the utmost sympathy.

---

[4] **disparity:** a difference; inequality

[c] **bow-windows:** windows that stick out from a wall and form a curve

(continued)

"With the exception of the heel of a Dutch cheese— which is not adapted to the wants of a young family"—said Mrs. Micawber, "there is really not a scrap of anything in
85 the larder. I was accustomed to speak of the larder when I lived with papa and mama, and I use the word almost unconsciously. What I mean to express is, that there is nothing to eat in the house."

"Dear me!" I said, in great concern.

90 I had two or three shillings of my week's money in my pocket—from which I presume that it must have been on a Wednesday night when we held this conversation—and I hastily produced them, and with heartfelt emotion begged Mrs. Micawber to accept of them as a loan. But that lady,
95 kissing me, and making me put them back in my pocket, replied that she couldn't think of it. . . .

At last Mr. Micawber's difficulties came to a crisis, and he was arrested early one morning, and carried over to the King's Bench Prison in the Borough. He told me, as he went
100 out of the house, that the God of day had now gone down upon him—and I really thought his heart was broken and mine too. But I heard, afterwards, that he was seen to play a lively game at skittles, before noon.

Section 2

On the first Sunday after he was taken there, I was to
105 go and see him, and have dinner with him. I was to ask my way to such a place, and just short of that place I should see such another place, and just short of that I should see a yard, which I was to cross, and keep straight on until I saw a turnkey[d]. All this I did; and when at last I did see a turnkey
110 (poor little fellow that I was!), and thought how, when Roderick Random was in a debtors' prison, there was a man there with nothing on him but an old rug, the turnkey swam before my dimmed eyes and my beating heart.

---

[d] **turnkey:** a person who keeps the keys to a prison; a jailer

(continued)

Comprehend It

Draw a box around the paragraph where Mrs. Micawber explains why she is so worried. Then explain her problem.

_____

_____

_____

_____

How does David try to help Mrs. Micawber?

_____

_____

_____

_____

Take Note

Draw a box around the sentence that describes how Mr. Micawber's difficulties "came to a crisis." What happens to him, and how does he react?

_____

_____

_____

_____

_____

_____

_____

_____

Comprehend It

Where does David move after Mr. and Mrs. Micawber are both living in prison?

_____

_____

_____

Mr. Micawber was waiting for me within the gate, and we
115 went up to his room (top story but one), and cried very much.
He solemnly conjured me, I remember, to take warning by
his fate; and to observe that if a man had twenty pounds
a-year for his income, and spent nineteen pounds nineteen
shillings and sixpence, he would be happy, but that if he
120 spent twenty pounds one he would be miserable. After which
he borrowed a shilling of me for porter, gave me a written
order on Mrs. Micawber for the amount, and put away his
pocket-handkerchief, and cheered up.

At last Mrs. Micawber resolved to move into the prison,
125 where Mr. Micawber had now secured a room to himself. So
I took the key of the house to the landlord, who was very glad
to get it; and the beds were sent over to the King's Bench,
except mine, for which a little room was hired outside the
walls in the neighbourhood of that Institution, very much
130 to my satisfaction, since the Micawbers and I had become
too used to one another, in our troubles, to part. The Orfling
was likewise accommodated with an inexpensive lodging in
the same neighbourhood. Mine was a quiet back-garret[e]
with a sloping roof, commanding a pleasant prospect of
135 a timberyard; and when I took possession of it, with the
reflection that Mr. Micawber's troubles had come to a crisis
at last, I thought it quite a paradise.

All this time I was working at Murdstone and Grinby's
in the same common way, and with the same common
140 companions, and with the same sense of unmerited
degradation as at first. But I never, happily for me no doubt,
made a single acquaintance, or spoke to any of the many boys
whom I saw daily in going to the warehouse, in coming from
it, and in prowling about the streets at meal-times. I led the
145 same secretly unhappy life; but I led it in the same lonely,
self-reliant [5] manner. The only changes I am conscious of
are, firstly, that I had grown more shabby, and secondly, that
I was now relieved of much of the weight of Mr. and Mrs.
Micawber's cares; for some relatives or friends had engaged

---

[5] **self-reliant:** independent; able to take care of oneself

[e] **back-garret:** an attic to the rear of the house

(continued)

150 to help them at their present pass, and they lived more
comfortably in the prison than they had lived for a long while
out of it. I used to breakfast with them now, in virtue of some
arrangement, of which I have forgotten the details. I forget,
too, at what hour the gates were opened in the morning,

155 admitting of my going in; but I know that I was often up
at six o'clock, and that my favourite lounging-place in the
interval was old London Bridge, where I was wont to sit in
one of the stone recesses, watching the people going by, or to
look over the balustrades at the sun shining in the water, and

160 lighting up the golden flame on the top of the Monument. . . .

By way of going in for anything that might be on the
cards, I call to mind that Mr. Micawber, about this time,
composed a petition to the House of Commons, praying for
an alteration in the law of imprisonment for debt. I set down

165 this remembrance here, because it is an instance to myself
of the manner in which I fitted my old books to my altered
life, and made stories for myself, out of the streets, and out of
men and women; and how some main points in the character
I shall unconsciously develop, I suppose, in writing my life,

170 were gradually forming all this while.

1 There was a club in the prison, in which Mr. Micawber,
as a gentleman, was a great authority. 2 Mr. Micawber had
stated his idea of this petition to the club, and the club had
strongly approved of the same. Wherefore Mr. Micawber

175 (who was a thoroughly good-natured man, and as active a
creature about everything but his own affairs as ever existed,
and never so happy as when he was busy about something
that could never be of any profit to him) set to work at the
petition, invented it, engrossed it on an immense sheet of

180 paper, spread it out on a table, and appointed a time for all
the club, and all within the walls if they chose, to come up to
his room and sign it.

3 When I heard of this approaching ceremony, I was so
anxious to see them all come in, one after another, though I

185 knew the greater part of them already, and they me, that I

Comprehend It

How is David's life the same after he joins the Micawbers in prison? How does it change?

_____

_____

_____

_____

_____

_____

Comprehend It

A petition is a document that people write when they want leaders to change a law or rule. The House of Commons is like the United States Senate or House of Representatives.

In his petition, what is Mr. Micawber asking for leaders to change?

_____

_____

_____

_____

Make an inference about the kind of people who belonged to the club.

_____

_____

_____

_____

(continued)

Text Connection 6 (continued)

Comprehend It

Who is going to sign Mr. Micawber's petition?

_____

_____

_____

_____

Make an inference about why the Captain reads the petition aloud.

_____

_____

_____

_____

_____

_____

_____

got an hour's leave of absence from Murdstone and Grinby's, and established myself in a corner for that purpose. As many of the principal members of the club as could be got into the small room without filling it, supported Mr. Micawber in
190 front of the petition, while my old friend Captain Hopkins (who had washed himself, to do honour to so solemn an occasion) stationed himself close to it, to read it to all who were unacquainted with its contents. 4 The door was then thrown open, and the general population began to
195 come in, in a long file: several waiting outside, while one entered, affixed his signature, and went out. To everybody in succession, Captain Hopkins said: "Have you read it?"—"No."—"Would you like to hear it read?" If he weakly showed the least disposition to hear it, Captain Hopkins,
200 in a loud sonorous voice, gave him every word of it. 5 The Captain would have read it twenty thousand times, if twenty thousand people would have heard him, one by one. I remember a certain luscious roll he gave to such phrases as "The people's representatives in Parliament assembled," "Your
205 petitioners therefore humbly approach your honourable house," "His gracious Majesty's unfortunate subjects," as if the words were something real in his mouth, and delicious to taste; Mr. Micawber, meanwhile, listening with a little of an author's vanity, and contemplating (not severely) the spikes
210 on the opposite wall.

(continued)

Text Connection 6 (continued)

Identify It: Adverbs, Adverbial Phrases, and Adverbial Clauses

Read each numbered sentence.

Decide if the underlined words contain an adverb (Adv.), an adverbial phrase (Adv. Phrase), or an adverbial clause (Adv. Clause).

Check the column below.

	Adv.	Adv. Phrase	Adv. Clause
1.	❏	❏	❏
2.	❏	❏	❏
3.	❏	❏	❏
4.	❏	❏	❏
5.	❏	❏	❏

When my thoughts go back, now, to that slow agony of my youth, I wonder how much of the histories I invented for such people hangs like a mist of fancy over well-remembered facts! When I tread the old ground, I do not wonder that

215 I seem to see and pity, going on before me, an innocent romantic boy, making his imaginative world out of such strange experiences and sordid [6] things!

---

[6] **sordid:** wretched; shameful

Text Connection 7

Comprehend It

What happened on the ship's trip from Europe?

_____

_____

Take Note

As you review **"My First View of Ellis Island"** you should:

• Underline details about what Edward sees from the ship.

My First View of Ellis Island

1   My first impressions of the new world will always remain etched in my memory, particularly that hazy October morning [in 1907] when I first saw Ellis Island. The steamer *Florida* was fourteen days out of Naples. It was filled
5   to capacity with sixteen hundred natives of Italy. It had <u>weathered</u> one of the worst storms in our captain's memory; and glad we were, both children and grown-ups, to leave the open sea. We were glad to come at last through the Narrows into the Bay.

Use the Clues A:

• Read lines 1–9.

• Reread the underlined word **Florida**.

• Check the box that best defines the underlined word.

• What does the word **Florida** mean in this context?

  ❏ a city

  ❏ a ship

  ❏ a state

• Reread the underlined word **weathered**.

• Check the box that best defines the underlined word.

• What does the word **weathered** mean in this context?

  ❏ stormy

  ❏ forecasted

  ❏ survived

• Underline the context clues that helped you with your answers.

(continued)

Text Connection 7 (continued)

10 My mother, my stepfather, my brother Giuseppe, and my two sisters, Liberta and Helvetia, were happy that we had come through the storm safely. We <u>clustered on the foredeck</u> for <u>fear of separation</u> and looked with wonder on this miraculous land of our dreams.

Use the Clues B:

- Read lines 10–14.
- Reread the underlined phrase **clustered on the foredeck**.
- Check the box that best defines the underlined phrase.
- What does the phrase **clustered on the foredeck** mean in this context?
  - ❏ gathered at the front of the ship
  - ❏ hugged each other
  - ❏ viewed the shoreline
- Reread the underlined phrase **fear of separation**.
- Check the box that best defines the underlined phrase.
- What does the phrase **fear of separation** mean in this context?
  - ❏ motion sickness
  - ❏ being afraid of the storm
  - ❏ being afraid of losing each other
- Underline the context clues that helped you with your answers.

(continued)

Unit 28

Comprehend It

Describe the other passengers on the *Florida*.

_____

_____

_____

_____

_____

How did Edward feel on seeing the Statue of Liberty?

_____

_____

Comprehend It

How do you know that New York City was very different from the family's hometown in Italy?

_____

_____

_____

15   Giuseppe and I held tightly to stepfather's hands. Liberta and Helvetia clung to mother. Passengers all about us were crowding against the rail. Jabbered conversation, sharp cries, laughs, and cheers—a steadily rising din [1] filled the air. Mothers and fathers lifted up the babies so that they, too,

20 could see the Statue of Liberty.

    I looked at that statue with a sense of bewilderment [2], half doubting its reality. It loomed shadowy through the mist. It brought silence to the decks of the *Florida*. This was a symbol of America. This was an enormous expression of

25 what we had all been taught was the inner meaning of this new country. It inspired awe [3] in the hopeful immigrants. Many older persons among us were burdened with a thousand memories of what they were leaving behind. They had been openly weeping ever since we began our final

30 approach toward the unknown. Now somehow steadied, I suppose, by the concreteness of the symbol of America's freedom, they dried their tears.

    Directly in front of the *Florida*, half visible in the haze, rose an even greater challenge to the imagination.

35   "Mountains!" I cried to Giuseppe. "Look at them!"

    "They're strange," he said, "why don't they have snow on them?" He was craning his neck and standing on tiptoe to stare at the New York skyline.

    Stepfather looked toward the skyscrapers and smiled. He

40 assured us that they were not mountains but buildings. They were "the highest buildings in the world."

_____

[1] **din:** a loud, persistent noise

[2] **bewilderment:** confusion; puzzlement

[3] **awe:** a feeling of great admiration or respect

(continued)

Every side of the harbor offered its marvels. Tugs, barges, sloops, lighters, sluggish freighters, and giant ocean liners moved in different directions. They managed to dart in

45 and out and up and down without colliding [4]. They spoke to us through the varied sounds of their whistles. The *Florida* replied with a deep echoing voice. Bells clanged through our ship. This caused a new flurry among our fellow passengers. Many of these people had come from provinces

50 far distant from ours. They were shouting to one another in dialects strange to me. Everything combined to increase our excitement. We rushed from deck to deck, fearful lest we miss the smallest detail of the scene.

Finally the *Florida* veered to the left. It turned northward

55 into the Hudson River. Now the incredible buildings of lower Manhattan came very close to us.

The officers of the ship, mighty and unapproachable beings they seemed to me, went striding up and down the decks shouting orders. They drove the immigrants before

60 them. [1] Scowling and gesturing, they pushed and pulled the passengers. They herded us into separate groups as though we were animals. A few moments later we came to our dock, and the long journey was over.

Comprehend It

How did the officers of the ship make Edward feel?

_____

_____

_____

---

[4] **colliding:** crashing; hitting against something with force

(continued)

Text Connection 7 (continued)

Comprehend It

What is the main message of the poem?

_____

_____

_____

_____

The New Colossus

Not like the brazen [5] giant of Greek fame	A
65 With **2** <u>conquering</u> limbs astride from land to land;	B
Here at our sea-washed, sunset gates shall stand	B
A mighty woman with a torch, whose flame	A
Is the **3** <u>imprisoned</u> lightning, and her name	A
Mother of Exiles [6]. From her beacon-hand	B
70 Glows world-wide welcome; her mild eyes command	B
The air-bridged harbor that twin cities frame,	A
"Keep, ancient lands, your storied pomp!" cries she	C
With silent lips. *"Give me your tired, your poor,*	D
Your huddled masses **4** *<u>yearning to breathe free</u>,*	C
75 *The wretched refuse of your* **5** *<u>teeming</u> shore,*	D
Send these, the homeless, tempest-tossed to me,	C
*I lift my lamp beside the golden door!"**	D

Identify It: Participles and Participial Phrases

Read each numbered underlined section.

Check the correct box to indicate if the underlined words are participles acting as adjectives (P), or are participles in participial phrases (PP).

For each item, write the noun that is being described on the line.

	P	PP	
1.	❏	❏	_____
2.	❏	❏	_____
3.	❏	❏	_____
4.	❏	❏	_____
5.	❏	❏	_____

Adapted from "When I First Saw Ellis Island" by Edward Corsi
Poem "The New Colossus" by Emma Lazarus

---

[5] **brazen:** shocking and annoying

[6] **exiles:** deportees; refugees

*The section of the poem in italics appears on a plaque on the base of the Statue of Liberty.

Amigo Brothers

by Piri Thomas

Take Note: Rising Action

As you review the story, identify events that contribute to its rising action. Record information about these events in the boxes below.

Section 1

Viewing Each Other

1   *Human beings are competitive by nature. In families, children experience sibling rivalry. As we grow up and participate in academic, athletic, and social interaction, we are always encouraged to try our best. The result of our efforts*
5   *brings about our natural human competitive nature.*

Some humans, the best among us, view each other differently. They don't see others merely as competitors; rather, they rise above competition. In this story, a pair of 17-year old friends from Manhattan's lower east side teach us to view
10   *each other first as human beings, and only secondarily as competitors.*

Antonio Cruz and Felix Varga were both seventeen years old. They were so together in friendship that they felt themselves to be brothers. They had known each other since
15   childhood, growing up on the lower east side of Manhattan in the same tenement building on Fifth Street between Avenue A and Avenue B.

(continued)

Antonio was fair, <u>lean</u>, and <u>lanky</u>, while Felix was dark, <u>short</u>, and <u>husky</u>. Antonio's hair was always falling over his
20 eyes, while Felix wore his black hair in a natural Afro style.

Use the Clues A:

- Read lines 19–21. Use contrast clues and your knowledge of antonyms to determine the meanings of the words **lean** and **lanky**.

  If Felix is short, Antonio must be _____.

  If Felix is husky, Antonio must be _____.

  Lean and lanky means:

  a) tall and heavy

  b) tall and thin

  c) short and heavy

  Circle the transition word that signals the contrast.

Each youngster had a dream of someday becoming lightweight champion of the world. Every chance they had the boys worked out, sometimes at the Boys Club on 10th Street and Avenue A and sometimes at the pro's gym on
25 14th Street. Early morning sunrises would find them running along the East River Drive, wrapped in sweat shirts, short towels around their necks, and handkerchiefs Apache style around their foreheads.

(continued)

While some youngsters were into <u>street negatives</u>,
30 Antonio and Felix slept, ate, rapped, and dreamt positive.
Between them, they had a collection of *Fight* magazines
second to none, plus a scrapbook filled with torn tickets
to every boxing match they had ever attended, and some
clippings of their own. If asked a question about any given
35 fighter, they would immediately zip out from memory banks
divisions, weights, records of fights, knock-outs, technical
knock-outs, and draws or losses.

Use the Clues B:

- Read lines 30–38. Use contrast clues to determine the meaning of the phrase **street negatives**.

- **Street negatives** include:

  a) illegal behavior

  b) unsafe actions

  c) poor choices

  d) all of the above

  Underline the contrast clues that helped you determine your answer. Circle the transition word that signals the contrast.

Comprehend It

How would you characterize Antonio and Felix's interest in boxing?

_____

_____

(continued)

Text Connection 8 (continued)

Comprehend It

What are Antonio's and Felix's strengths in boxing?

_____

_____

_____

Take Note: Rising Action

What is the initiating event?

_____

_____

_____

_____

Comprehend It

Why did Antonio and Felix feel a wall rising between them?

_____

_____

_____

_____

Each had fought many <u>bouts</u> representing their community and had won two gold-plated medals plus a silver
40 and bronze medallion. The difference was in their style. Antonio's lean form and long reach made him the better boxer, while Felix's short and muscular frame made him the better slugger. Whenever they had met in the ring for sparring sessions, it had always been hot and heavy.

> ### Use the Clues C:
>
> • Read lines 39–45. Use substitution clues to determine the meaning of the word **bouts**.
>
> • In this context, **bouts** means:
>
> a) a period of time
>
> b) periods of illness
>
> c) boxing matches
>
> d) arguments
>
> Underline the synonym that helped you determine your answer.

45   Now, after a series of elimination bouts, they had been informed that they were to meet each other in the division finals that were scheduled for the seventh of August, two weeks away—the winner to represent the Boys Club in the Golden Gloves Championship Tournament.
50   The two boys continued to run together along the East River Drive. But even when joking with each other, they both sensed a wall rising between them.
    One morning less than a week before their bout, they met as usual for their daily work-out. They fooled around with a
55 few jabs at the air, slapped skin, and then took off, running lightly along the dirty East River's edge.
    Antonio glanced at Felix, who kept his eyes purposely straight ahead, pausing from time to time to do some fancy leg work while throwing one-twos followed by upper cuts to
60 an imaginary jaw. Antonio then beat the air with a barrage [1]

_____

[1] **barrage:** a heavy outpouring

(continued)

of body blows and short devastating lefts with an overhand jaw-breaking right.

After a mile or so, Felix puffed and said, "Let's stop a while, bro. I think we both got something to say to each other."

65 Antonio nodded. It was not natural to be acting as though nothing unusual was happening when two *ace-boon buddies*[a] were going to be blasting each other within a few short days.

They rested their elbows on the railing separating them from the river. Antonio wiped his face with his short towel.

70 The sunrise was now creating day.

Felix leaned heavily on the river's railing and stared across to the shores of Brooklyn. Finally, he broke the silence.

"Man, I don't know how to come out with it."

Antonio helped. "It's about our fight, right?"

75 "Yeah, right." Felix's eyes squinted at the rising orange sun.

"I've been thinking about it too, *panin*[b]. In fact, since we found out it was going to be me and you, I've been awake at night, pulling punches on you, trying not to hurt you."

"Same here. It ain't natural not to think about the fight.

80 I mean, we both are *cheverote*[c] fighters and we both want to win. But only one of us can win. There ain't no draws in the eliminations."

Felix tapped Antonio gently on the shoulder. "I don't mean to sound like I'm bragging, bro. But I wanna win, fair and square."

85 Antonio nodded quietly. "Yeah. We both know that in the ring the better man wins. Friend or no friend, brother or no."

Felix finished it for him. "Brother, Tony, let's promise something right here. Okay?"

"If it's fair, *hermano*[d], I'm for it." Antonio admired the courage

90 of a tug boat pulling a barge five times its welterweight size.

"It's fair, Tony. When we get into the ring, it's gotta be like we never met. We gotta be like two heavy strangers that want the same thing and only one can have it. You understand, don'tcha?"

---

[a] **ace-boon buddies:** best friends

[b] **panin:** pal, buddy

[c] **cheverote:** cool, fine

[d] **hermano:** brother

Take Note: Rising Action

Record information about the rising action of the story.

_____

_____

Comprehend It

Summarize the dilemma that Antonio and Felix find themselves in.

_____

_____

_____

_____

(continued)

95   "*Sí*, I know." Tony smiled. "No pulling punches. We go all the way."

    "Yeah, that's right. Listen, Tony. Don't you think it's a good idea if we don't see each other until the day of the fight? I'm going to stay with my Aunt Lucy in the Bronx. I can use
100 Gleason's Gym for working out. My manager says he got some sparring partners with more or less your style."

    Tony scratched his nose pensively [2]. "Yeah, it would be better for our heads." He held out his hand, palm upward. "Deal?"

    "Deal." Felix lightly slapped open skin.

105   "Ready for some more running?" Tony asked lamely.

    "Naw, bro. Let's cut it here. You go on. I kinda like to get things together in my head."

    "You ain't worried, are you?" Tony asked.

    "No way, man." Felix laughed out loud. "I got too much
110 smarts for that. I just think it's cooler if we split right here. After the fight, we can get it together again like nothing ever happened."

    The amigo brothers were not ashamed to hug each other tightly.

115   "Guess you're right. Watch yourself, Felix. I hear there's some pretty heavy dudes up in the Bronx. *Sauvecito*[e], okay?"

    "Okay. You watch yourself too, *sabe*[f]?"

    Tony jogged away. Felix watched his friend disappear from view, throwing rights and lefts. Both fighters had a lot
120 of psyching up to do before the big fight.

Section 2

    The days in training passed much too slowly. Although they kept out of each other's way, they were aware of each other's progress via the ghetto grapevine.

    The evening before the big fight, Tony made his way to
125 the roof of his tenement. In the quiet early dark, he peered over the ledge. Six stories below the lights of the city blinked

---

[2] **pensively:** thoughtfully

[e] **sauvecito:** take it easy; be cool

[f] **sabe:** You know?

(continued)

and the sounds of cars mingled with the curses and the laughter of children in the street. He tried not to think of Felix, feeling that he had succeeded in psyching his mind.

130 But only in the ring would he really know. To spare Felix hurt, he would have to knock him out, early and quick.

Up in the South Bronx, Felix decided to take in a movie in an effort to keep Antonio's face away from his fists. The flick was *The Champion* with Kirk Douglas, the third time Felix
135 was seeing it.

The champion was getting the daylights beat out of him. He was saved only by the sound of the bell.

Felix became the champ and Tony the challenger.

The movie audience was going out of its head. The champ
140 hunched his shoulders grunting and sniffing red blood back into his broken nose. The challenger, confident that he had the championship in the bag, threw a left. The champ countered with a dynamite right.

Felix's right arm felt the shock. Antonio's face,
145 superimposed on the screen, was hit by the awesome force of the blow. Felix saw himself in the ring, blasting Antonio against the ropes. The champ had to be forcibly restrained [3]. The challenger fell slowly to the canvas.

1 When Felix finally left the theatre, he had figured out
150 how to psyche himself for tomorrow's fight. 2 It was Felix the Champion vs. Antonio the Challenger.

He walked up some dark streets, deserted except for small pockets of wary-looking kids wearing gang colors. Despite the fact that he was Puerto Rican like them, they eyed him as
155 a stranger to their turf. Felix did a fast shuffle, bobbing and weaving, while letting loose a torrent of blows that would demolish whatever got in its way. 3 It seemed to impress the brothers, who went about their own business.

Finding no takers, Felix decided to split to his aunt's.
160 Walking the streets had not relaxed him, neither had the fight flick. All it had done was to stir him up. He let himself

---

[3] **restrained:** stopped from moving freely

(continued)

Comprehend It

Why does Antonio want to knock Felix out early in the match?

_____

_____

_____

Take Note: Rising Action

Record information about the rising action of the story.

_____

_____

_____

165   quietly into his Aunt Lucy's apartment and went straight to bed, falling into a fitful sleep with sounds of the gong for Round One.

4 Antonio was passing some heavy time on his rooftop. How would the fight tomorrow affect his relationship with Felix? After all, fighting was like any other profession. Friendship had nothing to do with it. A gnawing doubt crept in. He cut negative thinking real quick by doing some speedy

170 fancy dance steps, bobbing and weaving like mercury. **5** The night air was blurred with perpetual motions of left hooks and right crosses. Felix, his _amigo_[g] brother, was not going to be Felix at all in the ring. Just an opponent with another face. Antonio went to sleep, hearing the opening bell for the

175 first round. Like his friend in the South Bronx, he prayed for victory, via a quick clean knock-out in the first round.

Identify It: Simple or Complex Sentences

Read each numbered sentence.

Decide if it is a simple (S) or complex (C) sentence.

Put an X in the correct column.

	S	C
1.	❏	❏
2.	❏	❏
3.	❏	❏
4.	❏	❏
5.	❏	❏

    Large posters plastered all over the walls of local shops announced the fight between Antonio Cruz and Felix Vargas as the main bout.

180   The fight had created great interest in the neighborhood. Antonio and Felix were well liked and respected. Each had his own loyal following.

_____

[g] **amigo:** friend

(continued)

Antonio's fans had unbridled faith in his boxing skills. On the other side, Felix's admirers trusted in his dynamite-
185 packed fists.

Felix had returned to his apartment early in the morning of August 7th and stayed there, hoping to avoid seeing Antonio. He turned the radio on to *salsa* music sounds and then tried to read while waiting for word from his manager.
190 The fight was scheduled to take place in Tompkins Square Park. It had been decided that the gymnasium of the Boys Club was not large enough to hold all the people who were sure to attend. In Tompkins Square Park, everyone who wanted could view the fight, whether from ringside or
195 window fire escapes or tenement rooftops.

The morning of the fight Tompkins Square was a beehive of activity with numerous workers setting up the ring, the seats, and the guest speakers' stand. The scheduled bouts began shortly after noon and the park had begun filling up
200 even earlier.

The local junior high school across from Tompkins Square Park served as the dressing room for all the fighters. Each was given a separate classroom with desk tops, covered with mats, serving as resting tables. Antonio thought he
205 caught a glimpse of Felix waving to him from a room at the far end of the corridor. He waved back just in case it had been him.

The fighters changed from their street clothes into fighting gear. Antonio wore white trunks, black socks, and
210 black shoes. Felix wore sky blue trunks, red socks, and white boxing shoes. Each had dressing gowns to match their fighting trunks with their names neatly stitched on the back.

The loudspeakers blared into the open windows of the school. There were speeches by dignitaries, community
215 leaders, and great boxers of yesteryear. Some were well prepared, some improvised on the spot. They all carried the same message of great pleasure and honor at being part of such a historic event. This great day was in the tradition of champions emerging from the streets of the lower east side.

Comprehend It

Describe the atmosphere of the event.

_____

_____

_____

_____

_____

(continued)

Take Note: Rising Action

Record information about the rising action of the story.

_____

_____

_____

_____

220 Interwoven with the speeches were the sounds of the other boxing events. After the sixth bout, Felix was much relieved when his trainer Charlie said, "Time change. Quick knock-out. This is it. We're on."

Waiting time was over. Felix was escorted from the 225 classroom by a dozen fans in white T-shirts with the word FELIX across their fronts.

Antonio was escorted down a different stairwell and guided through a roped-off path.

As the two climbed into the ring, the crowd exploded 230 with a roar. Antonio and Felix both bowed gracefully and then raised their arms in acknowledgement.

Antonio tried to be cool, but even as the roar was in its first birth, he turned slowly to meet Felix's eyes looking directly into his. Felix nodded his head and Antonio 235 responded. And both as one, just as quickly, turned away to face his own corner.

Bong—bong—bong. The roar turned to stillness.

"Ladies and Gentlemen, *Señores y Señoras*."

The announcer spoke slowly, pleased at his bilingual 240 efforts.

"Now the moment we have all been waiting for—the main event between two fine young Puerto Rican fighters, products of our lower east side.

"In this corner, weighing 134 pounds, Felix Vargas. And 245 in this corner, weighing 133 pounds, Antonio Cruz. The winner will represent the Boys Club in the tournament of champions, the Golden Gloves. There will be no draw. May the best man win."

The cheering of the crowd shook the window panes of 250 the old buildings surrounding Tompkins Square Park. At the center of the ring, the referee was giving instructions to the youngsters.

"Keep your punches up. No low blows. No punching on the back of the head. Keep your heads up. Understand. Let's 255 have a clean fight. Now shake hands and come out fighting."

(continued)

Both youngsters touched gloves and nodded. They turned and danced quickly to their corners. Their head towels and dressing gowns were lifted neatly from their shoulders by their trainers' nimble fingers. Antonio crossed himself. Felix
260 did the same.

Section 3

BONG! BONG! ROUND ONE. Felix and Antonio turned and faced each other squarely in a fighting pose. Felix wasted no time. He came in fast, head low, half hunched toward his right shoulder, and lashed out with a straight left. He missed
265 a right cross as Antonio slipped the punch and countered with one-two-three lefts that snapped Felix's head back, sending a mild shock coursing through him. If Felix had any small doubt about their friendship affecting their fight, it was being neatly dispelled [4].
270 Antonio danced, a joy to behold. His left hand was like a piston pumping jabs one right after another with seeming ease. Felix bobbed and weaved and never stopped boring in. He knew that at long range he was at a disadvantage. Antonio had too much reach on him. Only by coming in close could
275 Felix hope to achieve the dreamed-of knockout.

Antonio knew the dynamite that was stored in his *amigo* brother's fist. He ducked a short right and missed a left hook. Felix trapped him against the ropes just long enough to pour some punishing rights and lefts to Antonio's hard
280 midsection. Antonio slipped away from Felix, crashing two lefts to his head, which set Felix's right ear to ringing.

Bong! Both *amigos* froze a punch well on its way, sending up a roar of approval for good sportsmanship.

Felix walked briskly back to his corner. His right ear
285 had not stopped ringing. Antonio gracefully danced his way toward his stool none the worse, except for glowing glove burns, showing angry red against the whiteness of his midribs.

---

[4] **dispelled:** caused to go away

(continued)

Take Note: Rising Action

Record information about the rising action of the story.

_____

_____

_____

"Watch that right, Tony." His trainer talked into his ear. "Remember Felix always goes to the body. He'll want you to
290 drop your hands for his overhand left or right. Got it?"

Antonio nodded, spraying water out between his teeth. He felt better as his sore midsection was being firmly rubbed.

Felix's corner was also busy.

"You gotta get in there, fella." Felix's trainer poured water
295 over his curly Afro locks. "Get in there or he's gonna chop you up from way back."

Bong! Bong! Round two. Felix was off his stool and rushed Antonio like a bull, sending a hard right to his head. Beads of water exploded from Antonio's long hair.

300 Antonio, hurt, sent back a blurring barrage of lefts and rights that only meant pain to Felix, who returned with a short left to the head followed by a looping right to the body. Antonio countered with his own flurry, forcing Felix to give ground. But not for long.

305 Felix bobbed and weaved, bobbed and weaved, occasionally punching his two gloves together.

Antonio waited for the rush that was sure to come. Felix closed in and feinted with his left shoulder and threw his right instead. Lights suddenly exploded inside Felix's head as
310 Antonio slipped the blow and hit him with a pistonlike left, catching him flush on the point of his chin.

Bedlam broke loose as Felix's legs momentarily buckled. He fought off a series of rights and lefts and came back with a strong right that taught Antonio respect.

315 Antonio danced in carefully. He knew Felix had the habit of playing possum when hurt, to sucker an opponent within reach of the powerful bombs he carried in each fist.

A right to the head slowed Antonio's pretty dancing. He answered with his own left at Felix's right eye that began
320 puffing up within three seconds.

Antonio, a bit too eager, moved in too close and Felix had him entangled into a rip-roaring, punching toe-to-toe slugfest that brought the whole Tompkins Square Park screaming to its feet.

(continued)

325   Rights to the body. Lefts to the head. Neither fighter was giving an inch. Suddenly a short right caught Antonio squarely on the chin. His long legs turned to jelly and his arms flailed out desperately. Felix, grunting like a bull, threw wild punches from every direction. Antonio, groggy, bobbed

330 and weaved, evading [5] most of the blows. Suddenly his head cleared. His left flashed out hard and straight, catching Felix on the bridge of his nose.

    Felix lashed back with a haymaker right off the ghetto streets. At the same instant, his eye caught another left hook

335 from Antonio. Felix swung out trying to clear the pain. Only the frenzied screaming of those along ringside let him know that he had dropped Antonio. Fighting off the growing haze, Antonio struggled to his feet, got up, ducked, and threw a smashing right that dropped Felix flat on his back. Felix

340 got up as fast as he could in his own corner, groggy but still game. He didn't even hear the count. In a fog, he heard the roaring of the crowd, who seemed to have gone insane. His head cleared to hear the bell sound at the end of the round. He was very glad. His trainer sat him down on the stool.

345   In his corner, Antonio was doing what all fighters do when they are hurt. They sit and smile at everyone.

    The referee signaled the ring doctor to check the fighters out. He did so and then gave his okay. The cold water sponges brought clarity to both *amigo* brothers. They were rubbed

350 until their circulation rang free.

    Bong! Round three—the final round. Up to now it had been tic-tac-toe, pretty much even. But everyone knew— there would be no draw and that this round would decide the winner.

355   This time, to Felix's surprise, it was Antonio who came out fast, charging across the ring. Felix braced himself but couldn't ward off the barrage of punches. Antonio drove Felix hard against the ropes.

Comprehend It

Describe how Antonio and Felix have done in the fight so far.

_____

_____

_____

_____

_____

---

[5] **evading:** avoiding; dodging

(continued)

360   The crowd ate it up. Thus far the two had fought with *mucho corazón*[h]. Felix tapped his gloves and commenced his attack anew. Antonio, throwing boxer's caution to the winds, jumped in to meet him.

       Both pounded away. Neither gave an inch and neither fell
365 to the canvas. Felix's left eye was tightly closed. Claret red blood poured from Antonio's nose. They fought toe-to-toe.

       The sounds of their blows were loud in contrast to the silence of a crowd gone completely mute.

       Bong! Bong! Bong! The bell sounded over and over again.
370 Felix and Antonio were past hearing. Their blows—continued to pound on each other like hailstones.

       Finally the referee and the two trainers pried Felix and Antonio apart. Cold water was poured over them to bring them back to their senses.

375   They looked around and then rushed toward each other. A cry of alarm surged through Tompkins Square Park. Was this a fight to the death instead of a boxing match?

       The fear soon gave way to wave upon wave of cheering as the two *amigos* embraced [6].

380   No matter what the decision, they knew they would always be champions to each other.

       BONG! BONG! BONG! "Ladies and Gentlemen, *Señores and Señoras*. The winner and representative to the Golden Gloves Tournament of Champions is . . . "

385   The announcer turned to point to the winner and found himself alone. Arm in arm the champions had already left the ring.

---

[6] **embraced:** hugged

[h] **mucho corazón:** a lot of heart

Cell Phones for Teens: A Good Call for Safety?

1   Imagine this: It's a frigid, rainy winter night. Your teenager is riding in a car. The car gets a flat tire on an <u>infrequently</u> patrolled highway. The nearest call box is two miles away. Now imagine this: Your teenager has a cell

5 phone. The scenario [1] looks a lot less frightening, doesn't it? This is just one of many potentially dangerous situations in which a cell phone is <u>indispensable</u>. Every young person should have a cell phone when he or she is out alone.

Take Note

Read the essay through once. Then reread it.

Find and underline each of the following parts of the essay. Then label each in the margin.

1. the writer's **statement of position**

2. two reasons why all kids should have cell phones (label each **reason**)

3. an **anticipated objection**

4. the writer's **call to action**

Use the Clues

- Read lines 1–8. Note the underlined words **infrequently** and **indispensable**.

- Use information that you've learned about prefixes and suffixes to match words with their definitions.

a) frequently	not often
b) infrequently	often
c) dispensable	not essential
d) indispensable	essential

---

[1] **scenario:** a description of events

(continued)

Unit 29

Text Connection 9 (continued)

Take Note

Find the writer's claim that most parents now work outside the home. Then draw a box around the fact or example that the writer uses to support this idea.

10 In fact, because of the realities of family life today, cell phones should be standard [2] pocket gear for all young people. The majority of parents now work outside the home. This means that more and more kids must spend at least part of the day alone. According to the United States Census Bureau, one out of five children between the ages of 5 and 14 has no 15 adult supervision for at least part of the day. These kids need to be able to get in touch with their parents at a moment's notice. Even kids whose parents do not work outside the home have reason to carry cell phones. Murphy's law says, "Anything that can go wrong probably will go wrong." This 20 statement isn't always true. Still, unexpected problems do arise: a missed bus, a problem with a pet, sudden stomach flu at a baseball game. Difficulties requiring adult assistance [3] are part of life. Without a cell phone, a child in one of these situations may be miserably stuck.

25 **1** Many parents will take issue with the proposition **that** kids need cell phones. **2** **They** see cell phones as expensive time-wasters. **3** **Some** will argue that cell phones and the rate [4] plans that come with them are too expensive.

4 **Others** will assert that the phones are loaded with gadgets 30 such as digital cameras and ring options. These options have no benefit in the area of personal safety.

The objections are valid [5]. They should not stand in the way of cell phones becoming safety equipment for kids, however. **5** Cell phone companies need to listen to these 35 concerns and take **them** as a call to action. The giants of the wireless networks should get busy designing and marketing an affordable bare-bones cell phone and calling plan. Instead of just targeting young people with eye-popping features

---

[2] **standard:** commonly accepted as norm; usual

[3] **assistance:** aid; help in doing something

[4] **rate:** a cost of something; amount

[5] **valid:** convincing; sound

(continued)

and flashy advertising campaigns, they should work to
40 make safety-first cell phones available and affordable for
all families. Yes, cellular titans [6], even if you don't have a
teenager who is out and about at night, you'll sleep better
knowing that you've done something to make a positive
difference for families everywhere.

Identify It: Pronouns

Read sentence 1.

Determine if the bold word is a nominative, an object, or a relative pronoun.

Copy the pronoun under the correct heading.

Follow the same procedure for sentences 2–5.

	Nominative Pronoun	Object Pronoun	Relative Pronoun
1.			
2.			
3.			
4.			
5.			

Determine which of the pronouns you wrote are indefinite pronouns. Copy them on this line:

_____

---

[6] **titans:** powerful companies and those who run them

A Call to Poetry

1   **1** *A call can come in the form of a ringing telephone.* **2**
A call can be an inner voice that suddenly inspires you. **3** *Or,*
a call can be an unseen force that draws you forward into a
new world. The poems that follow explore what it means to be
5 *called in different ways. As you read each poem, ask yourself*
these questions: What kind of call is the poet describing? How
is the poet affected by receiving it?

Use the Clues:

- Read the sentences numbered 1, 2, and 3. Use meaning signals to determine the meaning of the word **call** in each sentence.

- Read each sentence below.

- Match each numbered sentence with the sentence below that uses the same meaning for the word **call**.

- Write the sentence number in the blank.

- Underline the meaning signal in each numbered sentence.

    _____ From childhood, she felt a **call** to be a teacher.

    _____ You have a **call** on line one.

    _____ A **call** of the sea lures turtles into the surf.

    _____ An emergency **call** awakened the family.

(continued)

Postscript
By Naomi Shihab Nye

1.

I wish I had said nothing.

10 Had not returned the call.

Had left the call dangling [1], a shirt from one pin.

And settled into the deep pink streaks of sundown
without a single word flying from my mouth.
the thousand small birds of January

15 in their smooth soaring cloud
finding the trees.

2.

Or if I had to say something,
only a tiny tiny thing. A well-shaped phrase.
Smoothed off at the edges like a child's wooden

20   cow.
That nobody would get a splinter from.

Take Note

- Circle **call** in line 11. Underline what the call is compared to.

- Circle **word** in line 13. Underline the words in the same line that compare a word to a bird.
  This is a _____.
  _____ metaphor
  _____ simile

- Find and underline another image of birds.

- Find a simile and draw a box around it.

[1] **dangling:** hanging uncertainly; remaining unresolved

(continued)

Take Note

- Reread lines 29–33. Circle a word that shows that the poet has used a metaphor to compare the speaker's body to a prison.

- Then go back and reread lines 29–33. Circle a word that supports this image of someone in prison.

- Review lines 23–38. Box two words that suggest the speaker is recalling his youth.

- Underline the things the speaker would do before his calling.

The Calling
By Luis J. Rodriguez

The calling came to me
while I languished [2]
25 in my room, while I
whittled away my youth
in jail cells
and damp *barrio* fields

It brought me to life,
30 out of captivity [3],
in a street-scarred
and tattooed place
I called body.

Until then I waited silently,
35 a deafening clamor [4] in my head,
but voiceless to all around;
hidden in America's eyes,
a brown boy without a name.

I would sing into a solitary
40 tape recorder,
music never to be heard.
I would write my thoughts
in scrambled English;
I would take photos in my mind—
45 plan out new parks,
bushy green, concrete free,
new places to play
and think.

---

[2] **languished:** became downcast; pined

[3] **captivity:** confinement

[4] **clamor:** a loud, noisy outcry

(continued)

Waiting.
50 Then it came.
The calling.
It brought me out of my room.
It forced me to escape
night captors
55 in street prisons.

It called me to war,
to be writer,
to be scientist
and march with the soldiers
60   of change.

It called me from the shadows,
out of the wreckage
of my barrio—from among those
who did not exist.

65 I waited all of 16 years
for this time.

Somehow, unexpected,
I was called.

Take Note

• Draw a box around an example of personification. What thing or idea is being personified?

_____

_____

(continued)

Unit 29

Take Note

• Circle the word **silence** in line 73. Then underline the words the speaker uses to describe silence.

Story from Bear Country
By Leslie Marmon Silko

70 You will know
    when you walk
    in bear country
    By the silence
    flowing swiftly between the juniper trees

75 by the sundown colors of sandrock
    all around you.

    You may smell damp earth
    1 scratched away
    from yucca roots

80 You may hear snorts and growls
    2 slow and massive sounds
    from caves
    in the cliffs high above you.

    It is difficult to explain

85 how they call you
    All but a few who went to them
    left behind families
            grandparents
            and sons

90   a good life.
    The problem is
    you will never want to return
    their beauty will overcome your memory
    like winter sun

95 3 melting ice shadows from snow
    and you will remain with them
    locked forever inside yourself
            your eyes will see you
            dark shaggy and thick.

(continued)

100   We can send bear priests
      4 <u>loping after you</u>
      their medicine bags
      bouncing against their chests
      5 <u>Naked</u> legs painted black
105   bear claw necklaces
      rattling against
      their capes of blue spruce.

      They will follow your trail
      into the narrow canyon
110   through the blue-gray mountain sage
      to the clearing
      where you stopped to look back
      and saw only bear tracks
      behind you.

115   When they call
      faint ⁵ memories
      will writhe ⁶ around your heart
      and startle you with their distance.
      But the others will listen
120   because bear priests sing
      beautiful songs
      They must
      if they are ever to call you back.

Take Note

- Underline details that describe the bear priests. Based on this description, who might you compare bear priests to?

  _____

  _____

  _____

  _____

- Draw a box around lines 111–114. What do you think that bear tracks might symbolize here?

  _____

  _____

  _____

  _____

  _____

  _____

  _____

---

⁵ **faint:** unclear; weak

⁶ **writhe:** twist and turn

(continued)

Take Note

- Underline the lines that suggest that the person referred to as **you** is a man who is hiking.

- Draw a box around lines 129–133 and 137–141. Whose voice do you think the hiker is hearing if he is all alone?

_____

_____

_____

_____

They will try to bring you
125   step by step
back to the place you stopped
and found only bear prints in the sand
where your feet had been.

Whose voice is this?
130   You may wonder
hearing this story when
after all
you are alone
hiking in these canyons and hills
135   while your wife and sons are waiting
back at the car for you.

But you have been listening to me
for some time now
from the very beginning in fact
140   and you are alone in this canyon of stillness
not even cedar birds flutter.
See, the sun is going down now
the sandrock is washed in its colors
Don't be afraid
145   we love you
          we've been calling you
          all this time

(continued)

150

Go ahead
turn around
see the shape
of your footprints
in the sand.

Identify It: Adjectives and Participial Phrases

Read each numbered word or words.

Decide if it is an adjective (A) or participial phrase (PP).

Put an X in the correct column.

Write the noun that is being described beside the X.

	A	PP	
1.	☐	☐	_____
2.	☐	☐	_____
3.	☐	☐	_____
4.	☐	☐	_____
5.	☐	☐	_____

Postscript, from *19 Varieties of Gazelle* by Naomi Shihab Nye
"The Calling," from *Cool Salsa* edited by Lori M. Carlson
"Story from Bear Country," from *Storyteller* by Leslie
Marmon Silko

Text Connection 11

Comprehend It

Read the first paragraph. What do you know about Kibuka?

_____

_____

_____

_____

_____

Kibuka went back to the Headquarters to see if the young man who replaced him needed advice. Make an inference about why Kibuka did this.

_____

_____

_____

_____

The Pig:
An Individual Dilemma
Part I

By Barbara Kimenye

1   1 Old Kibuka had long believed that retirement was no sort of life for a man like himself, who would, so he <u>modestly</u> believed, pass for not a day over forty-five. He had held a responsible post at the Ggombolola Headquarters,
5 until the Government had sent somebody from the Public Service Commission to nose around the offices and root out all employees over retirement age. 2 Then the next thing Kibuka knew, despite his <u>youthfully</u> dyed hair, he had a pension [1], a Certificate of Service, but no longer a job.

10   He still worried about the state his filing system must be in today, for having once called in at the Headquarters, merely to see if the youngster who had replaced him needed any advice or help, he had been appalled at the lack of order. 3 Papers were scattered everywhere, confidential folders
15 were open for all the world to read, and his successor was flirting <u>madly</u> with some pin-brained girl at the other end of the <u>newly</u> installed telephone.

_____

[1] **pension:** regular payment made by a business or government to a retired person

(continued)

Text Connection 11 (continued)

Use the Clues

- Read the sentences numbered 1, 2, and 3. Note the underlined words **modestly**, **youthfully**, **madly** and **newly**.

- Use information that you have learned about suffixes to match words with their definitions.

a) modestly	like crazy
b) youthfully	humbly
c) madly	in a young way
d) newly	recently

- What question do these adverbs answer?

_____

Comprehend It

Reread lines 1–28. Then summarize how Kibuka feels about retirement.

_____

_____

_____

_____

_____

_____

_____

The visit had not been anything near a success, for not even his former colleagues showed anything but superficial
20 interest in what Kibuka had to say.

So there he was, destined to waste the remainder of his life in the little cottage beside the Kalasanda stream, with plenty indeed to look back on, but not very much to look forward to, and his greatest friend, Yosefu Mukasa, was away
25 in Buddu County on business.

The self-pitying thought "I might as well be dead" kept recurring in his mind as he pumped his pressure stove to boil a kettle of tea. Then the noise of a car, grinding its way along the narrow, uneven track, heading in his direction, sent
30 him eagerly to the door. 1 It was his eldest grandson who climbed out of the battered Landrover. A tall, loose-limbed young man in a khaki shirt and blue jeans. Old Kibuka practically choked with happiness as his frail fingers were squeezed in a sinewy grip, and the bones of his shoulders
35 almost snapped under an affectionate hug.

"What a wonderful surprise! Come in, my boy. 2 I was just making a cup of tea."

(continued)

Take Note

Draw a box around the event in the plot that changes Kibuka's life. In the margin, label this event **initiating event**.

Comprehend It

Why does Kibuka's grandson bring him the piglet?

_____

_____

_____

_____

What details show that Kibuka views the piglet not as a meal but as a pet?

_____

_____

_____

_____

_____

_____

_____

"Grandfather, this is a very short visit. I'm afraid I can't stay more than a few minutes." The boy's voice was musically
40 deep, very much like his grandfather's once had been, before the tremor of age had changed it. 3 "I just came to see how you are getting on, and I brought you a present."

"That's very kind of you, son!" The unexpected visit and now a present: in a matter of seconds Kibuka had completely
45 reversed his opinion that life was no longer worth living. He was aglow [2] with excitement.

"Yes. 4 It's one of the piglets from the Farm School. The sow doesn't seem able to feed this new litter, so I thought you might like one for eating; it should make an excellent meal."

50 The boy strode back to the Landrover and returned with a black, squealing bundle under his arm.

Kibuka was more delighted than ever. 5 He had never seen so small a pig before, and he spent a good ten minutes marveling at its tiny twinkling eyes, its minute hoofs, and
55 its wisp of a tail. When his grandson drove away, he waved happily from the doorstep, the piglet clutched tenderly to his chest.

Identify It: Simple, Compound, or Complex Sentences

Reread sentence 1.

Determine whether it is a simple sentence, a compound sentence, or a complex sentence.

Put an X in the correct column.

Complete sentences 2–5 in a similar manner.

	Simple	Compound	Complex
1.	❏	❏	❏
2.	❏	❏	❏
3.	❏	❏	❏
4.	❏	❏	❏
5.	❏	❏	❏

[2] **aglow:** delighted; radiating excitement

(continued)

He had told his grandson that he would take the creature up to the Mukasas and ask Miriamu to prepare it as a special
60 "welcome home" supper for Yosefu, but he soon sensed a certain reluctance within himself to do this, because the piglet followed him about the house or squatted trustingly at his feet each time he sat down. Moreover, it obviously understood every word Kibuka said to it, for, whenever
65 he spoke, it listened gravely with its dainty forefeet placed lightly upon his knee.

By nightfall Kibuka was enchanted with his new companion, and would have as much considered eating it as he would consider eating the beloved grandson who had
70 given it to him. He fed the piglet little scraps of food from his own plate, besides providing it with a rich porridge mixture. Nevertheless, within a few days it was clear that the pig's appetite was increasing out of all proportion to its size, and Kibuka had to resort to collecting matoke peelings[a] in an old
75 bucket from his friends and nearest neighbors.

The news that Kibuka was keeping a pig, the first ever actually reared in Kalasanda, caused something of a sensation. In no time at all there was little need for him to cart the bucket from house to house, because the women and
80 children, on their way to draw water from the stream, made a practice of bringing the peelings and food scraps with them as part of the excuse for calling on him, and being allowed to fondle the animal and discuss its progress as if it were a dear relative with a delicate hold on life.

85 No pig had ever had it so good. Fortunately, it proved to be a fastidiously clean creature, and for this reason Kibuka allowed it to spend its nights at the foot of his bed, although he was careful not to let his neighbors know of this. The pig, naturally enough, positively flourished in this cozy
90 atmosphere of good will and personal attention. From a squealing bundle small enough to be held in one hand, it quickly developed into a handsome, hefty porker with eyes

---

[a] matoke peelings—banana or plantain peels

Comprehend It

How do you think Kibuka feels about having so many visitors come to see the pig? Why do you think that?

_____

_____

_____

_____

_____

_____

(continued)

Text Connection 11 (continued)

Take Note

Draw a box around the sentence that signals the beginning of problems Kibuka has with the pig.

Take Note

Reread lines 95–128. Draw an X in the margin next to each problem that the pig causes for Kibuka.

which held the faintest glint of malice [3] even when it was at its most affectionate with Kibuka.

95   However, as the weeks went by, its rapid growth was accompanied by a variety of problems. For instance, it required more and more food, and, having been reared on the leavings of every kitchen in Kalasanda, was inclined to turn up its enormous snout at the idea of having to root in
100 the shamba[b] whenever it felt like something to eat. Every time it started to kick its empty dish about noisily, pausing now and then to glare balefully at old Kibuka and utter snorts of derision [4], the old man was driven to taking up his bucket and trudging forth to see if any scraps in the village
105 had been overlooked.

Also, while Kibuka had at first secretly enjoyed the warmth of a cuddly little piglet lying across his feet each night, he found himself at a distinct disadvantage when that same piglet acquired a bulk of some fifty or so pounds, and
110 still insisted upon ponderously hoisting itself onto his bed as of right. Worse still, along with the weight, the piglet also produced a snore which regularly kept poor Kibuka awake until dawn. It was a grave decision he was finally called upon to make, yet one on which he simply dare not waver: in
115 future, the pig would have to stay outside, tethered to a tree.

Who suffered most, Kibuka or his pig, would be hard to tell, for the animal's lamentations, continuing throughout the night, were equal in strength to the black remorse [5] and wealth of recrimination churning in Kibuka's bosom.
120 That pig never knew how often it was near to being brought indoors and pacified with a bowl of warm milk.

---

[3] **malice:** in a manner of causing intentional harm

[4] **derision:** belittling; ridicule

[5] **remorse:** strong feeling of sadness or guilt

[b] shamba—garden or field where food is grown

(continued)

Text Connection 11 (continued)

During the day it still was free to roam about until, that is, it adopted the irritating habit of falling into the stream. There it would be, placidly ambling after Kibuka as he
125 pottered in his small shamba, or gently napping in the shade of a coffee tree, and then, for no apparent reason, off it would go to the water's edge, and either fall or plunge in before anybody could say "bacon."

The Kalasanda stream had no real depth; many
130 Kalasandans often bathed there or waded in; but sometimes, after a drop or two of rain, the current had more strength, and was quite capable of sweeping a child off its feet. The pig seemed always to choose such times for its immersion, and there wasn't anything anybody could really do as it spluttered
135 and floundered with its hoofs flaying madly, and terror written plainly across its broad, black face.

At first, Kibuka would rush back and forth along the bank, calling frantically in the hope that it would struggle towards him, but what usually happened in the end was that
140 a particularly strong eddy would sweep it round the bend into a thicket of weeds and rushes, and then the children playing there would have a good half-hour's fun driving it home.

This happened so often that Kibuka was forced to keep
145 the pig tethered day and night. He visualized the time when no children would be playing in the reeds, and the pig would perhaps become entangled, dragged under and drowned.

By way of compensation he decided upon a regular evening walk for the animal, so by and by Kalasanda became
150 accustomed to the sight of Kibuka, slight yet patriarchal in his kanzu and black waistcoat[c], sedately traversing the countryside with a huge black pig at the end of a rope, and only strangers saw anything out of the ordinary in it. Without doubt, these walks were a source of great pleasure
155 and exercise to the pig, who found them a wonderful

Take Note

Reread lines 148–168. Draw an X in the margin next to each new problem that the pig causes for Kibuka.

---

[c] **kanzu and black waistcoat:** traditional long cotton garment and black vest worn by Bugandan males

(continued)

change from the all too familiar view of Kibuka's shamba. Unfortunately, the same could not be said of their effect on old Kibuka. To be frank, Kibuka's corns were killing him, and the excruciating pain of every step sometimes brought
160 tears to his eyes. Still, he tried to bear his discomfort with stoic[6] fortitude, for, as he said to Daudi Kulubya, who showed concern over his limp, it was always the same before the heavy rains; in fact, his corns were as good as a barometer when it came to forecasting the weather. But he
165 was always glad to return home, where he could sit for an hour with his poor feet in a bowl of hot water and try to keep his mind off the small fortune he was spending on corn plasters brought to Kalasanda by the peddlers in the market.

Reprinted from *Kalasandra Revisited* by Barbara Kimenye

---

[6] **stoic:** indifferent; showing little or no reaction

Text Connection 12

The Pig:
An Individual Dilemma
Part II

by Barbara Kimenye

Take Note

Look for the event that solves Kibuka's problem. Then label it **climax** in the right margin

1 How long this <u>state of affairs</u> would have continued is anybody's guess. There were occasions when Kibuka actually entertained the <u>notion</u> of <u>parting</u> with his pet at the first good offer from a <u>reputable</u> farmer or butcher. And yet,
5 one trusting glance or look of affection from that waddling <u>hunk of pork</u> was enough for him to feel ashamed of what he regarded as his own treachery[1].

Use the Clues

- Read lines 1–7.

- Reread the underlined words and phrases: **state of affairs**, **notion**, **parting**, **reputable**, and **hunk of pork**.

- Think about the meaning of each. Use context clues in the story to help you.

- Match each word or phrase with its definition listed below.

- Use a dictionary for help if needed.

a) state of affairs	separating
b) notion	idea
c) parting	situation
d) reputable	pig
e) hunk of pork	trustworthy

- Reread the paragraph, substituting the definitions for the underlined words.

---

[1] **treachery:** betrayal; disloyalty

(continued)

Text Connection 12 (continued)

Comprehend It

How does Kibuka feel right after the pig's death?

_____

_____

The end came at last in the most unlikely manner. One minute there was Kibuka contemplating the sunset, and,
10 incidentally, giving his feet a rest by one of the obscure paths leading to the Sacred Tree, while the pig scratched happily at the root of a clump of shrubs, its head hidden by foliage [2], while its carcass, broadside on, barricaded the path, and then, seconds later, there was the snarl of a motorcycle engine,
15 the horrible grinding of brakes, followed by a whirling kaleidoscope of disaster. Kibuka, pig, bike and rider seemed to explode in all directions. Each had a momentary vision of the others sailing through the air.

When Kibuka eventually dared to open his eyes and
20 cautiously move each limb, he was relieved to find he was still in one piece, although one shoulder felt painfully bruised and there was blood on both his hands. The rider, whom he now recognized as a certain Nathaniel Kiggundu, did not appear to have fared very badly either. He was staggering
25 out of a tangled mass of weeds, wiping mud off his face, and fingering a long tear in the knee of his trousers.

Somewhere from behind the hedge came the raucous cries of a pig in distress, and it was in this direction that both men headed, once they had regained their bearings. They
30 were only just in time to see the injured animal give up the ghost and join its ancestors in that heavenly piggery which surely must exist somewhere above. There was scarcely a mark on it, but its head lay at a strange and awkward angle, so it can be safely assumed that it died of a broken neck.

35　1 Old Kibuka was terribly upset, and the accident had left him in a generally shaky condition. He sat down beside the dead animal and wondered what would happen next. Nathaniel Kiggundu, however, seeing Kibuka was comparatively unhurt, showed more concern over his
40 motorcycle, which lay grotesquely twisted in a ditch. The inevitable [3] crowd collected almost as soon as the pig

---

[2] **foliage:** leaves of plants and trees

[3] **inevitable:** certain; predictable

(continued)

Text Connection 12 (continued)

expired, so there was much coming and going, first to stare at the fatal casualty, then to stare at the motorbike. Nantondo kept up a running commentary, her version of how the
45 accident happened, although nobody believed she had seen it, and by the time Musisi the Ggombolola Chief arrived on the scene, she had fully adopted the role of Mistress of Ceremonies.

After taking a statement from Kiggundu, Musisi
50 approached Kibuka and insisted upon taking him home in the Landrover. **2** "You don't look at all well, Sir. Come. **3** You can make your statement in the morning, when you have had a rest."

"But I can't leave my pig here." **4** Kibuka refused to
55 budge from the spot.

5 "Well, I can put it in the back of the Landrover, if you like. Only it would be better to have the butcher cut it up, because I don't think pork will keep for long in this weather."

Identify It: Simple, Compound, or Complex Sentences

Reread sentence 1.

Determine whether it is a simple sentence, a compound sentence, or a complex sentence.

Put an X in the correct column.

Complete sentences 2–5 in a similar manner.

	Simple	Compound	Complex
1.	❏	❏	❏
2.	❏	❏	❏
3.	❏	❏	❏
4.	❏	❏	❏
5.	❏	❏	❏

The idea of eating the pig had never entered Kibuka's
60 mind. While sitting beside the body, he had been seriously

(continued)

Take Note

Underline the sentences that explain what happens to the pig after the accident. In the margin, label this **resolution**.

Text Connection 12 (continued)

Comprehend It

How does Kibuka sleep the night after the accident?

_____

_____

_____

Why is Musisi going to Yosefu's house?

_____

_____

_____

Why does Kibuka go along with him?

_____

_____

considering just whereabouts in the shamba he could bury it. Now he opened his mouth to tell Musisi in no uncertain terms that eating one's good friends was a practice reserved for barbarians; and then, he suddenly had a clear picture
65 of himself struggling to dig a grave. He was sure no Kalasandans would want to help him do it. Then came the realization of the effect a perpetual[4] reminder of his porking friend in his shamba would have on him. He did not think he could stand it. Far better, indeed, to let the past bury
70 itself and, besides, why deprive his fellow villagers of a tasty treat? They were, after all, the people who had nourished the creature on their leftovers.

"Very well. Get somebody to carve it up and share it out among the people who eat pork, and do be sure to send a
75 whole back leg up to the Mukasas," he said at last, suddenly feeling too weary[5] to care.

"Musa the butcher won't do it," Nantondo piped. "He's a Muslim."

"Well, I'll take it along to the Ggombolola Headquarters
80 and ask one of the *askaris*[a] to carve it up. Anybody who wants pork must go there at about seven o'clock tonight," declared Musisi, and ordered two of the onlookers to help him lift the carcass into the back of his vehicle.

Back at his cottage, Kibuka rubbed his injured shoulder
85 with a concoction he used to cure most of his ailments, be they loose bowels or a sore throat, and then sat brooding over a cup of tea. He went to bed very early and awoke the next day to find the sun well risen. He decided he had had the best night's sleep he had enjoyed for many a month. Musisi
90 arrived as Kibuka was leaving home to see if the leg of pork had been safely delivered to Yosefu and Miriamu.

_____

[4] **perpetual:** continuing forever; constant
[5] **weary:** tired; fatigued
[a] askaris: police officers

(continued)

"No, I'm taking the meat there now, Sir," Musisi said. "Would you care to come with me?"

Kibuka gladly accepted the lift, although he declined the
95 lump of pork Musisi had brought for him, personally. "You have it, son. I'm not a great lover of pork."

Miriamu went into raptures over the leg of pork, and Yosefu showed the keenest interest in the details of the accident. They pressed both Kibuka and Musisi to stay to
100 lunch, but Musisi had to leave to attend a committee meeting in Mmengo, so only Kibuka remained. He and Yosefu, who lately had not seen as much of each other as usual, had plenty to discuss, and lunch was an exhilarating meal.

"I must say, you really are a wonderful cook!" Kibuka told
105 Miriamu, helping himself to more food. Miriamu preened herself, shyly. "Well, that pork was as tender as a chicken, and very tasty, too!"

There was a moment of dismay [6] when Kibuka realized he was eating and thoroughly enjoying the succulence of his
110 late friend, but it quickly passed, and he continued piling his plate with meat, smiling to himself at the knowledge that there would be no need to take a walk in the late afternoon; he could have a good nap instead.

Reprinted from *Kalasandra Revisited* by Barbara Kimenye

Take Note

• Write **conclusion** in the margin next to the last part of the story.

• Underline the sentence that describes Kibuka's reaction to the news that he has been eating pork for lunch.

---

[6] **dismay:** shock; disappointment

Resources

Resources

ē
1. me
2. these
3. see
4. eat
5. chief
6. happy
7. key
8. ___

ĭ
1. sit
2. gym
3. build

ā
1. baby
2. make
3. rain
4. play
5. ___
6. ___
7. ___
8. great
9. ___

ĕ
1. pet
2. head

ă
1. cat

ī
1. item
2. time
3. pie
4. my
5. ___

ŏ
1. fox
2. ___
3. ___
4. tough
5. ___

ə
1. about
2. lesson
3. elect
4. definition
5. circus

ŭ
1. cup
2. ___
3. ___
4. dog
5. ___

aw
1. ___
2. ___
3. ___
4. ___
5. ___

ō
1. go
2. vote
3. boat
4. shop
5. toe

ŏŏ
1. ruby
2. put
3. tube
4. ___
5. ___
6. ___
7. ___

ōō

er
her
fur
sir

ar
cart

or
sport

oi	oy
oil	boy
ou	ow
out	cow

Consonant Chart

Mouth Position

Type of Consonant Sound	Lips	Lips/Teeth	Tongue Between Teeth	Tongue Behind Teeth	Roof of Mouth	Back of Mouth	Throat
Stops	/ b / / p /			/ t / / d /		/ k / / g /	
Fricatives		/ f / / v /	/ th / / t̲h̲ /	/ s / / z /	/ sh /		/ h /
Affricatives					/ j / / ch /		
Nasals	/ m /			/ n /		/ ng /	
Lateral				/ l /			
Semivowels	/ w / / hw /			/ r /	/ y /		

Divide It Checklist

Steps for Syllable Division	Example: disconnected
First, check the word for prefixes and suffixes. Circle them. Next, look at the rest of the word:	(dis)connect(ed)
1. Underline the **first** vowel. Write a **v** under it.	(dis)connect(ed)
2. Underline the **next** vowel. Write a **v** under it.	(dis)connect(ed)
3. Look at the letters **between** the vowels. Mark them with a **c** for consonant.	(dis)connect(ed)
4. Look at the pattern and divide according to the pattern.	(dis)con/nect(ed)
5. Place a diacritical mark over the vowels. Cross out the **e** at the end of final silent **e** syllables. Listen for schwa in the unaccented syllable, cross out the vowel, and place a ə symbol above it.	(dis)con/nect(ed)
Finally, blend each syllable and read the word.	disconnected

Diacritical Marks and Symbols

Diacritical marks and **symbols** are used to indicate the correct sound for the vowel graphemes.

breve / brĕv /	ă	short vowel phonemes
macron	ā	long vowel phonemes
circumflex	âr	**r**-controlled phonemes
schwa	ə	schwa phoneme

Pattern	How to Divide	Examples
VCCV	**vc / cv** • Divide between the consonants. • The first syllable is closed. • The vowel sound is short.	năp/kĭn **VCCV**
VCV	**v/cv** • **Usually**, divide after the first vowel. • The first syllable is open. • The vowel sound is long. **Note:** If the first vowel is followed by an **r**, the syllable is **r**-controlled. or **vc/v** • If the first division does not result in a recognizable word, divide after the consonant. • The first syllable is closed. • The vowel sound is short.	sī/lə̆nt **VCV** mâr/kĕt **V CV** nĕv/êr **VCV**
VCCCV	• vc/ccv or vcc/cv • Divide before or after the blend or digraph. • Do not split the blend or digraph.	ăth/lēte **VCCCV**
VV	• v/v • Divide between the vowels if they are not a vowel team or diphthong. • The first syllable is open. • The vowel sound is long.	nē/ŏn **VV**
c + le	• /cle • Count back three and divide.	crā/dle 321

Check It: Reasons/Examples Checklist

IDEAS AND CONTENT

☐ Is my position clearly stated?

☐ Did I give three reasons for evidence?

☐ Did I tell how the reasons support my topic?

ORGANIZATION

☐ Did I stick to the topic?

☐ Did I sequence my ideas?

☐ Did I end with a conclusion sentence?

CONVENTIONS

☐ Did I punctuate correctly?

☐ Did I capitalize correctly?

☐ Did I spell correctly?

☐ Did I use complete sentences?

Writer's Checklist

1. PRE-WRITING

Did I:
- ☐ Identify what kind of writing I am doing?
- ☐ Think about who my audience is?
- ☐ Generate a list of words and ideas to get me started?
- ☐ Determine what I need to know and gather the resources I need?
- ☐ Decide how my writing should be organized?
- ☐ Create an outline or other framework to organize my ideas?

2. WRITING A FIRST DRAFT

Did I:
- ☐ Write in pencil to make revising easier?
- ☐ Write from my notes or outline?
- ☐ Let my thoughts roll, without getting hung up on details?
- ☐ Keep my audience and purpose in mind as I wrote?

3. REVISING

I Used (check one):
- ☐ the **Checklist for Revising** (if I am revising my work independently)
- ☐ the **Peer Writing Review** (if I am revising with a peer)

4. PROOFREADING AND PUBLISHING

Did I:
- • Punctuate sentences correctly?
  - ☐ capitalize first word
  - ☐ capitalize proper nouns
  - ☐ use correct end marks
- • Check my spelling?
  - ☐ words with endings (doubling, drop *e*, change *y*, advanced doubling)
  - ☐ easily confused words (*there, their*)
  - ☐ place names
  - ☐ longer words
- • Check sentence structure?
  - ☐ run-ons and fragments
  - ☐ verb tense
- • Make a clean, correct, final copy of my work?

Checklist for Revising

Read your writing with a critical eye. Check to make sure you have done each thing below. Make any necessary revisions.

IDEAS AND DEVELOPMENT: *My writing has...*

- ☐ an introduction, body, and conclusion
- ☐ clear main ideas or clear story events
- ☐ enough details or facts to make my ideas interesting and well supported

ORGANIZATION: *My writing has...*

- ☐ a strong beginning that will grab my readers' interest
- ☐ an ending that won't leave my readers hanging
- ☐ a logical flow of ideas
- ☐ transition and signal words
- ☐ no repeated ideas
- ☐ no sentences that are off the topic

VOICE: *I have used...*

- ☐ language that fits my audience
- ☐ my personal voice

SENTENCE FLUENCY: *I have included...*

- ☐ a variety of sentence lengths
- ☐ different kinds of sentence types

WORD CHOICE: *I have made sure to use...*

- ☐ colorful adjectives
- ☐ specific nouns and verbs
- ☐ phrases that create pictures in readers' minds

Peer Writing Review

IDEAS AND DEVELOPMENT

- Is the draft focused on the assigned topic?
- Does the draft include an introduction, body paragraphs, and a conclusion?
- Are the main ideas or main events easy to understand?
- Are there enough details to make the ideas clear and well supported?

Things That Work Well:

_____

_____

_____

Things You Might Improve:

_____

_____

_____

ORGANIZATION AND FLOW

- Does the beginning catch your interest? How can it be improved?
- Do the ideas flow in an order that makes sense?
- Has the writer used transition words to help make the flow of ideas clear? Give examples.
- Does the writing have a strong ending? How could the ending be stronger?

Things That Work Well:

_____

_____

_____

Things You Might Improve:

_____

_____

_____

STRONG SENTENCES

- Has the writer used a variety of sentence types? Give examples.
- If any sentences seem unclear, how can they be improved?
- Has the writer used specific verbs and nouns? What are some examples of these?
- Has the writer used colorful adjectives to create pictures in readers' minds? Can any be added or changed?

Things That Work Well:

_____

_____

_____

Things You Might Improve:

_____

_____

_____

Six Elements of Poetry

Element of Poetry	Definition	Example	Unit
thought			
imagery			
mood			
melody			
meter			
form			

Word Fluency 1

	Correct	Errors
1st Try		
2nd Try		

carriage	machine	shoes	pigeon	marriage	surgeon	shoes	carriage	pigeon	surgeon	10
shoes	carriage	marriage	machine	surgeon	pigeon	machine	surgeon	shoes	carriage	20
machine	surgeon	pigeon	carriage	shoes	marriage	shoes	marriage	carriage	surgeon	30
pigeon	shoes	marriage	surgeon	machine	carriage	pigeon	carriage	surgeon	machine	40
surgeon	marriage	pigeon	carriage	machine	carriage	machine	surgeon	pigeon	shoes	50
shoes	surgeon	carriage	machine	pigeon	marriage	pigeon	shoes	carriage	machine	60
carriage	machine	shoes	marriage	surgeon	pigeon	shoes	surgeon	carriage		70
surgeon	shoes	carriage	pigeon	machine	shoes	pigeon	machine	marriage	surgeon	80
pigeon	surgeon	shoes	marriage	carriage	machine	surgeon	carriage	pigeon	shoes	90
marriage	shoes	carriage	machine	pigeon	shoes	pigeon	surgeon	carriage	machine	100

Word Fluency 2

Correct	Errors
1st Try	
2nd Try	

10	20	30	40	50	60	70	80	90	100
judge	niece	judge	rice	judge	cent	center	rice	excess	except
fudge	nice	fudge	niece	cent	except	judge	fudge	judge	center
rice	judge	niece	fudge	excess	center	cent	excess	except	rice
race	excess	rice	cent	except	rice	race	center	niece	judge
niece	fudge	nice	judge	center	judge	except	center	except	excess
nice	center	cent	except	race	nice	fudge	cent	rice	niece
excess	rice	center	excess	niece	race	niece	except	nice	cent
except	cent	except	race	nice	fudge	excess	judge	center	race
center	race	excess	nice	fudge	niece	rice	race	cent	nice
cent	except	race	center	rice	excess	nice	niece	race	fudge

Word Fluency 3

	Correct	Errors
1st Try		
2nd Try		

general	generous	manage	message	stage	oxygen	strange	village	voyage	origin	10
manage	strange	general	village	generous	voyage	message	origin	stage	oxygen	20
strange	message	manage	generous	general	stage	village	oxygen	voyage	origin	30
generous	stage	strange	message	manage	origin	general	voyage	oxygen	village	40
village	voyage	stage	oxygen	strange	generous	manage	message	general	origin	50
message	oxygen	voyage	strange	stage	origin	village	generous	manage	general	60
stage	village	message	oxygen	voyage	manage	strange	general	origin	generous	70
oxygen	strange	stage	manage	origin	general	generous	message	voyage	village	80
strange	general	generous	village	stage	voyage	oxygen	manage	origin	message	90
voyage	stage	strange	general	oxygen	message	origin	village	generous	manage	100

Word Fluency 4

	Correct	Errors
1st Try		
2nd Try		

Words	Count
eligible illegible passive positive receptive recessive explicit implicit precede exceed	10
passive explicit eligible implicit illegible precede exceed positive receptive recessive	20
explicit positive passive illegible receptive eligible implicit recessive precede exceed	30
illegible receptive positive explicit passive exceed eligible precede recessive implicit	40
implicit precede receptive explicit exceed illegible passive positive eligible exceed	50
positive recessive recessive precede receptive exceed implicit passive illegible eligible	60
receptive recessive exceed explicit passive exceed explicit eligible exceed illegible	70
recessive explicit precede illegible eligible exceed illegible exceed precede implicit	80
explicit illegible recessive positive passive precede recessive passive positive exceed	90
precede explicit positive recessive receptive exceed exceed implicit illegible passive	100

Correct	Errors	
		1st Try
		2nd Try

based on "Stonehenge: Secrets of an Ancient Circle"

Stonehenge has puzzled people for thousands of years.   8
This circle of large, upright stones in southern England   17
is one of the world's great mysteries. It holds the secrets   28
of an ancient people. Over time, discoveries have been   37
made about how it was built. Why it was built remains   48
a puzzle.   50

What do we know about the Ancient Circle? One fact   60
that we know about Stonehenge is that it was built over   71
a period of 2,000 years. Scientists believe that its   80
construction had three stages.   84

The building of Stonehenge began around 5,000 years   92
ago. Starting about 3100 BC, a circular ditch was dug.   102
Dirt from the ditch was piled up into a bank, or henge.   114
Within the bank, fifty-six holes were dug. There may   123
have been a wooden building inside the circle. Not many   133
stones were used in the first stage.   140

Stage Two began about 2500 BC. The builders built   149
more wooden structures in the circle. They built an   158
avenue into the circle. They also set up pillars of stone.   169
They used bluestones, named for their color. These are   178
the smaller stones we still see today.   185

Stage Three began about 2100 BC. During this stage,   194
most of the stones we see today were placed. In Stage   205
Three, they brought in even bigger stones. Five sets of   215
two sandstone pillars were set up. How did they get the   226
stones in an upright position? How did they lift the top   237
stones into place? We are not sure. The heaviest stones   247
weighed about 45 tons. *(That's 90,000 pounds!)*   254

Word Fluency 1

	Correct	Errors
1st Try		
2nd Try		

movement	movie	four	prove	movement	move	movie	prove	lose	four	**10**
four	move	movement	lose	movie	movement	four	move	four	prove	**20**
movement	four	move	prove	move	prove	movie	prove	movement	lose	**30**
lose	movement	four	movie	four	lose	four	movement	move	movie	**40**
move	movie	movement	four	lose	movie	four	prove	lose	movement	**50**
lose	four	move	movie	prove	move	lose	movie	four	prove	**60**
four	move	movement	prove	movement	prove	move	prove	movement	four	**70**
movement	prove	lose	movie	move	movement	lose	move	movie	lose	**80**
move	movie	four	movement	four	move	four	prove	movie	movement	**90**
lose	four	movement	movie	lose	prove	move	movie	four	move	**100**

Word Fluency 2

	Correct	Errors
1st Try		
2nd Try		

avenue	argue	fruit	juice	pool	proof	stood	took	group	tour	10
fruit	stood	avenue	took	argue	group	juice	tour	pool	proof	20
stood	juice	fruit	argue	avenue	pool	took	proof	group	tour	30
argue	pool	stood	fruit	juice	avenue	group	proof	took		40
took	group	pool	proof	stood	fruit	avenue	juice	avenue	tour	50
juice	proof	group	stood	proof	tour	took	argue	fruit	avenue	60
pool	took	juice	proof	group	fruit	stood	avenue	tour	argue	70
proof	stood	fruit	tour	avenue	argue	juice	group	took		80
stood	avenue	argue	took	pool	argue	proof	fruit	tour	juice	90
group	pool	stood	avenue	proof	juice	tour	took	argue	fruit	100

Word Fluency 3

	Correct	Errors
1st Try		
2nd Try		

10	look	loose	suit	soup	food	foot	stood	spoon	cool	cook
20	food	foot	look	stood	loose	cool	suit	cook	soup	spoon
30	look	loose	food	suit	foot	cook	cool	spoon	stood	soup
40	suit	food	loose	cook	look	spoon	stood	soup	foot	cool
50	look	cook	stood	spoon	cool	soup	food	foot	loose	suit
60	cook	spoon	cool	suit	look	foot	soup	loose	stood	stood
70	look	cool	cook	cook	spoon	loose	stood	food	suit	foot
80	suit	loose	stood	cool	cook	look	spoon	foot	soup	food
90	stood	look	spoon	food	loose	foot	suit	cool	cool	soup
100	spoon	cool	suit	look	stood	food	cook	soup	foot	loose

	Correct	Errors
1st Try		
2nd Try		

heredity integrity academic analytic object except occupy obtain continue conceit	10
academic occupy heredity obtain integrity continue analytic conceit object except	20
occupy analytic academic integrity heredity object obtain except continue conceit	30
integrity object occupy analytic academic conceit heredity continue except obtain	40
obtain continue object except occupy integrity academic analytic heredity conceit	50
analytic except continue occupy object conceit obtain integrity academic heredity	60
object obtain analytic except continue academic occupy heredity conceit integrity	70
except occupy object academic analytic heredity integrity conceit continue obtain	80
occupy heredity integrity obtain object continue except academic analytic conceit	90
continue object occupy heredity except analytic conceit obtain integrity academic	100

Passage Fluency 1

	Errors	Correct
1st Try		
2nd Try		

based on "Tsunamis"

What are tsunamis? They are giant waves. Most are   9
caused by earthquakes. But landslides can cause them   17
too. So can volcanic eruptions.   22

The earth's crust is split into large pieces. These are   32
called plates. Plates make up the continents. They   40
make up the seafloor. Sometimes, the edges of the   49
plates rub against each other. Sometimes, the edge of   58
one plate pushes down. It can push under the edge of   69
another plate. This movement is slow. Usually, it's   77
a few centimeters a year. Sometimes, there is a faster,   87
bigger shift. An earthquake results. Suddenly, one   94
ocean plate pushes under another. When this happens,   102
the upper crust springs up. It displaces vast amounts of   112
water. A huge wave is born.   118

The wave's energy travels fast. It can travel at the   128
speed of a jet. But the movement happens below the   138
surface. In the deep ocean, it's hard to see. Then the   149
wave nears the shore. The shoreline is much more   158
shallow. The wave gains height. Some tsunamis come   166
in as giant waves. Others come in as strong floods.   176

Scientists are finding better ways to predict these deadly 185
waves. Stations in the Pacific record earthquake activity. 193
They measure changes in sea level. They detect changes   202
in water pressure. These changes can warn of a tsunami.   212

We cannot avoid tsunamis. But we can build more   221
warning systems. We can be better prepared for the   230
next one.   232

	Correct	Errors
1st Try		
2nd Try		

#										
10	billion	million	opinion	union	religion	region	opinion	billion	union	region
20	opinion	billion	religion	million	region	union	million	region	religion	billion
30	million	region	opinion	union	religion	billion	opinion	religion	billion	region
40	union	religion	million	billion	region	opinion	union	billion	region	million
50	region	opinion	union	million	billion	region	union	religion	union	religion
60	opinion	region	billion	union	religion	million	billion	union	billion	million
70	billion	million	religion	opinion	region	union	opinion	region	religion	billion
80	region	opinion	billion	union	million	religion	million	billion	region	region
90	union	religion	opinion	million	billion	region	opinion	billion	union	religion
100	religion	opinion	billion	union	million	union	religion	opinion	billion	million

Word Fluency 2

Correct	Errors
1st Try	
2nd Try	

guide	guise	grey	they	boulder	shoulder	receive	deceive	veil	vein	10
grey	receive	guide	deceive	guise	veil	they	vein	boulder	shoulder	20
receive	they	grey	guise	guide	boulder	deceive	shoulder	veil	vein	30
guise	boulder	receive	they	grey	vein	guide	veil	shoulder	deceive	40
deceive	veil	boulder	shoulder	receive	guise	grey	they	guide	vein	50
they	shoulder	veil	receive	boulder	vein	deceive	guise	grey	guide	60
boulder	deceive	they	shoulder	veil	receive	grey	guide	vein	guise	70
shoulder	receive	boulder	grey	guise	they	veil	shoulder	deceive		80
receive	guide	guise	deceive	boulder	veil	shoulder	grey	vein	they	90
veil	boulder	receive	guide	shoulder	they	vein	deceive	guise	grey	100

Word Fluency 3

	Correct	Errors
1st Try		
2nd Try		

nation	notion	social	special	partial	patient	artificial	associate	amino	chili	10
social	artificial	nation	associate	notion	amino	special	chili	partial	patient	20
artificial	special	social	notion	nation	partial	associate	patient	amino	chili	30
notion	partial	artificial	special	social	chili	nation	amino	patient	associate	40
associate	amino	partial	patient	artificial	notion	social	special	nation	chili	50
special	patient	amino	artificial	partial	chili	associate	notion	social	nation	60
partial	associate	special	patient	amino	social	artificial	nation	chili	notion	70
patient	artificial	partial	social	chili	nation	notion	special	amino	associate	80
artificial	nation	notion	associate	partial	amino	patient	social	chili	special	90
amino	partial	artificial	nation	patient	special	chili	associate	notion	social	100

Word Fluency 4

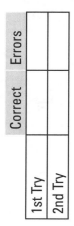

	Correct	Errors
1st Try		
2nd Try		

Words	Count
attach attract adopt admit submit package passage direction duration	10
adopt package attach passage attract direction adapt duration admit submit	20
package adapt adopt attract attach admit passage submit direction duration	30
attract admit package adapt adopt duration attach direction submit passage	40
passage direction admit submit package adapt adopt attract attach duration	50
adapt submit direction admit duration package attract adopt attach	60
admit passage adapt submit direction adopt package attach duration attract	70
submit package admit adapt attach attract duration direction passage	80
package attach attract passage admit direction submit adopt adapt duration	90
direction admit package submit adapt duration passage attract adopt	100

Errors		
Correct		
	1st Try	2nd Try

based on "Wolf Society"

In a wolf society, each member has its own social   10
standing, or rank. Every wolf pack has two leaders.   19
One is male. One is female. These are called the   29
alpha pair. They decide where the pack goes. They   38
decide when the pack hunts. They usually are the   47
only wolves in the pack allowed to have pups. Alpha   57
wolves keep their ears and tails raised. This shows   66
their rank. They bare their teeth. They growl. This   75
threatens the lesser wolves.   79

Beneath the alpha pair are beta wolves. To show   88
their lower rank, beta wolves often keep their tails   97
hanging down. They keep their ears flat. If a beta   107
wolf approaches an alpha wolf, it puts its tail between   117
its legs. This signals that it knows who is the boss.   128

At the bottom of the social structure is the omega wolf.   139
The omega wolf is often mistreated by the rest of the   150
pack. Omega wolves are not allowed to get close to   160
the rest of the pack. They must eat last, after the others   172
have had their fill. Omega wolves keep their tail between   182
their legs most of the time. This signals their low rank.   193

The wolves in a pack work together as a family unit.   204
They hunt together. They play together. They protect   212
their territory together. Wolf packs raise the young of   221
the alpha pair as a group.   227

Wolves act in certain ways depending on their rank   236
within a pack. These behaviors guarantee their place   244
in the pack and their survival in the wild.   253

Word Fluency 1

	Correct	Errors
1st Try		
2nd Try		

10	aunt	brought	view	caught	aunt	bought	brought	caught	view
20	view	caught	aunt	source	brought	aunt	source	view	caught
30	aunt	view	caught	bought	caught	bought	view	brought	source
40	source	aunt	brought	view	source	source	aunt	bought	brought
50	caught	brought	view	source	source	view	brought	caught	aunt
60	source	view	caught	brought	bought	source	view	source	caught
70	view	bought	caught	caught	brought	aunt	source	bought	view
80	aunt	caught	brought	source	brought	source	brought	caught	aunt
90	caught	brought	view	aunt	view	brought	bought	caught	brought
100	source	view	brought	bought	brought	view	source	bought	caught

	Correct	Errors
1st Try		
2nd Try		

10	saturate	century	statue	situate	grew	new	straw	saw	cause	sauce
20	grew	new	saturate	straw	century	cause	statue	situate	sauce	saw
30	saturate	century	grew	statue	new	sauce	cause	saw	straw	situate
40	statue	grew	century	sauce	saw	saturate	straw	situate	new	cause
50	saturate	sauce	straw	saw	situate	cause	grew	new	century	statue
60	sauce	saw	cause	situate	new	saturate	saw	statue	situate	straw
70	cause	saturate	sauce	situate	saw	situate	saturate	new	statue	new
80	statue	century	straw	cause	new	century	statue	saw	cause	statue
90	straw	saturate	saw	grew	century	grew	saw	situate	cause	sauce
100	saw	cause	saturate	straw	grew	situate	sauce	new	situate	century

Word Fluency 3

	Correct	Errors
1st Try		
2nd Try		

draw	drew	virtuous	flew	virtual	graduate	educate	congratulate	10
few	graduate	drew	educate	flew	congratulate	virtuous	virtual	20
graduate	few	draw	drew	virtuous	educate	educate	congratulate	30
drew	virtuous	few	congratulate	draw	educate	virtual	educate	40
educate	educate	virtuous	drew	few	draw	draw	congratulate	50
flew	educate	virtual	graduate	drew	few	flew	draw	60
virtuous	virtual	educate	few	graduate	congratulate	drew	drew	70
virtual	few	draw	congratulate	drew	flew	educate	educate	80
graduate	drew	virtuous	educate	virtual	few	congratulate	flew	90
educate	graduate	virtual	flew	congratulate	educate	drew	few	100

	Correct	Errors
1st Try		
2nd Try		

actual gradual neutral natural medial medical progress regress audition audience **10**

neutral progress actual regress gradual audition natural audience medial medical **20**

progress natural neutral gradual actual medial regress medical audition audience **30**

gradual medial progress natural neutral audience actual audition medical regress **40**

regress audition medial medical progress gradual neutral natural actual audience **50**

natural medical audition progress medial audience regress gradual neutral actual **60**

medial regress natural medical audition neutral progress actual audience gradual **70**

medical progress medial neutral audience actual gradual natural audition regress **80**

progress actual gradual regress medial audition medical neutral audience natural **90**

audition medial progress actual medical natural audience regress gradual neutral **100**

Passage Fluency 1

Correct	Errors	
		1st Try
		2nd Try

based on "A View of the Eye"

Your eye is a ball about one inch in diameter. 10
Most of the ball is covered by a tough white 20
bag. This is called the *sclera*, or the white of the 31
eye. At the front of the ball is a hole that lets in 44
light. This hole is called the *pupil*. It appears 53
as a black dot in the middle of your eye. 63

Like a window, your eye has a curtain to control 73
the amount of light that enters it. The colored 82
ring around the pupil acts like a curtain. It is 92
called the *iris*. In dim light, the iris opens to let 103
in more light. In bright light, the iris closes to 113
let in less light. 117

The pupil is covered with a clear layer of skin 127
called the *cornea*. Behind the cornea is a clear 136
disk called the *lens*. The job of the lens and the 147
cornea is to gather light and focus it on a special 158
spot at the back of the eye. This spot is called 169
the *retina*. 171

The retina is a special layer of cells about the 181
size of a nickel. If you thought of the eye as a 193
movie camera, the retina would be the film in 202
the camera. When you take a picture with a 211
camera, you must develop the film. To develop 219
this film, the light focused onto the retina is 228
changed into nerve impulses. These impulses 234
are sent to the brain through the *optic nerve*. 243
The brain develops the impulses into visual 250
images. 251

Word Fluency 1

	Correct	Errors
1st Try		
2nd Try		

oh	straight	whole	whom	whose	wolf	whole	oh	whom	wolf	10
whole	oh	whose	straight	wolf	whom	straight	wolf	whole	oh	20
straight	wolf	whom	oh	whole	whose	whole	oh	wolf	wolf	30
whom	whose	whole	wolf	straight	oh	wolf	whom	oh	straight	40
wolf	whole	whom	whose	oh	straight	oh	whom	whole	whole	50
whole	wolf	oh	straight	whom	whose	whole	oh	straight	wolf	60
oh	straight	whose	whole	wolf	whom	whose	wolf	oh	whose	70
wolf	whose	whom	straight	whole	straight	whom	straight	whole	wolf	80
whom	wolf	whose	oh	straight	wolf	oh	oh	whom	whole	90
whole	whose	oh	straight	whom	whose	whom	whom	wolf	straight	100

Word Fluency 2

	Correct	Errors
1st Try		
2nd Try		

10	talk	salt	halt	hall	world	work	wall	tall	all	also
20	world	work	talk	wall	salt	all	halt	also	hall	tall
30	talk	salt	world	halt	work	also	all	tall	wall	hall
40	halt	world	salt	also	talk	tall	wall	hall	work	all
50	talk	also	wall	all	world	hall	salt	work	salt	halt
60	also	tall	all	tall	hall	work	world	salt	world	wall
70	all	talk	also	hall	tall	salt	wall	tall	halt	work
80	halt	salt	wall	all	also	talk	tall	also	world	world
90	wall	talk	tall	world	salt	work	halt	all	also	hall
100	tall	all	halt	talk	world	hall	also	hall	work	salt

Word Fluency 3

	Correct	Errors
1st Try		
2nd Try		

water	watch	always	already	walk	warm	forward	qualify	word	quality	10
always	forward	water	qualify	watch	word	already	quality	walk	warm	20
forward	already	always	watch	water	walk	qualify	warm	word	quality	30
watch	walk	forward	already	always	quality	water	qualify	warm	word	40
word	qualify	walk	warm	forward	watch	always	already	water	quality	50
already	word	warm	forward	walk	quality	word	watch	always	water	60
walk	word	walk	forward	qualify	always	forward	word	quality	watch	70
warm	forward	always	always	quality	water	watch	already	word	qualify	80
forward	watch	walk	word	walk	qualify	warm	always	quality	already	90
qualify	forward	warm	water	quality	warm	word	quality	watch	always	100

Word Fluency 4

	Correct	Errors
1st Try		
2nd Try		

structure	fracture	juncture	rupture	entrance	excellence	semiannual	convenience	confidence	semiannual	10
juncture	semiannual	structure	convenience	fracture	confidence	rupture	semiannual	entrance	excellence	20
semiannual	rupture	juncture	fracture	structure	entrance	convenience	excellence	confidence	semiannual	30
fracture	entrance	semiannual	rupture	juncture	semiannual	structure	confidence	excellence	convenience	40
convenience	confidence	entrance	excellence	semiannual	fracture	juncture	rupture	structure	semiannual	50
rupture	excellence	confidence	semiannual	entrance	semiannual	convenience	fracture	juncture	structure	60
entrance	convenience	rupture	excellence	confidence	juncture	semiannual	structure	semiannual	fracture	70
excellence	semiannual	entrance	juncture	semiannual	structure	fracture	rupture	confidence	convenience	80
semiannual	structure	fracture	convenience	entrance	confidence	excellence	juncture	semiannual	rupture	90
confidence	entrance	semiannual	structure	excellence	rupture	semiannual	convenience	fracture	juncture	100

Correct	Errors
1st Try	
2nd Try	

based on "Advertisements: It's Your Call"

How much do you know about advertising? Chances are	9
that you already know a lot. An average American sees	19
or hears 560 advertisements each day!	25
Ads come in many forms. One form is the print ad.	36
Print ads use pictures and words to persuade readers	45
to buy products and services. Other ads are broadcast on	55
the radio. Between songs, companies try to sell products	64
and services. TV is another medium filled with ads.	73
Shows are frequently interrupted for commercials.	79
Some companies even pay to have their products appear	88
in the shows themselves. This strategy is called product	97
placement. It is a way for companies to slip their products	108
into consumers' minds.	111
Advertising is often aimed at young people. Young	119
people spend billions of dollars every year. They also	128
influence how their parents spend money. It is important	137
to look critically at ads that are aimed at you. While	148
ads do inform you about products, they also try to	158
persuade you to buy them. Advertisers try to make you	168
think that buying their product will make you happy and	178
improve your life. Of course, not many products will	187
really do this.	190
How can you look at ads critically? When you see or	201
hear a commercial, think about what its message is. Think	211
about who created it. Think about what they want you to	222
do or buy. Also, think about the strategy the ad is using to	235
grab your attention. Recognizing these strategies will	242
make it easier for you to evaluate products in ads.	252

Word Fluency 1

	Correct	Errors
1st Try		
2nd Try		

behalf bouquet broad mountain sew shepherd broad behalf mountain shepherd	10
broad behalf sew bouquet shepherd mountain bouquet shepherd broad behalf	20
bouquet shepherd mountain behalf broad sew behalf shepherd	30
mountain sew broad shepherd bouquet mountain behalf shepherd bouquet	40
shepherd broad mountain sew behalf bouquet shepherd mountain broad	50
broad shepherd behalf bouquet mountain sew mountain behalf bouquet	60
behalf bouquet sew broad shepherd mountain broad shepherd sew behalf	70
shepherd sew behalf mountain bouquet broad mountain bouquet broad shepherd	80
mountain shepherd broad sew behalf bouquet shepherd behalf mountain broad	90
broad sew behalf bouquet mountain sew mountain shepherd behalf bouquet	100

Word Fluency 2

	Correct	Errors
1st Try		
2nd Try		

chronic	scene	chorus	clique	enough	tough	opaque	zero	zebra	scent	10
chorus	opaque	chronic	zero	scene	zebra	clique	scent	enough	tough	20
opaque	clique	chorus	scene	chronic	enough	zero	tough	zebra	scent	30
scene	enough	opaque	clique	chorus	scent	chronic	zebra	tough	zero	40
zero	zebra	enough	tough	opaque	scene	clique	chronic	chronic	scent	50
clique	tough	zebra	opaque	enough	scent	zero	scene	chorus	chronic	60
enough	clique	tough	zebra	chorus	chronic	opaque	scent	scent	scene	70
tough	opaque	enough	chorus	scent	chronic	clique	zebra	zero	zero	80
opaque	chronic	scene	enough	zero	chorus	tough	chorus	scent	clique	90
zebra	enough	opaque	chronic	tough	clique	scent	zero	scene	chorus	100

Word Fluency 3

	Correct	Errors
1st Try		
2nd Try		

conditions	continued	scholar	school	telephone	telegraph	photograph	microphone	science	scientists	10
scholar	photograph	conditions	microphone	continued	science	school	scientists	telephone	telegraph	20
photograph	school	scholar	continued	conditions	telephone	microphone	telegraph	science	scientists	30
continued	telephone	photograph	school	scholar	scientists	conditions	microphone	telegraph	science	40
science	microphone	telephone	telegraph	photograph	continued	scholar	school	conditions	scientists	50
school	telegraph	microphone	photograph	telephone	scientists	science	continued	scholar	conditions	60
telephone	science	school	telegraph	microphone	scholar	photograph	conditions	scientists	continued	70
telegraph	photograph	telephone	scholar	scientists	conditions	continued	school	science	microphone	80
photograph	conditions	continued	science	telephone	microphone	telegraph	scholar	scientists	school	90
microphone	telephone	photograph	conditions	telegraph	school	scientists	science	continued	scholar	100

Word Fluency 4

	Correct	Errors
1st Try		
2nd Try		

facility	fidelity	corrosion	excursion	compliance	continuance	persistent	resistant	corruption	obstruction	**10**
corrosion	persistent	facility	resistant	fidelity	corruption	excursion	obstruction	compliance	continuance	**20**
obstruction	excursion	corrosion	fidelity	facility	compliance	resistant	continuance	corruption	persistent	**30**
fidelity	compliance	persistent	excursion	corrosion	obstruction	facility	corruption	continuance	resistant	**40**
resistant	corruption	compliance	continuance	persistent	fidelity	corrosion	excursion	facility	obstruction	**50**
excursion	continuance	corruption	obstruction	compliance	persistent	resistant	fidelity	corrosion	facility	**60**
compliance	resistant	excursion	continuance	corruption	corrosion	obstruction	facility	persistent	fidelity	**70**
continuance	persistent	compliance	corrosion	obstruction	facility	fidelity	excursion	corruption	resistant	**80**
persistent	facility	fidelity	resistant	compliance	corruption	continuance	corrosion	obstruction	excursion	**90**
corruption	compliance	persistent	facility	continuance	excursion	obstruction	resistant	fidelity	corrosion	**100**

based on "The Eighteenth Camel"

Errors		
Correct		
	1st Try	2nd Try

A tale is told of a certain wealthy Bedouin who,   10
upon his death, left seventeen camels. These were   18
to be divided among three sons. The first son was   28
to get half of the camels. The second would get   38
a third. The third son would get one-ninth of the lot.   49

By such a division, the first son would get eight and   60
a half camels. The second son would get five and   70
two-thirds camels. The third son would inherit only   78
one and eight-ninths of a camel. The situation seemed   87
impossible to solve. None of the sons would sell his   97
share to the others. Tempers flared. Angry words   105
were spoken.   107

Now, in the area lived a wealthy Arabian woman.   116
Distressed by the fighting, she offered the brothers one   125
of her own camels. She hoped it would help to settle   136
the dispute.   138

They now had eighteen camels to share. The first son   148
received his half. This consisted of nine camels. The   157
second son received six camels—his one-third share.   165
And the last son received two camels, one-ninth of   174
the eighteen.   176

To their surprise, they found that there was one camel   186
left. So they returned the woman's camel with their thanks.   196

Without her camel, the inheritance would not have been   205
peacefully resolved. It seemed that she had done   213
nothing—for she had neither lost nor gained an animal.   223
But the woman was a wise individual. An individual   232
can be a catalyst. The catalytic effect had great value.   242
Its worth was greater than any other gift she might have   253
given to the brothers.   257

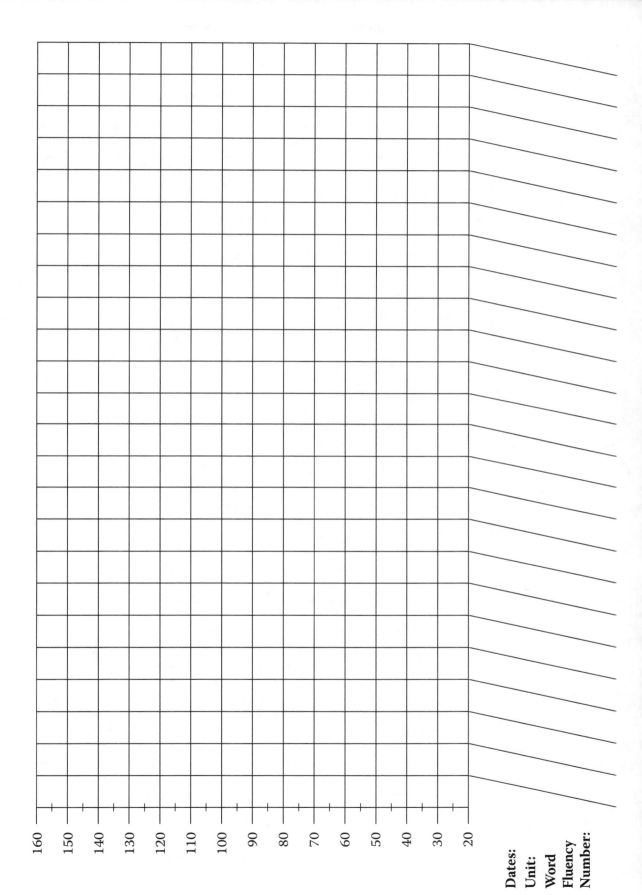

Word Fluency Chart

160
150
140
130
120
110
100
90
80
70
60
50
40
30
20

Dates:

Unit:

Word
Fluency
Number:

Fluency Charts

Correct Phrases Per _____

Dates: _____

Number: _____

	160	150	140	130	120	110	100	90	80	70	60	50	40	30	20

Essential Word Cards

Unit 25

carriage	machine	marriage
pigeon	shoes	surgeon

Unit 26

four	lose	move
movement	movie	prove

Unit 27

billion	carriage	million
opinion	region	religion

Unit 28

aunt	bought	brought
caught	source	view

Unit 29

oh	straight	whole
whom	whose	wolf

Unit 30

behalf	bouquet	broad
mountain	sew	shepherd

Word Building Letter Cards

Unit 25

| c | g | -dge | | | | |

Unit 26

| oo | oo | ou | ue | ui | |

Unit 27

| ui | ou | ey | ei | ei | |

Unit 28

| au | aw | eu | ew | | |

Unit 29

| wa | al | all | walk | war | wor | qua |

Unit 30

| ph | gh | sc | ch | | | |

Unit 25	Unit 25	Unit 25
post	**-ible**	**plic**
Unit 25	Unit 25	Unit 25
vid	**-ive**	**vis**
Unit 25	Unit 25	Unit 25
plex	**cede**	**pli**
Unit 25	Unit 25	Unit 25
cess	**pon**	**ceed**

Unit 25	Unit 25	Unit 25
pound	**pos**	**cred**
Unit 26	Unit 26	Unit 26
ob-	**-ity**	**ten**
Unit 26	Unit 26	Unit 26
vert	**oc-**	**-ic**
Unit 26	Unit 26	Unit 26
tin	**vers**	**of-**

Unit 26	Unit 26	Unit 26
tain	**op-**	**cept**

Unit 26	Unit 26	
cap	**ceit**	

Unit 27	Unit 27	Unit 27
ad-	**-tion**	**sist**

Unit 27	Unit 27	Unit 27
flect	**ac-**	**-sion**

Morphemes for Meaning and Challenge Morphemes

Unit 27 **sta**	Unit 27 **flex**	Unit 27 **af-**
Unit 27 **-age**	Unit 27 **stit**	Unit 27 **gen**
Unit 27 **ag-**	Unit 27 **mis**	Unit 27 **al-**
Unit 27 **mit**	Unit 27 **an-**	Unit 27 **ap-**

Unit 27	Unit 27	Unit 27
ar-	**as-**	**at-**
Unit 27	Unit 27	Unit 27
sub-	**suc-**	**suf-**
Unit 27	Unit 27	Unit 27
sug-	**sup-**	**sus-**
Unit 28	Unit 28	Unit 28
anti-	**-al**	**fer**

Unit 28	Unit 28	Unit 28
spir	mal-	-ial
Unit 28	**Unit 28**	**Unit 28**
tend	capit	-ual
Unit 28	**Unit 28**	**Unit 28**
tens	capt	tent
Unit 28	**Unit 28**	**Unit 28**
aud	grad	gress

Unit 29	Unit 29	Unit 29
semi-	**-ure**	**struct**
Unit 29	Unit 29	Unit 29
frac	**-ance**	**rupt**
Unit 29	Unit 29	
junct	**-ence**	

Bank It

Student _____ Date_____

Sound-Spelling Correspondences

Student _____ Date_____

Sound-Spelling Correspondences

Bank It

Student _____ Date _____

Prefixes

Bank It

Student _____ Date_____

Roots

Student _____ Date _____

Roots

Bank It

Student _____ Date _____

Roots

(blank lined table section)

(blank lined table section)

Bank It

Student _____ Date_____

Roots

Bank It

Student _____ Date _____

Suffixes

Student _____ Date _____

Suffixes

Student _____ Date _____

Suffixes

Sources

Unit 25

Circle Poems Take Many Forms

Neihardt, John G. 1961. *Black Elk Speaks: Being the Life Story of a Holy Man of the Oglala Sioux.* Lincoln, NE: University of Nebraska Press. Copyright © 1932, 1959, 1972 by John G. Neihardt. Copyright © 1961 by the John G. Neihardt Trust. Copyright © 2000 by the University of Nebraska Press. Used by permission of the University of Nebraska Press.

Prelutsky, Jack. 1994. "I Was Walking in a Circle," from *A Pizza the Size of the Sun.* New York: Greenwillow Books. Text copyright © 1996 by Jack Prelutsky. Used by permission of HarperCollins Publishers.

Wright, Richard. 1998. "716," *Haiku: This Other World.* New York: Arcade Publishing. Used by permission. Copyright © 1998 by Ellen Wright. Reprinted from *Haiku: This Other World* by Richard Wright, published by Arcade Publishing, New York, New York.

Wright, Richard. 1998. "745," *Haiku: This Other World.* New York: Arcade Publishing. Used by permission. Copyright © 1998 by Ellen Wright. Reprinted from *Haiku: This Other World* by Richard Wright, published by Arcade Publishing, New York, New York.

Circles in Nature

Cummings, E.E. 1994. "who knows if the moon's," from G.J. Firmage (Ed.), *E.E. Cummings Complete Poems 1904–1962.* New York: Liveright. Copyright 1923, 1925, 1951, 1953, © 1991 by the Trustees for the E. E. Cummings Trust. Copyright © 1976 by George James Firmage. Used by permission of Liveright Publishing Corporation.

Esbensen, Barbara J. 1996. "circles," from *Echoes for the Eye: Poems to Celebrate Patterns in Nature.* New York: HarperCollins Publishers. Text Copyright © 1996 by Barbara Juster Esbensen. Used by permission of HarperCollins Publishers.

Markham, Edwin. 1913/1915. "Outwitted," from *The Shoes of Happiness and Other Poems.* Garden City, N.Y.: Doubleday, Page & Company.

Unit 26

The House on Mango Street

Cisneros, Sandra. 1994. *The House on Mango Street.* New York: Alfred A. Knopf. Used by permission of Susan Bergholz Literary Services.

The Rules of the Game

Tan, Amy. 1989. "The Rules of the Game," from *The Joy Luck Club.* Copyright © 1989 by Amy Tan. Used by permission of G.P. Putnam's Sons, a division of Penguin Group (USA), Inc.

Tan, Amy. 1989. *The Joy Luck Club.* Copyright © by Amy Tan. Excerpt digitalized by permission of the author and the Sandra Dijkstra Agency.

Tsunamis

National Oceanic and Atmospheric Administration. 2005. "Tsunamis," from the NOAA Web site. http://www.noaa.gov/tsunamis. html (accessed March 10, 2005).

Owen, James. 2005. "Tsunami Family Saved by Schoolgirl's Geography Lesson," From *National Geographic News* (January 18, 2005) from the National Geographic Web site. http://news. nationalgeographic.com/news/2005/01/ 0118_050118_tsunami_geography_lesson.html (accessed March 10, 2005).

_____. 2005. "Girl, 10, used geography lesson to save lives," from *Telegraph,* from the Web site. http://www.telegraph.co.uk/news/ main.jhtml?xml=/news/2005/01/01/ugeog. xml&sSheet=/portal/2005/01/01/ixportaltop.html (accessed March 10, 2005).

Wiseman, Paul. 2005. "Politics Enters Plan for Tsunami Warning System," from *USA Today*, from the *USA Today* Web site. http://www.usatoday.com/news/world/2005-03-02-tsunami-warning-system_x.htm (accessed March 10, 2005).

_____. 2005. "Tsunami risk areas being mapped," from *Phuket Gazette*, from the *Phuket Gazette* Web site. http://www.phuketgazette.net/news/index.asp?id=4075 (accessed March 10, 2005).

National Geographic News. 2005. "The Deadliest Tsunami in History?" from the National Geographic Web site. http://news.nationalgeographic.com/news/2004/12/1227_041226_tsunami.html (accessed March 10, 2005).

Pendick, Daniel. 2005. "A Deadly Force," from PBS Online. http://www.pbs.org/wnet/savageearth/tsunami/index.html (accessed March 10, 2005).

The Museum of Unnatural Mystery. 2005. "Tsunami: Deadly Waves," from the Web site. http://www.unmuseum.org/tsunami.htm (accessed March 10, 2005).

Unit 27

Wolf Society

_____. 2005. "Eastern Timberwolf, Canis lupus lycaon, Connecticut Pack," from the Web site http://www.clcookphoto.com/grrsnap.htm (accessed March 17, 2005).

_____. 2004. "Pack Life," from the Wolf Guide Web site. http://www.aboutwolves.org/thewolf/packlife.htm (accessed March 17, 2005).

_____. 2005. "Communication and Social Order Within a Wolf Pack: Howling," from the Web site http://canidae.ca/WCOMM.HTM (accessed March 15, 2005).

_____. 2005. "Alpha Status, Dominance, and Division of Labor in Wolf Packs: Results and Discussion," from the USGS: Northern Prairie Wildlife Research Center Web site. http://www.npwrc.usgs.gov/resource.mammals.alstat/alpst.htm (accessed March 15, 2005).

_____. 2005. "Social Organization," from the Web site http://www.bio.davidson.edu/people.vecase/Behavior/Spring2004/porter/Social%20Organization.htm (accessed March 15, 2005).

_____. 2005. "Wolf Families," from the International Wolf Center Web site. http://www.wolf.org/wolves/learn/justkids.kids_wolf_families.asp (accessed March 15, 2005).

_____. 2004. "About the Wolf," from The Wolf Society of Great Britain Web site. http://www.wolfsociety.org.uk/education.general/about-the-wolf.htm (accessed March 15, 2005).

_____. 1998. "Wolf Wisdom: Packs," from the WERC Web site. http://www.wolfcenter.org.Hertel/html/Packs.html (accessed March 15, 2005).

David Copperfield

Dickens, Charles. 1849. "Chapter 11: I Begin Life on My Own Account, and Don't Like It," from *The Complete Works of Charles Dickens* Web site. http://www.dickens-literature.com(accessed March 30, 2005).

Unit 28

A View of the Eye

Allison, Linda. 1987. "Eye See: Experiments With Seeing," from *Brown Paper School Book: Blood and Guts* by The Yolla Bolly Press. Copyright © 1976 by The Yolla Bolly Press. By Permission of Little, Brown and Co., Inc.

_____. "How the Eye Works" http://www.bausch.com/us/vision/concerns/eyeworks.jsp (accessed April 13, 2005).

My First View of Ellis Island

Corsi, Edward. 1935. "The First Time I Saw Ellis Island," from *In the Shadow of Liberty, American Quilt Teacher's Theme Guide.* New York: Scholastic, Inc. Copyright © 1993 by Instructional Publishing Group. Used by permission of Ayer Company Publishers.

Lazarus, Emma. 1883. "The New Colossus," from *Emma Lazarus, The New Colossus (1883)*, from the Web site http://wroads.virginia.edu/~CAP/LIBERTY/lazarus.html (accessed April 1, 2005).

Amigo Brothers

Thomas, Piri. 2002. "Amigo Brothers," adapted from *Stories From El Barrio*. Copyright © 1978 by Piri Thomas. Reprinted by permission of the author. All rights reserved.

Unit 29

Advertisements: It's Your Call

_____. 2005. "Cell Phones Catering To Kids," from the CBS News Web site. http://www.cbsnews.com/stories/2005/03/31/earlyshow/series.main684359.shtml (accessed April 21, 2005).

Smith, Hedrick. 2005. "National Statistics: Snapshots of Work and Family in America," from *Juggling Work and Family* on the PBS Web site. http://www.pbs.org/workfamily/discussion_snapshots.html (accessed April 21, 2005).

Gaudin, Sharon. 2001. "Cell phone facts and statistics," from the NetworkWorldFusion Web site. http://www.nwfusion.com/research/2001/0702featside.html (accessed April 21, 2005).

A Call to Poetry

Rodriguez, Luis J. 1989. "The Calling," from *Poems Across the Pavement*. San Fernando, CA: Tia Chucha Press. Reprinted by permission of Luis J. Rodriguez. All rights reserved.

Silko, Leslie Marmon. 1981. "Story From Bear Country," from *Storyteller*. Copyright © 1981 by Leslie Marmon Silko. Reprinted from *Storyteller* by Leslie Marmon Silko. New York, N.Y.: Seaver Books. Used by permission of Seaver Books.

Nye, Naomi Shihab. 2002. "Postscript," from *19 Varieties of Gazelle: Poems of the Middle East*. Text copyright © 2002 by Naomi Shihab Nye. New York, N. Y.: Greenwillow Books, an imprint of HarperCollins Publishers. Used by permission of HarperCollins Publishers.

Unit 30

The Eighteenth Camel

Schmidhauser, Thelma. "The Eighteenth Camel," from *Cricket Magazine* (November), vol. 30, no. 13. Cricket Magazine Group, 315 Fifth Street, Peru, IL 61354-0300. Copyright © 2002 by Thlema Schmidhauser. Reprinted by permission.

The Pig: An Individual Dilemma

Kimenye, Barbara. 1965. "The Pig," from *Kalasanda Revisited*. Copyright © 1965. By Barbara Kimenye. Published by Oxford University Press, Eastern Africa. Used by permission of Barbara Kimenye.